S0-AVV-053

The Quiet Revolution:

Grass Roots of Today's Wilderness Preservation Movement

The Quiet Revolution:

Grass Roots of Today's Wilderness Preservation Movement

With an Introduction by Orville L. Freeman
(Former Secretary of Agriculture)

Donald N. Baldwin

PRUETT PUBLISHING COMPANY

Boulder, Colorado

ISBN: 0-87108-062-1

Library of Congress Card Catalog Number: 72-90480

First Edition

Pruett Publishing Company
Boulder, Colorado 80302
Printed in the United States of America
by
Pruett Press, Incorporated

To Arthur Hawthorne Carhart

In memory of Dr. Baldwin, who passed away during production of the book to which he was so totally dedicated.

INTRODUCTION

by Orville L. Freeman (Former Secretary of Agriculture)

The idea of wilderness — a primitive sanctuary undisturbed by the works of man, where civilized man may find solitude for brief periods — has been around for centuries *as an idyllic dream in the minds of poets* and philosophers. It remained a dream until one Federal agency — the Forest Service of the Department of Agriculture assisted at its birth, nurtured it through infancy, defended it, sometimes against formidable odds, gave it form and substance, and made the dream a reality. Forty-five years after the idea was born, the United States Congress enacted and President Lyndon Johnson on September 3, 1964 signed into law the *National Wilderness Preservation System.* Thereby the United States of America became the only country on the face of the earth to so set apart some of its lands as wilderness sanctuaries — and every American citizen may take enormous pride, as I do, in this single fact. Today our Wilderness System contains 10.2 million acres. When the law was enacted in 1964, 9.1 million acres, under the jurisdiction of the Forest Service, became part of that system, because for those 45 years the agency had been reserving certain lands for just such purposes.

A federal agency is made up of people. So, at some point some one individual had to give the wilderness idea form and substance. Historian, Dr. Donald Baldwin set out to find the origin and trace the early development of the Wilderness concept. He has succeeded, and all of us who know something of Wilderness are indebted to him for that accomplishment.

In most circumstances, if one individual is credited, another must be discredited. This is not the case here, for recognition is accorded to many Forest Service officers and others who labored mightily in the cause of Wilderness.

I have before me a newspaper story from the *Albuquerque Journal of* June 4, 1972, which names as the "Father of the Wilderness concept" Aldo Leopold, Yale graduate, patron saint of the Wilderness Society, and a noted conservation philosopher who died in 1948. This is conventional conservation wisdom. But as Dr. Baldwin brought to light, it is only partially true.

As Assistant District Forester of District 3 (now Region 3), consisting of Arizona and New Mexico, Aldo Leopold was the first to submit a formal Wilderness proposal regarding the Gila Wilderness of the Gila National Forest in Southwestern New Mexico. His proposal was dated October 2, 1922. That proposal was approved finally by District Forester Frank C. W. Pooler, June 3, 1924, and the Gila became the first wilderness area to be established in the entire National Forest System.

It is worth noting here that Aldo Leopold never claimed to have originated the Wilderness concept. That story has grown up since his death.

For millions of Americans who enjoy forest recreation and for those who journey into a Wilderness, a new and authentic hero emerges from the pages of Dr. Baldwin's book.

He is none other than Arthur Hawthorne Carhart, now of Lemon Grove, California — landscape architect, recreation planner, raconteur, and distinguished conservation author.

By no means is Arthur Carhart's name new to conservationists or to those who have read his numerous books. What is new is the central, pioneering role Arthur Carhart played a half century ago, as the first landscape architect ever employed by the Forest Service of the Department of Agriculture. Under the working title of recreation engineer, the young landscape architect Carhart *felt the emotions, thought out beginning principles, made the plans, and applied the de facto concept of wilderness — first on the San Isabel and White River National Forests of Colorado in 1919, and then on the Boundary Waters Canoe Area of Minnesota, in 1921, a good two to three years ahead of the Aldo Leopold proposal of 1922.*

So, in the 1920's a Government agency responded to a new idea, explored and championed it over sometimes raucous opposition and ultimately saw it make history. It is to the great credit of the Forest Service that its leadership, with few deviations, fought hard and successfully for the wilderness idea.

When Arthur Carhart is asked about the beginnings of the Wilderness concept, he invariably names a number of other people — associates, supervisors, supporters — who also played key roles in getting the early de facto principles established. But Dr. Baldwin's book clearly documents the fact that the original thinking and planning was the work of Carhart himself.

As Secretary of Agriculture, I had the rare privilege of exploring some of our primitive and wilderness areas along with my wife, Jane, my friend Edward P. Cliff, then Chief of the Forest Service, and other Forest Service officers. The Bob Marshall Wilderness of Montana, the North Cascades Primitive Area in Washington State, the Middle Fork of the Salmon River in the Idaho Primitive Area and the Sawtooth Primitive Area in Idaho were all wilderness areas that we thoroughly enjoyed. By the time this is published, Congress, hopefully, will have classified the Sawtooth as a Wilderness Area.

Between 1961 and the passage of the Wilderness Act in 1964, I exercised my administrative authority as Secretary of Agriculture to reclassify four National Forest Primitive Areas as wilderness, added 72,216 acres to the Boundary Waters Canoe Area and stiffened the requirements for use of that area. During the same period, the Chief of the Forest Service, under delegated authority, reclassified five primitive areas into the more restrictive Wild Area category and created three new wild areas not previously classified as "primitive." (At that time Wilderness areas of less than 100,000 acres were called Wild Areas.) These actions added up to over two and one-half million acres or about one-fourth of the present National Wilderness Preservation System. It is paradoxical that the Wilderness Act, with its procedural and legislative requirements, actually slowed down the establishments of Wilderness areas in the National Forests. As I look back on it, nothing I did in the eight years I served as Secretary of Agriculture gives me more satisfaction than these actions to expand and protect our nation's wilderness areas.

As a boy and then as Governor of Minnesota and Secretary of Agriculture, I became familiar with the Boundary Waters Canoe Area. Here in this superb canoe-wilderness of the Superior National Forest, the young recreation engineer Arthur Carhart in 1921 first raised the flag of "no road-building," thus inducing the labor pains that were part of the birth of Wilderness itself. The controversies over it that began a half century ago still go on today. While it is not pure wilderness, its uniqueness led to its being included in the Wilderness System.

To backpack, ride horseback or canoe deep into Wilderness, far from the sights and sounds of civilization is something one must experience. It can't be related to the uninitiated. It is the soul-satisfying serenity of feeling one with nature and the natural world which was once man's home. It is the realization of the ascendancy of God's handiwork over that of man's. It is to go home again to the security of a unique world.

If we are to preserve our planet and keep it habitable, Wilderness could be one of those elements that will help us do it.

However, we must keep in mind a *balance* among the various resources. That is a key word. Wilderness will remain for a long time the domain of relatively few people. We also must be concerned about the "many" in our society. This, I thought, was a strong point with Forest Service Chief Edward P. Cliff. Contrary to what some of his critics believed, Cliff was always a strong supporter of the wilderness idea. However, he maintained unflinchingly a balanced approach to the use of all the nation's resources.

Victor Hugo said, "No force on earth is so powerful as an idea whose time has come." If we assume that the wilderness idea was one of those whose time had come, it came to the White River National Forest of Northwest Colorado in the early summer of 1919. To the calm, clear waters of a high-mountain lake, it came knocking at the doors of Arthur Carhart's mind. There at Trapper's lake he heard the singing serenity of pure solitude. In the unheard melodies of another dimension, the voice of wilderness spoke, and previous plans for that National Forest were turned around, and recreation planning on the National Forests of America would never quite be the same again.

Historian Donald Baldwin has rendered a high service to the history of wilderness, to the agency that had the wisdom to preserve it, and to the man who initially did most to give the whole idea form and substance.

Orville L. Freeman

PREFACE

The preparation of this book was, *inter alia*, a long lesson in patience and humility. Early in the research process it became necessary for the author to seek the counsel of a host of individuals who gave freely of their accumulated experience. More acknowledgments than can be made here are owed to the countless persons who furnished indispensable and intelligent assistance to the author. Historical research is never the work of one person alone, and this author acknowledges a debt of gratitude to all those whose *expertise* in their chosen fields was shared generously, and from whose non-routine aid he profited greatly. In that regard, the author wishes especially to express his profound gratitude to the late Dr. Harold H. Dunham, the professor in charge of the dissertation. Dr. Dunham will always be remembered as a Gentleman of the Old School whose keen, perceptive mind he kindly placed at the author's disposal.

To whom does one dedicate his book? Initially, the author's thoughts led directly to his dear wife, the late Eleanore Bender Baldwin, who was his sweetheart, constant companion, and source of great strength through the years of study and research. Then he recalled that Eleanore and he had earlier decided that Arthur Hawthorne Carhart was the only logical choice. The hours the author spent in fruitful conversation with Mr. Carhart are without number and cannot be repaid with laudatory phrases. He is entitled to special thanks because he provided not only inspiration, but he frequently offered suggestions as to additional sources. And the general help of his staff, particularly Mrs. Roberta Winn, at the Conservation Library Center, Denver Public Library, was indeed extraordinary.

The personal papers of Arthur Hawthorne Carhart, a former Forest Service employee, were extensively explored. They were particularly useful in tracing his contributions to the progress made in the introduction and acceptance of the wilderness concept, in showing the *Zeitgeist* of the 1920's, and in revealing some of the political maneuverings of the era as well. The chief sources used in this study were available only because Carhart had the foresight to preserve them. His collection comprised the *sine qua non* of this research. But special credit is also due to the Denver Public Library Commission and to Librarian John T. Eastlick, for their support in the inauguration of the Conservation Library Center in which those documents are stored, and to the present Librarian, Henry G. Shearouse, for his continuing interest in expanding that collection now under the able supervision of Miss Kay Collins.

Much of the primary material for this research was gleaned from the official files of the Forest Service, United States Department of Agriculture, located variously in Colorado, Minnesota, and New Mexico. The author visited the following Forest Service offices: Regional Forester's Office, Region 2, Denver, Colorado; Forest Supervisor's Office, White River National Forest, Glenwood Springs, Colorado; Meeker Forest Ranger Station, Meeker, Colorado; Regional

Forester's Office, Region 9, Milwaukee, Wisconsin. He also examined the Forest Service files in storage at the National Archives, General Services Administration, Federal Records Center, Denver, Colorado.

On-the-spot investigations were conducted at places calculated to yield information pertinent to this inquiry, such as Trappers Lake in Colorado's White River National Forest. The author also made photographic reproductions of selected materials with portable equipment. In this manner numerous documents were microfilmed for leisurely or repeated reference. Permission to employ this procedure was readily obtained from custodians of the records and documents copied.

The Library of Congress, The Superintendent of Documents, The State Historical Society of Colorado, The State of New Mexico Records Center and Archives, The Library of the Colorado State University at Fort Collins, and The Mary Reed Library at the University of Denver, were among the many institutions drawn upon during the course of this investigation. Mrs. Alys Freeze, Head of the Western History Department of the Denver Public Library, and Librarians of that Department brought numerous secondary accounts to the attention of the author. Lastly, I cannot minimize the gratitude I feel for the decision of Fred Pruett to publish this work, and the cooperation I received from his Editor and Staff. As to any factual or other misteaks that may have krept in, I admit freely: *Peccavi.*

Most dissertations are not written with the idea of reaching a "recreational reading" market. The basic research for this book was done to satisfy the requirements for the Doctor of Philosophy degree in History. While it was being readied for publication certain revisions were indicated and necessary. How to keep the updated account free from biases and preconceptions was ever present. After much soul-searching, it seemed wiser to leave the vast body of the findings in the original language the author shall call "Dissertationese," a rather staid, sometimes stilted, encyclopedic, but, nevertheless, *factual* reporting style. Inasmuch as this is *not* a romantic novel about love or sex it may enjoy a restricted appeal to a select group of readers in its present, *i.e.,* largely original and "scholarly" format. To increase its marketability an alternative was to employ the contemporary idiom, replete with "salty" phrases and earthy four-letter words; in short, the entire book could and should, perhaps, have been rewritten in a more popular vein. *Zum Beispiel*: there could have been a chapter or two about "Unimproved Women in the Roadless Wilderness"; or "The Untouched Virgin Forest"; or, would you believe, a book entitled, "Undeveloped Parts of Your Establishment," (Short Title: "UP Your Establishment"). But then the author reminded himself of the scholarly community, his professional responsibilities, and dreading the supercilious eyebrows, reluctantly relented. Instead, he shall rely on the intelligence of the reading public interested primarily in *facts* about this—*"my land"* and *"your land."*

Some years ago, the following intriguing "Foreword to the Second Edition," appeared in *The Common Background of Greek and Hebrew Civilizations*, by Cyrus H. Gordon:

> On details here and there differences of interpretation are justified and welcome, but on the main issues the answer is clear. Accordingly, I do not divide the critics into my supporters and opponents but only into those who catch on fast and those who need more time.

To those who may consider some of the interpretations about the chronological position of Aldo Leopold heretical, the author hastens to apologize and adds that he attempted to report just the facts historical. Objectivity, however elusive, however unattainable, was something for which he strove most earnestly. The reader, of course, will evaluate the data furnished and arrive at his own conclusions.

Since June 1965, when the basic study was made available to the Denver Regional Office of the U. S. Forest Service, it has been in continuous use locally and in the Chief Forester's Office in Washington, D.C., as a daily reference tool. When the author became interested in the broad subject of wilderness over a decade ago there existed no easy manual or reference book (in or out of the U. S. Forest Service) to guide him in his quest for dependable data in convenient size. Now that "Environment" has become a household word, anyone whose interest has been whetted by the current furor over the wilderness issue will find this brief survey useful as an introductory text or manual—a kind of springboard to further study of the subject in depth. The selected bibliography should help point the way.

There is no such thing as a complete investigation. Neither is there such a thing as *the* history of the wilderness preservation movement. The history of wilderness preservation has numerous facets. This is but one of them.

D. N. B.

Denver, Colorado:
May, 1972

TABLE OF CONTENTS

LIST OF FIGURES

PROLOGUE: EVERYBODY TALKS BUT NOBODY DOES ANYTHING

The genesis and implementation of ideas relating to conservation of America's natural heritage have been, too frequently, viewed as products of the Progressive and New Deal periods. In general this association of conservationism with progressivism and the era of reform in the 1930's is certainly correct. This association is, however, invalid in the case of the conversion of long-current and widely entertained philosophic attitudes favorable to the preservation of wilderness areas to a workable plan for accomplishing that end. The "wilderness concept" was first translated into a functional plan and actual results during the years from 1919 to 1933, a period not noted for its progressivism and reformist spirit. And the source of this initiative lay within, not a reformist association, but a bureaucratic organization, the United States Forest Service. The prime mover within that organization in this regard was a man, Arthur H. Carhart, whose principal drive came not only from general conservationist sentiments, but from the orientations derived from his profession of landscape architecture.

The central purpose of this study is to document answers to the following questions: What is meant by the term "wilderness concept" and how did it originate in the United States? When, where, and how was it first applied? How did it get embodied in authoritative regulations, national in their application? What actual results were obtained by the end of the period here under consideration (1919-1933)? Was the idea of the preserved wilderness merely "a poem, yet unwritten,"[1] as it was recently described? Or was the achievement of the 1920's an important first step in the creation of a national wilderness preservation system?

In providing at least partial answers to the foregoing queries, the following discussion will trace the origin and evolution of a recreation policy in the National Forests of the western United States from World War I to the New Deal. It will show how Forest recreation was stimulated by certain farsighted members of the United States Forest Service and such powerful, interacting forecs as increased population,[2] prosperity, assembly line automobile production, and the "good roads" movement. These latter influences, it will be demonstrated in turn, supported the demand for preserving "wilderness areas." The creation of such areas called for zoning of National Forest lands under regional management plans, and the entire development culminated in the embodiment of these plans in the law establishing the National Wilderness Preservation System in 1964.[3]

It should be emphasized that the genesis of a workable plan for the preservation of wilderness areas emerged through the evolution of national forest recreation policies within the U. S. Forest Service, but that there was delay in the acceptance of such a plan, largely due to the lack of understanding and communication between various units and personnel of that same service. The Service's responsibilities for scientific timber production and watershed protection led many of its chief administrators to assign a very low priority to recreational use of the Forests. A similar lack of perspective caused contention between the Forest Service and the National Park Service over the use of federal funds for the development of recreational facilities within the National Forests.[4] The ultimate blending of different fields of professional learning, particularly those embracing forestry and landscape architecture, furnished the impetus to overcome these shortcomings. Professionally trained foresters and landscape architects met in the United States Forest Service following World War I. Both kinds of professionally trained men were then engaged to help administer the National Forests in accordance with a stated mission established by Congress.

Establishing a federal agency does not bring a full solution to the problem which the agency is to handle. In interpreting and applying the law under which it operates, the agency may find that it lacks sufficient power or encounters such conditions that it may be unable to carry out the basic assignment for which it was created. This generalization may be illustrated in the case of the United States Forest Service. This Service was created February 1, 1905, during the period of the conservation movement, under the aegis of Gifford Pinchot and Theodore Roosevelt, in order to prevent waste and undesirable exploitation in the National Forests. Contrary to some assertions that the Forests and their natural resources were thus protected by the "creation of an effective policy,"[5] waste and exploitation were curtailed but not ended.

There were, however, many Americans who took comfort in the great progress which had been made in the field of conservation and considered the problem solved for all time. This view appeared to more perceptive minds to be illusory. The Forest Service had in its leadership and in its ranks men of great stature, men who fought for ideals and who struggled to promote proper growth and development of the Service program. But, in the 1920's, the hoped for full conservation of the multiple opportunities for use of the National Forest was hampered by the limited mission given to the Service by Congress, a mission that was dominated by a timber-management emphasis.

For the purpose of this study a precise definition of the term "wilderness" cannot be given, but a general explanation of what this elusive word has come to mean in debates over the use of the National Forests should prove helpful. Probably the most complete analysis of this meaning may be found in the monumental twenty-seven-volume report to the President and to the Congress in January, 1962, by the Outdoor Recreation Resources Review Commission (hereafter cited as ORRRC), especially in *Study Report 3*.[6] This report reflected the fact that there was an ambiguity in the meaning of the term wilderness, which could not be overcome. In other words, there was a "blurred distinction between the physical reality of wilderness as real estate and the subjective values which human beings place on the stimulus of wilderness."[7] In Forest Service and conservationist terminology, a wilderness area has come to be broadly defined as one which remains in its natural, wild state, undisturbed by man-made roads and structures.

Just as Frederick Jackson Turner in 1893 was disturbed by the foreseeable consequences of the closing of the frontier,[8] there were men in the post-World War I period who found alarming the rapid diminution in the amount of wilderness land and who pointed to the need to protect the remaining superlative scenic areas for recreational use. This was a use for which the Congress had up until then allotted the Forest Service but little money, and for which the Service had even fewer plans or policies; such a use seemed at least visionary, if not irrational to many officials. Despite this view, the decade following World War I was epochal for the conservation movement in the United States, because it marked the beginning of a new and important stage. During the so-called period of "normalcy" a new brand of conservation was carried out.[9] The available historical literature on conservation in the roaring 1920's has not characterized this period as one of germination, or to use an apt phrase of Richard Hofstader for the 1930's, one in which a "new departure" was made.[10]

But, as early as 1919 Arthur H. Carhart, a landscape architect in the Denver office of the United States Forest Service, provided the first blueprint for practical development of recreational resources in the National Forests.[11] He worked even more notably, albeit frequently from behind the scenes, in influencing others in positions of authority and responsibility to further the cause of wilderness preservation. His papers, recently deposited in the Conservation Library Center and presently housed in the Denver Public Library, are a prime source for documenting his efforts to arouse the United States Forest Service and his contemporaries into taking forthright action to meet the changing needs in outdoor recreation for a growing nation. Many of the Carhart papers contain important threads for the cloth of conservation history; they record the role played by some of the lesser and unknown pioneer actors in the movement to preserve America's forest heritage. These documents serve to illustrate why Carhart more aptly than any of his contemporaries might be considered "Father of the Wilderness Concept."

An authority on conservation recently noted that there now exist numerous biographies and historical monographs which analyze and describe the conservation problems in our National Forests and our National Parks.[12] The present study will therefore mention briefly, and then only where necessary for the sake of continuity, the basic developments which led to early conservation measures.[13]

Despite the abundance of treatises on conservation, there is a dearth of literature on the topic of outdoor recreation. Ralph Greenhouse and William Matheson undertook a survey of the written materials in this field during the period September 8 to Novemebr 20, 1959. They found that the outline prepared for them by the General Reference and Bibliography Division of the Library of Congress "assumed the existence of a substantial body of material relating rather directly to outdoor recreation." Nevertheless, they lamented that it proved to be of little value to them. Their disillusionment grew as the actual hunt progressed and the "true situation—that the field (if it is yet that) of outdoor recreation has been but sketchily treated." They reported, "The card catalog of the Library of Congress, a central source for any bibliographer, contains no subject heading OUTDOOR RECREATION."[14] In spite of such deficiencies, the present study will concern itself primarily with that phase or type of outdoor recreation requiring "wilderness" as an essential ingredient.

Finally, irrespective of the rather extensive amount of writing on the subject of "wilderness" published by conservation organizations, there remains a wide gap in the accounts of the origin and initial applications of the wilderness concept which needs to be bridged. The *lacuna* referred to is not the cleavage between the "right use" of John Muir[15] and the "wise use" of Gifford Pinchot.[16] Rather, it is the absence of the detailed facts concerning the genesis and first applications of the wilderness concept during the period 1919-1924. These early actions will be documented in chronological sequence, beginning with the application at Trappers Lake, Colorado, in 1919, which set a precedent. The second such application occurred in the Superior National Forest, Minnesota, in 1921, and the third in the Gila National Forest, New Mexico, in 1924. It is the first two applications which have not previously been accounted for in the historical accounts of the evolution of the wilderness concept.

A thorough examination of materials prepared by the Forest Service and conservation organizations has disclosed that the available accounts began with the third, and omitted any reference to the first two. According to a 1963 Forest Service pamphlet, for example, "nearly 40 years ago" the Forest Service had pioneered in preserving America's wilderness heritage "led by Aldo Leopold."[17] Continuing it stated:

> The forest Service pioneered this concept in the 1920's. Studies of wild lands on the National Forests began, and in 1924 a large part of what is now the Gila Wilderness in New Mexico was set aside as a special

> area for the preservation of wilderness. The Gila, the Nation's first designated wilderness, contains 500,000 acres of primitive American lands astride the Mogollon Rim and Diablo mountain ranges.[18]

Though historically and factually *erroneous*, the foregoing account is only one of many about the origin of the wilderness concept which has apparently been accepted among conservationists.

One of the earliest published articles to proclaim that *incorrect* data was a 1940 publication of The Wilderness Society that likewise traced

> Wilderness Areas from their formal beginning in the mind and on the pen point of Aldo Leopold to the achievement by Robert Marshall of a practical new wilderness system in the National Forests.[19]

Moreover, Harvey Broome stated, "Unquestionably, Aldo Leopold was the Jeremiah of wilderness thinking."[20] Broome explained that in 1925 Leopold had written an article about the value of wilderness,[21] from which Robert Marshall had quoted five years later.[22] But if Leopold was the prophet of the wilderness movement," Broome asserted, "Marshall was the first to suggest organization."[23]

In this connection, it is instructive to note what Aldo Leopold himself claimed when he attempted to trace the "origin and ideals of wilderness areas."[24] In 1940 he wrote:

> I will here attempt to cover the history of the wilderness movement in the southwest prior to 1926. I suppose subsequent events are too well known to require comment.
>
> The earliest action I can find in my files is a letter dated September 21, 1922, notifying the District Forester that the establishment of a wilderness area on the head of the Gila River, in the Gila National Forest. I

> suppose one may assume a prior "incubation period" of a year or two. I take it, then, that the movement in the Southwest must have started about 1920.
>
> This assumption is further corroborated by the publication, in 1921, of my paper, "The Wilderness and Its Place in Forest Recreational Policy" . . . In 1924 the action stage was reached. I have a map dated March 31 showing the Gila area boundaries as originally proposed by me and as approved by District Forester F. C. W. Pooler. I do not know when Washington finally added its approval.[25]

Leopold then considered this question:

> How widely had the idea spread by 1924? I offer in evidence the resolutions passed by the National Conference on Outdoor Recreation (Jour. Forestry, October, 1924) which contain no mention of wilderness.[26]

It has been stated above that the *original application of the wilderness concept occurred in 1919,* followed by *a second such step in 1921. These and other pertinent actions took place prior to and during the "incubation period" referred to by Leopold.* Furthermore, they helped pave the way, by 1929, for the first nationwide regulation and protection given to such areas selected for wilderness protection by the Washington office of the Forest Service. Until July 12, 1929, when the Forest Service issued its "Regulation L-20: Primitive Areas," these areas were identified under the authority of the District Foresters, and did not require the approval of the Washington office. Thus, they were subject to no uniform management plan.[27]

Regulation L-20 gave final authority for the creation of Primitive Areas to the Chief of the Forest Service, and thus created the possibility of a unified and nationwide protection of wilderness values in national forests. Between 1929 and 1933, this opportunity was utilized to identify sixty-three potential primitive areas within the National Forests, and formally to establish eleven of them. By 1939, seventy-three such areas had been so established. It was not until 1939 that new regulations[28] superseded that of 1929. Thus, the accomplishments of the New Deal in extending the preservation of recreational values in the National Forests, were based upon authority and methods of procedure and actual examples which were created during the Republican ascendancy.

While developments concerning wilderness areas subsequent to 1933 are relatively well-documented, only skeleton accounts of the events during the years 1919 through 1933 appear in documents consulted during the course of this investigation.[29] It is true that in the case of the ORRRC Report, a truly impressive array of information is included, and the criticism of deficiency of detail cannot readily be made. On the other hand, valuable and pertinent information contained in the personal files of Arthur H. Carhart are not included in that Report.

Study Report 27 dealing with the historical development of outdoor recreation is so cryptic that it is misleading, and it stands in part uncorroborated by evidence appearing in other portions of the report; hence it might also be classified as incomplete.[30] Information appearing in ORRRC reports, as for example in the section entitled "The Gila Wilderness: A Case History," is supplemented in what follows by additional data found in the sources for those reports.[31]

In the chapters that follow, the history of the development of the "wilderness concept" from an idea to a working program in the years before the New Deal will be presented in detail.

CHAPTER I

HEAD FOR THE WOODS

What was the status of "recreation" in National Forests of the United States in the years immediately prior to, during and after World War I? What if anything was being done to preserve wilderness conditions in this period? A laconic answer to the first question—germinating; to the second—not much. This chapter will illustrate the fact that while there had been recognition of the value of National Forests for recreation prior to 1919, there existed no active program for their development for such a purpose, and that no practical plan or policy regarding the preservation of wilderness values in the National Forests had been formulated or even proposed.

Increasing Recreational Uses Prior to and During World War I (1914-1918)

On the eve of World War I, Forest Service officials noted the increasing use of National Forests as playgrounds. The minutes of a Forest Supervisors' conference held in Denver,

Colorado, January 29-February 3, 1917, gave significant evidence of the origin and growing awareness of the recreational uses of the National Forests among Forest Service personnel.[1] The Chairman of the conference was Smith Riley, the District Forester. At the morning session of Wednesday, January 31st, Q. R. Craft, the District Fiscal Agent, noted that "twelve years ago tomorrow" the Forest Service had been transferred from the Interior Department to the Department of Agriculture, and that in 1905 the rank and file had little grasp of what it meant. Gifford Pinchot, Riley, and a few others, however, had "realized fully what it meant," and Craft lauded the "great strides" which had been made and pointed to the accomplishments which could be expected in the succeeding twelve years. He confessed that he hoped to "get the vision better of what is possible in the future" than he had had twelve years before. Of one thing he seemed certain:

> . . . we know that this western country is bound to increase wonderfully in population and that means that every Forest officer must advance and keep pace with the development and need of these Forest resources. . . .[2]

At the same session, Wallace I. Hutchinson, in charge of the Information and Education Branch of the Denver District Office, spoke on the subject of "Popularizing the National Forests."[3] His statement contained one of the earliest clear-cut appeals *by a Forest Service officer* to "open up" our National Forests to the public for recreation. He also mentioned the incipient controversy between the Forest Service and the National Park Service, and the related dispute over the *alleged* use of the National Forests by "the poor man," and the maintenance of the National Parks for "the rich man." Hutchinson declared:

> Popularizing the National Forests—what do we mean by this phrase? Simply to make the mountain forests of the west the favorite vacation lands of people who

> take a summer outing—a place where everyone goes who is in search of outdoor life and enjoyment. The opening up of these vast areas and making them available for the use of the poor man as well as the rich is, I believe, a very practical problem. . . .[4]

He noted that the National Forests scattered from Maine to California and from the Gulf of Mexico to the Canadian Line were visited by 2,000,000 people in 1916, and that the seventeen National Forests of Colorado alone had received more than 600,000 visitors during the previous summer. He asked, "Did you ever stop to think that the greatest playgrounds in the United States are the National Forests . . . ?[5] Hutchinson prophesied that the number of visitors during 1916 was but the forerunner of the great wave of travel which would sweep through the west in increasing volume until at some future date "millions will be coming to our forests in search of outdoor recreation." He then made a plea:

> Isn't it about time we were waking up to the fact, and laying plans for the handling of these visitors in a business-like and efficient manner? Up to the present time there has been a tendency on the part of a good many Supervisors to consider recreation work as a kind of a side issue, to be handled at odd times when there is nothing much else to do. . . . This is an entirely mistaken idea, and one we should get away from at once. . . .[6]

Hutchinson added a remark which was not wholly accurate, when he said that the "Government too has suddenly awakened" to the fact that the recreation resources of "our National Parks and Forests" were one of the great assets of the country, and that the chances of development were "unlimited." The truth of the matter was that any appropriations specifically for the development of recreation resources were still years away.

Hutchinson then pursued another line of thought by asking: "Why is it that in these days we hear so much about the National Parks and so little about our National Forests? The answer is Publicity."[7] The National Park Service had gone into "the advertising game" in a thorough and comprehensive way, he suggested, and was getting the "backing of every possible publicity medium." He therefore suggested that the Forest Service should advertise also, and he outlined steps which the Service could take to popularize the National Forests.[8] The mass-production of the automobile was to help accomplish the goal of popularization. Undoubtedly there was design behind the fact that on January 31, 1917, the Forest Supervisors visited the Ford Plant in Denver and were escorted through all the departments. Yet increased automobile production since 1914 was enabling Americans to travel to the National Forests in search of recreation. "At that time," the minutes of the conference recorded, "the plant was putting out a car about every three minutes."[9]

Following the plant visit the meeting was reconvened. Arthur M. Cook, Forest Supervisor of the Routt National Forest, Colorado, spoke first and suggested that Hutchinson had "pretty nearly made a ten-strike" in the morning session. Cook then recalled what he had been taught as a "proper" definition of Forestry. The ideal was divided into three parts:

First— Protection for the resources of any Forest property.

Second— Production of timber and any other Forest products, such as forage, etc., and

Third— Development of forest resources for the purpose of pleasure.

It seemed to Cook "extremely timely at last" that, since the first two divisions of the ideal of the forester had made progress in the past few years, "we now come to give some heed to the third and last."[10]

Another answer to the question about recreation posed at the beginning of this chapter appeared in a 1918 pamphlet[11] prepared by Frank A. Waugh for the Forest Service. Waugh explained how in older countries public forests had existed for centuries with recreation in such areas as a recognized use. He noted that the original and primary purpose in the creation of public forests for recreation was seen most significantly in the ancient law of England, lasting from pre-Norman times until the reign of Charles II, when forests were legally defined as:

> A certain territorie of wooddy grounds and fruitfull pasture, priviledged for wild beastes and foules of Forest Chase and Warren to rest and abide in, in the safe protection of the King, for his princely delight and pleasure, which territorie of ground, so priviledged, is meered and bounded with irremoueable markes, meres, and boundaries, wether knowen by matter of record or else by prescription.[12]

Since he had been asked in 1917 by the Forester to make an extended examination of the existing conditions of recreation in the National Forest with recommendations for methods and general policies, Waugh had come to believe that the fundamental problem was one of releasing the great aesthetic and human values offered by the mountains, glaciers, lakes, streams, woods, and natural parks, and making the resources of the Forests accessible to visitors. He would make them "not merely accessible but intelligible and effective."[13]

Significantly, he stressed the need to place recreation in its proper place, along with all other utilities, in order to achieve the largest possible public benefit.[14] Waugh referred to the hundreds of miles of trails suitable for foot passengers and pack animals to be found in the National Forests east of the Mississippi, and similar trails in the mountains of Colorado, California, Oregon and Washington, along with other "hundreds of miles of roadway fit for wagon traffic and automobiling." He also mentioned the finished roads which

> lie far and tempting through the Forest . . . attracting the camper in his wagon and tourist in his automobile to linger for days and weeks at a time. . . .[15]

Waugh spoke of the "noblest of landscape in the National Forests," and suggested that where such landscapes can be preserved without sacrifice of other interests they should be firmly protected. He added that

> if in special areas this direct human value of the landscape can be shown to outweigh other economic values it obviously becomes good public policy to sacrifice the lesser interest to the greater.[16]

But Waugh was not talking about preserving the wilderness as the term was later understood. He referred to areas classed as National Monuments, which he noted, were created for the preservation of some natural wonder or some historic or prehistoric relic. Such objects and the land surrounding them were withdrawn by presidential proclamation from the usual status of public lands. These monuments were not intended for private use, nor for homesteading or mining, and were to be closed to commercial exploitation.[17]

In summarizing the employment policy of the Forest Service, Waugh pointed out that men trained in technical forestry had been placed in charge of sylvicultural operations, and men expert in the cattle industry in control of grazing activities, while mining engineers, land surveyors, lawyers, entomologists, and statisticians had been utilized in their fields of competence. Recreation, he suggested, was an essential and inescapable Forest utility, requiring the talents of the landscape engineer.[18] Among the conclusions Waugh reached was this astute one: "In this work the Forest Service should employ men suitably trained and experienced in recreation, landscape engineering, and related subjects."[19] This suggestion was implemented in the following year, when the Forest Service employed its first landscape architect.

Introduction of Landscape Architecture After World War I (1919)

The introduction of a landscape architect in 1919 brought new concepts of forest management into our National Forests. Application of landscape engineering principles in the Forests proved that Waugh's observations were correct. For the first time, men professionally trained in landscape architecture and those trained for forestry began to communicate, and the Forest Service began to plan for the preservation of aesthetic values. Not only did the Forest Service launch an active program for the development of forest recreation in 1919, but as a by-product gave birth to the basic formula for wilderness preservation, the exclusion of man-made structures in designated areas protected by a surrounding regional plan.

When the armistice was signed on November 11, 1918, American troops became eager to return to their homes and their peacetime occupations. This group included First Lieutenant Arthur H. Carhart of the Sanitary Corps, United States Army, stationed at Camp Meade, Maryland. While still in the Washington, D.C., area in December of that year, he applied first to the National Park Service, Department of the Interior, for employment as a Landscape Architect, but without success. Then he visited the main office of the Forest Service in the United States Department of Agriculture where he made the acquaintance of Edward A. Sherman, the Assistant Forester, who, like Carhart, was a graduate of Iowa College.

Carhart's background to 1918 had been unexceptional. He was born September 18, 1892, at Mapleton, Iowa, where he was educated in the public schools. In June, 1916, he was graduated from Iowa State College with a Bachelor of Science degree in Landscape Architecture. When he entered the United States Army in September, 1917, he had acquired approximately thirteen months of experience in greenhouses, nurseries, and related landscape operations, including a summer with the Shaw Botanical Garden at St. Louis, Missouri.[20]

Sherman accorded the applicant a warm reception. Carhart later recalled that "Sherman was a big man who looked a good deal like Abraham Lincoln."[21] Having no specific openings to offer, Sherman suggested that Carhart correspond directly with the various district offices of the Forest Service to determine their possible need for a landscape architect. How low a priority was given to "recreation" may be gauged by the following representative reply received by Lieutenant Carhart in response to his many separate applications for employment:

> Your letter of December 18 has been given careful consideration and I regret to say that at this time it is impossible for this District to employ a landscape architect. We realize that the time is coming when a man trained along this line will be needed, but for a period to come we will be occupied in getting our work back to normal conditions and in restoring to active duty the men now on military furlough. Until this is accomplished we cannot undertake plans calling for new men or opening up new lines of work.[22]

Carhart received equally discouraging replies from other districts, but the one from the Denver office of the Forest Service, District 2, permitted further negotiations. Carhart was informed that at the time there was no provision for the employment of a landscape engineer, but that while there was a good deal of work which really required the services of one, the Service had "heretofore had to depend upon engineers in other lines of work to furnish us the necessary instructions." The engineers also were responsible "for the direction of work involving not only scenic, trail and road location, but sanitation." The letter continued:

> In your statement of experience there is nothing indicating the extent of any training and experience you may

> have acquired in hydro-electric engineering, or highway engineering, and a letter has been addressed to Mr. E. A. Sherman, as suggested by you, making further inquiry concerning your qualifications. When a reply has been received from him, I shall be glad to correspond with you further.[23]

Faced with such demands for training and experience a less determined man probably would have sought employment elsewhere. But Carhart pursued the matter further, and in a letter from Assistant Forester Sherman was advised that the Forester had definitely approved the plan of securing a recreational engineer for the Denver office at a beginning salary of $1800 per annum. "You understand, of course," wrote Sherman, "the salary conditions and the fact that you must report for duty at Denver at your own expense." The letter closed by stressing some additional conditions of employment:

> After the examination has been held and the papers rated by the Civil Service Commission, they establish a register of eligibles. They will then ask us to make a permanent appointment . . . and will certify to us the names of the three men standing highest on the register. . . . If not one of the three highest, we would be forced to terminate your appointment and make a selection from among the three. It will probably take six months to . . . establish a register. I apprehend that you have sufficient sporting blood to run the risk of being one of the three topnotch men on the list. . . .[24]

From his home in Mapleton, Iowa, Carhart accepted the appointment, agreeing to report to Denver on March 1, 1919, to take up his duties as the first Recreational Engineer to be employed by the Forest Service on a fulltime, permanent basis. His duties were described as follows:

> A complete plan embodying the lines of work incident to this newly-created position has not yet been formulated. Nevertheless, it is now known that among your duties will be such as general sanitation work in the National forests with special reference to ranger stations, simple highway landscape improvement, and improving the present layout plans for as many of our permanent ranger stations as you can personally visit during the field season. As the library in this office on such subjects as these is rather limited, . . . bring with you any publications which . . . will be of service to you in the work. . . .[25]

Initial Efforts in Planning and Developing Forest Recreation Resources (1919)

By May, 1919, news of the work that Recreation Engineer Carhart had undertaken began to circulate throughout the Rocky Mountain Region of what was then District 2 (now Region 2) of the Forest Service, an area embracing some twenty-three million acres.[26] The map (Map 2) delineates the area.

In what was probably his first article boosting recreation in the National Forests, Carhart wrote in May, 1919:

> Recreation plans for the Forests of the District are getting a real start toward a comprehensive development plan. Not a surprising lot will be accomplished this season perhaps but the important thing, the beginning of a full utilization of Forest Recreation, commenced.[27]

He promised that better plans for development would be worked out by the next season for there would be all winter to draw them up. Also, the Recreation Engineer would have more complete knowledge of the opportunities for recreational work in the District. Drawing attention to the many delightful spots in the several Forests having unusual interest, he said that Jewel Cave National Monument in South Dakota, and the Wheeler National Monument[28] in Colorado were set aside as such because of their unique formations. But, he added, there were many less well known spots, perhaps not so spectacular as these two, that nevertheless had great scenic value. Carhart noted:

> Quite the greater part of these are now in the hands of the National Forests. In the older sections [of the nation] many have been taken up by some method of acquiring land because of this attractiveness and are not now available to the public unless admission is paid. If these areas can be set aside as recreational units their preservation for public use will be made easier.[29]

Carhart ended his article with a request that any natural phenomena having pronounced interest value, such as a waterfall, a cave, a lake, queer rock cliffs, a stream that dropped out of sight into a cavern, fossil rocks, unusual hot springs, unique forest conditions, and ruins of cliff or other dwellings, be reported to him for "consideration in this greater development of recreation in our forests."[30]

The District 2 *Bulletin* of May, 1919, also contained an item which stated that Carhart had recently taken up the work of Recreation Engineer in the District, and that "he is a good fellow, knows his business and is enthusiastic." The note urged that he be welcomed into the Service by sending him all the information he wanted.[31]

The "beauty engineer," as Carhart was quickly dubbed,[32] meanwhile continued to maintain contact with his friend Sherman in Washington. In reply to a letter from Carhart, Sherman wrote that he was very glad indeed to hear that conditions appeared favorable to the development of recreation in the National Forests in both Colorado and Wyoming, adding:

> I was particularly interested in your scheme for developing a system of camps for the city of Pueblo. The idea seems to me to be an excellent one and will no doubt meet with the approval of all persons who are able to visit the camps by automobile whether they be residents of Pueblo or of the plains country to the eastward. The establishment of such camps, I would say, will prove to be very popular with visitors from Kansas in particular who, no doubt, will come to this locality by automobile in increasing numbers. These camps ought to offer an attraction which will make them self-advertising.[33]

Sherman duly noted Carhart's suggestions regarding publicity, agreed fully that there was a big field for such publicity work in connection with the recreational use of the National Forests, but cautioned that "we must be careful in the beginning not to overdo this by advertising our wares too much before we are in condition to show them to good advantage." Sherman felt that the goods were "pretty well locked up in the storehouses," and that they had to "get them out" where they could be seen and used. This, he said, "we are going to accomplish through the roads we hope to have and the development work at camping places which we hope to secure."[34]

In the meantime, Carhart was working out "the system of camps" and was in the process of writing a sixty-four page report which he called a *General Working Plan, Recreational Development of the San Isabel National Forest, Colorado,* complete with attached maps of the locality.[35] Beginning in 1919 with this and other reports, articles and letters, Carhart's writings seemed to pyramid. A brief review of the San Isabel plan may be worthwhile.

In drafting the San Isabel National Forest Recreation Plan, Carhart said that his purpose was to embody in a convenient form the working plan for recreational development "as a matter of record." Sure of his ground he wrote further that:

> This larger plan is the first great regional plan that has been undertaken anywhere in the National Forests and it is bound to be a model for other like plans that will inevitably follow. . . .[36]

Perhaps by reason of hindsight it is easy to perceive the wisdom of what Carhart went on to say about large scale planning:

> The tendency is . . . to start with detail. It is more easily planned for, is more evident in its need and more easily grasped in its import. It is necessary [however] to start the plan for a Forest or large region of the Forest on a large scale in order that detail will not crowd out the big plan. . . .[37]

The 1919 San Isabel plan was rewritten and expanded by Carhart in 1920. The nature of his revision will be described later.

Also in the year 1919 when he became a truly itinerant Recreation Engineer, Carhart made a survey of the Superior National Forest in Minnesota. He travelled through the country now called the Boundary Waters Canoe Area by canoe, as did the early French *voyageurs* and *coureurs de bois*.[38] On this trip he made observations, and took photographs and extensive notes for the Forest Service. He embodied his findings in a *Preliminary Report* of 117 pages, with eighty-five pages of lively text and thirty-two magnificent photographs, carefully identified.[39] The copy of the report retained in the Carhart papers contained a later insertion which read as follows:

> This is the author's copy of the recreation plan for the Superior National Forest in Minnesota. This was the basic plan, a first step, toward the establishment of the famous Quetico-Superior roadless areas on both sides of the United States-Canada International Boundary. It is in the Quetico-Superior that most of the issues re-

garding the establishment of the "Wilderness Type" of public property were fought out.[40]

The report itself might warrant complete reproduction here because it stated so well Carhart's position, but limitations of space permit reference to only some of the salient points. Under the title "Preservation,"[41] Carhart asserted that the "first logical step" in any work of this type is to

> plan for preservation and protection of all of those things that are of values great enough to sacrifice a certain amount of economic return so there may be a greater total return from the aesthetic qualities.

This step was discussed severally under such additional headings as Game, Timber, Portage, and Ownership. He stressed the point that:

> It cannot be emphasized too strongly nor too repeatedly that immediate steps should be taken towards the right protection of all these points discussed. . . .

That the plan was practical and yet provided for wilderness protection through the exclusion of roads in the Forest, was shown under a section headed "Accessibility."[42] Attention is called here to the year in which these proposals were made—1919. Carhart remarked:

> Suffice it to say that good auto roads lead to the edge of this plan at many points, that railways touch the border in such a manner that they can carry much traffic to the boarders of the [planned area].

Aware of the limitations of this preliminary study, Carhart noted under a section headed "Recommendations for Study,"[43] that there was but one other National Forest in the District that

> has so many factors present combining to make the unit Forest a desirable recreational development and that Forest is now being studied and developed along those lines best suited. It is the San Isabel. . . .

He then added: "This plan does not take rank with the mere placing of camp sites. It goes far beyond that." Carhart further explained that in order to get "full return" from the Forest areas, in order to "correlate uses" so there will be no interference resulting in loss to the nation, and in order that

> This National Forest shall have its development based on sound foundations of a size commensurate with the importance of its recreational possibilities, *it is imperative that the planning reach what may be known for want of a better term as Forest Regional Planning* [italics supplied]. This is based on a regional-type area which has like attributes throughout its reaches.[44]

During 1921 Carhart revised this report as later discussion will show. The 1921 revision benefited by what Carhart called a "period of seasoning and maturing," and a return trip to the Superior National Forest.[45]

November, 1919, brought another article by the Recreation Engineer exalting the wonders of nature, and "selling" the recreational attractions of the forest. He pointed out that men in the field were often vague in their estimates of scenic attractions which they had come to take for granted, that they had lost sight of the many delightful, less magnificent places that would appeal to the person who had been confined to the city streets. He wondered how many men in close touch with nature had stopped during their field work to appreciate the landscape thoroughly. Carhart's penchant to become poetic was illustrated by his statement:

> Cloud banks above peaks one day in a way you never saw before, giving the mountain pinnacles a fluffy crown

> that whips and swirls with wind. Or snow blows on the high range and feathers the edges of the ridges. Perhaps the nightfall brings brilliant lightings in the west of the cloud banks above a range, and the whole tone scale between flaming orange and deepest mauve is run before the night finally draws the curtain of darkness. All these nature moods are a part of the landscape and a part that can be well studied and appreciated. . . .[46]

These early writings reveal Carhart's profound love for the wilderness and illustrate his sincerity in wanting to preserve it for mankind. In a romantic vein, he continued:

> Then don't look always for the smashing, the awe inspiring, the superlative, but look more for the nature tales that are everywhere laid before your eyes. If a seeker of play and rest comes to your district, don't run him to the edge of the most overwhelming outlook you have and then say "this is all" but point out the ferns, the little alpine phlox that clings to the high country meadows, show him where a squirrel has stored his hoard or point the way to some cozy little gulch where a tinkling fall of water will call and laugh to the visitor and the trees will hold out sheltering and welcoming limbs. . . .[47]

Without being didactic, Carhart was attempting to teach landscape appreciation to the foresters in much the same way that music students are taught to understand music. In masculine terms he urged in his summation:

> Get a good draft working in your nostrils, smell the hot sun on the pine needles, the tangy odor of the sage, the scent of the fire weed in full bloom. . . . Get off your ear muffs and hear the call of the jay, the splash of the jumping trout, the roar of a water fall. Brush the dust of habit away from your eyes and see the lacery of the pine needles, the vivid coloring of the cliff or wild flower,

> the majesty of the peaks. In other words take stock of the world in which you live. . . .[48]

Clearly, Carhart as a landscape architect brought with him to the Forest Service an attitude toward nature, the forests and wildlife which was to give birth to a management plan that ultimately helped, as will be demonstrated, to shape the National Wilderness Preservation System embodied in the Wilderness Act of 1964.[49]

On the basis of the Carhart-Sherman correspondence and the related documents thus far cited, certain conclusions may be formulated: Carhart was the first peripatetic planner of forest recreation in the National Forests in District 2. His plans were far-reaching in scope and implication. The San Isabel National Forest of Colorado appears to be the first Forest to receive the benefit of planned development of the unit forest by a competent, professional landscape architect. Colorado can claim this distinction in Forest recreation with pride.

CHAPTER II

TAKE ONE GIANT STEP FOR MANKIND

This chapter will describe recreational developments and wilderness preservation measures taken in our National Forests during the period 1919-1920. Emphasis will be placed on how the wilderness concept emerged through the early efforts to apply landscape architectural principles in areas of our National Forests selected for public convenience and recreation, and how the first application of the new concept was a *fait accompli* by 1919.

First De Facto Application of the Wilderness Concept at Trappers Lake, Colorado (1919)

The year 1919 was indeed a banner one for the Forest Service. In the summer of that year, Arthur H. Carhart was assigned to make a survey of the Trappers Lake area in the White River National Forest of Colorado. The purpose of the survey was to plot several hundred summer home sites on the lake shore and to plan a "through" road around the lake.

During July, 1919, operating out of what was then Scott Teague's camp located at the outlet of Trappers Lake, Carhart laid survey lines around the lake according to his instructions. In relating the account of what occurred at Trappers Lake, Carhart invariably includes the names of Paul J. Rainey and William McFadden. It seems that Rainey and McFadden were guests of Scott Teague at the lake, in July, 1919, so Carhart had a chance to meet them there. After a series of spirited talks together, Rainey and McFadden persuaded Carhart that the Forest Service should keep Trappers Lake in a wildland condition.[1] Carhart, in turn, then translated the idea into a functional plan through his landscape architectural training and his basic orientation toward nature and the unspoiled wilderness.

Upon his return to the district office in Denver, Carhart furnished his immediate supervisor, Carl J. Stahl, not only with the completed surveys but with the unsolicited comment that he opposed the plan of making homesites on the lake shore. This was not just a gratuitous aside, but Carhart's way of opposing further "improvement" where natural landscape would suffer. After some discussion, Stahl agreed with him that the Trappers Lake area should remain roadless and that the many applications for homesite permits around the Lake should not be honored. *This was an unprecedented step in Forest Service history*.

A 1915 law made it possible to obtain long term leases and permit construction of summer home sites in the National Forests for "Special Use."[2] By 1919 the backlog of applications for such sites had begun to plague the district office in Denver. Some of the men in the Forest Service were alarmed at the rate the back country was vanishing. To men like Stahl, Carhart's opposition to developing the Trappers Lake area merited further study and discussion with others in the Service who had similar problems. One such man was Aldo Leopold, then Assistant Forester of District 3, located in Albuquerque, New Mexico, who after hearing Stahl tell about the policy employed at Trappers Lake in District 2, became interested and wanted more information about it. Accordingly, Stahl arranged for Leopold and Carhart to hold a conference. Leopold visited the Denver District office on December 6, 1919, and met Carhart there. Following the day-long discussion, Leopold requested Carhart to reduce to writing some of the salient points which had been covered. What was to be simply a "Memorandum for Mr. Leopold, District 3," has become an historic document.[3]

A chain of events dating from 1919 to 1964 developed into what became known as the wilderness preservation movement. This movement culminated in 1964 with the passage of the Wilderness Act, as mentioned above, an achievement in law which made possible the program Carhart advocated in 1919.

Scrutinized from the perspective of over half a century, the full import of the document can be realized. It will be demonstrated that this memorandum reflected Jeffersonian democratic principles; it was a "radical" document because it ran contrary to accepted Forest Service policy; it was a "constitutional" document because it would "promote the general welfare, and secure the blessings of liberty to ourselves and our posterity," guaranteed to all the people.[4]

Because it is so pertinent to this study, much of the four-page memorandum sent *to* Assistant Forester Leopold in 1919 is given in Carhart's words as follows:

> This memorandum is to supplement some conversation between myself and Mr. Leopold, which happened on December 6th.
>
> There are no notes available in this office on this question, so it is thought best to incorporate in this form some observation relative to the problem discussed. The problem spoken of in this conversation was, how far

> shall the Forest Service carry or allow to be carried man-made improvements in scenic territories, and whether there is not a definite point where all such developments, with the exception of perhaps lines of travel and necessary sign boards, shall stop. The Forest Service, it seems to me, is obligated to make the greatest return from the total forests to the people of the Nation that is possible. This, the Service has endeavored to do in the case of timber, utilization, grazing, watershed protection and other activities. There is, however, a great wealth of recreational facilities and scenic values within the Forests, which have not been so utilized and at the present time the Service is face to face with a question of big policies, big plans, and big utilization for these values and areas.[5]

The next paragraph alluded to the "gospel of efficiency," the placing of dollar values on forest resources, which failed to assess other intangible but just as real values:

> Returns from the Forests cannot be counted in total in terms of dollars and cents in the case of the aesthetic qualities within the Forests, and it is therefore rather difficult to judge just how this greater utilization can best be accomplished. . . . It is, therefore, a concrete cash argument for utilization of scenic areas for the purpose of picnic grounds, summer homes, etc., as opposed to a preservation of the grounds in a natural state because of scenic qualities.[6]

Carhart then called attention to a current and "very hot" issue, that of government acquisition by purchase of land which had fallen over the years into private hands. The government has spent many millions of dollars since 1919 to regain such land,[7] and even in 1972, as this study is being readied for the press, additional land purchase negotiations between the government and private interests are in progress. Carhart's 1919 comments, therefore, remain pertinent:

> There enters in here a feature which has been long recognized by landscape architects and city planners, which has not come to the attention of the general public or men of other professions. . . . There are scenic values and recreational areas . . . which were never intended for private holdings. . . . In some areas . . . immense sums of money have been paid by municipalities, counties, and states, to secure shore lines on lakes or rivers, which had passed from under the control of the general public, and were held by individuals. . . .[8]

At this point he hammered at the fact that Americans no longer possessed "a chosen country, with room enough for our descendants to the hundredth and thousandth generation."[9] Carhart continued:

> There is a limit to the number of lands of shore line on the lakes; there is a limit to the number of lakes in existence; there is a limit to the mountainous areas of the world, and . . . there are portions of natural scenic beauty which are God made, and . . . which of a right should be the property of all people.
>
> There are . . . places in which the title is still vested . . . in the people of the Nation. If these areas are allowed to go into the hands of private individuals, or if they are even built on for summer home purposes, the use is in the measure restricted to individuals or a group. . . . The presence of a population, the monopolization of the scenery by those people living in those situations, react against the visitor in such a way that fullest return of scenic and aesthetic values is not realized . . . In Colorado . . . the great canon [sic] of the Big Thompson represents the case where private holdings defeat the beauties of the canon [sic]. . . . For me the aesthetic value . . . has been reduced not less than eighty percent. . . .[10]

With the vision of a statesman concerned for the interests

of future generations, Carhart claimed that forest treasures should be preserved and protected from the marring features of man-made structures, and that:

> These areas can never be restored to the original condition after man has invaded them, and the great value lying as it does in natural scenic beauty should be available, not for the small group, but for the greatest population. Time will come when these scenic spots, where nature has been allowed to remain unmarred, will be some of the most highly prized scenic features of the country. . . .[11]

The Forest Service should adopt a broad, farseeing attitude, he recommended, to meet the demands of the future, by doing all in its power to preserve these areas. Otherwise, he warned, "severe criticism will some day be meted out by the collective owners of this territory," meaning, of course, every United States citizen.

Then the memorandum took on the aspects of a "zoning" plan. "There are," Carhart noted, "other areas which are not necessarily superlative, but which should be preserved on this same basis." He advanced the point that:

> It is probable that great areas of *medium scenic*[12] [italics supplied] countries shall be preserved without any intrusion of civilization in order that there shall always be some great area to which the lover of the outdoors can turn without being confronted by a settlers cabin, country store, telephone pole, or other sign of frontier civilization. . . . In some individuals this desire for undeveloped country is especially marked. . . . Arctic Explorers . . . endure great hardships in these trips. . . . Our late ExPresident [Theodore] Roosevelt, Paul J. Rainey, and others, show this desire. . . . A big percentage of people of the United States have this craving . . . to a less marked extent. . . .[13]

The next paragraph contained the elements underlying the National Wilderness Preservation System. Carhart declared:

> I have jotted down *four different types of areas* [italics supplied], which should not contain summer homes, perhaps no camp sites, and other like developments. First of these is the superlative area; the second is the area unsuited for any camp and summer home development, such as the high ridge of a mountain range;third is the area which should be preserved for the group rather than the individual, such as lake shores, stream banks, or such a natural feature as medicinal springs; fourth group would include areas not in these three groups, but which represent those God made and of the greatest use for preservation of any owned by the Government. *There is no question in my mind but what there is a definite point in different types of country where man made structures should be stopped* [italics supplied].[14]

The remainder of the memorandum was devoted to suggesting alternative plans aimed at defining the stopping point and the areas to be preserved. Carhart believed that the whole responsibility could be taken by the Forest Service; or the Forest Service might ask the State to appoint an Art Commission; or a committee named by the National Society, formed to study rural planning and landscape architecture, might cooperate with the Service nationwide. While recognizing that the Service would probably have to take the entire initiative in the matter "immediately," the Recreation Engineer remarked that *"the question of how best to do this is perhaps the real question, rather than shall it be done* [italics supplied]."[15]

Here was a concept that was new to the world. When Carhart took up this crusade for wilderness preservation in the latter part of 1919 he faced formidable obstacles. His memorandum of December 10, 1919, the *first written word* concerning action by the United States Forest Service to preserve wilderness areas, became among other things the basis for a handbook written in 1961 and intended for land-use planners, managers and executives, committee and commission members, conservation leaders, and all who faced problems of wildland management.[16] In the handbook's foreword, written by the late Howard Zahniser, Executive Secretary of The Wilderness Society, the Editor of *The Living Wilderness*, Zahniser noted that though other conservationists advocated the designation of certain areas for preservation and protection in their natural condition, "Carhart looks beyond" the essential designations to "inclusive zoning plans" that would not only protect the remaining true wilderness but also would accommodate the demands that threatened the wilderness and strained the quality of wildness in all areas where it persisted.[17] Zahniser's comments in 1961 could have been applied to the 1919 memorandum with equal appropriateness.

Factors Affecting Support of the New Policy by Immediate Supervisors (1920)

Actually what Carhart advocated in 1919 was not so complicated as it was difficult to sell to his superiors. There were to be many disappointing episodes in the life of the "good and enthusiastic fellow" between the time he wrote the Memorandum for Mr. Leopold, District 3, and his 1961 authorship of *Planning for America's Wildlands.* A look at some of these episodes in 1920 would be pertinent.

At the request of Carl J. Stahl, Carhart's immediate supervisor, Carhart prepared a six-page memorandum[18] in which he reiterated substantially the plans outlined in the memorandum for Leopold, but with specific emphasis given to the plans for preserving Trappers Lake. Though repetitious, it is quoted here to illustrate the various steps Carhart took to introduce the new concept to the Forest Service. Carhart declared:

> There are a number of places with scenic values of such great worth that they are rightfully property of all people. They should be preserved for all time for the people of the Nation and the world. Trappers Lake is unquestionably a candidate for that classification. . . . If Trappers Lake is in or anywhere near in the class of superlatives, it should not have any cabins or hotels intruding in the lake basin. . . .[19]

He then pointed out how individuals naturally desired to "help themselves" to the best home sites they could obtain regardless of others, and how "this very greed undirected indirectly defeats its own purpose" by "destroying the very qualities" for which the individual located on the shore of the lake.[20] His next comment was most thought provoking:

> Human intellects and their perceptive powers are unable to withstand climaxes which are sustained. It is for this reason good plays, good music or good books bring one to a climax and then lead either to a quick logical conclusion or pass through a transitional stage to another climax.[21]

In Carhart's opinion, Trappers Lake was such a "smashing climax" that "if it were continually in view . . . the very intensity of it would make it displeasing to the individual." He pointed out that there was "no theory in this, it is proven," and that he had "experienced this reaction from sustained climax on Trappers Lake."[22] Expanding on the ideas found in the memorandum for Leopold and employing somewhat different language, Carhart claimed that the Forest Service could best return to the whole nation the existing beauty of Trappers Lake through a proper presentation of its scenic values.[23] His recommendation embodied a plan which would place summer homes "blocks from but within easy trail distance" of the lake, or a distance of less than half a mile, and reserve the whole lake area for the general use and enjoyment of the entire nation, "the nearby summer home people included."[24] This lake, he wrote, was one "comparatively untouched, the shores of which the Forest Service controls and can be wholly directed in development." Showing his awareness of the philosophy under which the Forest Service was operating at that time he closed by saying:

> This memorandum is submitted as a statement of my conclusions and to receive either approval or rejection before I do any actual work on [the] plan. I think the problem of sufficient magnitude and future importance that I wish to definitely place myself on record as favoring the type of development here suggested for the present situation, whatever type of plan may later be adopted.[25]

The approval of the plan to preserve Trappers Lake was not won by the single act of convincing Carl J. Stahl of the desirability of following such a course; there were other officials whose consent was needed. Those officials were Fred Morrell, Assistant District Forester, and A. S. Peck, District Forester. To convince them, Carhart prepared an eleven-page memorandum elaborating still further the plan for Trappers Lake.[26] Incidentally, at each level of authority in the chain of command Carhart was obliged to recapitulate and strengthen his argument for wilderness preservation, because the concept was new. A few highlights from his memorandum will illustrate how he emphasized the new approach to Forest management:

> The policy of recognizing the probability of such scenic units as Trappers Lake becoming so important as recreation grounds for universal use that . . . there has been suggested a plan to exclude all man made buildings with perhaps the exception of one publicly owned building such as the Fish Hatchery from the immediate lake basin. This plan has been approved on the basis of the

> general policy of the District towards scenic values of this magnitude. . . .[27]

Since camping would "produce the same effect as building summer homes," a "good large public camp" should be developed "along the stream at the outlet of the lake," and should be "entirely out of the lake picture and partially screened from the road."[28] The document then outlined developments recommended for the surrounding smaller lakes and streams as well as the relocation and improvement of certain of the existing "shacks" belonging to Teague:

> All architecture (if one can apply such a term to the shack-like tent houses in this camp) is of the poorest type. There should be here the best sort of design and no other construction should be allowed.[29]

Carhart continued to describe the camp conditions, particularly those aspects affecting vitally all the people down river who depended then as now on Trappers Lake for their domestic water supply. The former Army Sanitary Corps Officer recorded these deplorable details:

> The worst condition in the camp was with reference to the provision for human offal. The privies supplied were indescribable. There was no attempt made to keep them flyproof nor adequately house the seats. The construction was a mere board with holes in it placed over a pit and around this was a structure made of poles and gunny sacking with some building paper for the roof and sacking for a door. One of these dilapidated things was designed to serve the entire camp. As a result many of the men took to the woods. At one point I counted at one time eighteen stools of human feces within less than 150 feet of the lake and so situated that they would have been washed directly into the lake by a hard rain fall. The water of the lake and outlet stream is used for domestic purposes. The guests of the camp could not be

> blamed for using the great outdoors when the privy supplied was so filthy and inadequate. A flyproof privy of sufficient size to accommodate the guests of either sex should be built at a suitable place where there will be no chance of seepage draining to [the] water supply. . . .[30]

That Carhart was aware of the fact that he was "rocking the boat," as it were, was implicit in his summary remarks. Here he repeated his understanding that "the present policy" would disgruntle applicants for permits on the edge of Trappers Lake.[31]

A note from Carhart accompanying the memorandum explained that the "particular case was approved by Mr. Morrell and Mr. Stahl as outlined by this" memorandum and the note also requested Peck's comment.[32] The note and memorandum passed through Morrell's hands before being sent to Peck. Morrell added and initialed the following handwritten comment:

> I think Mr. Carhart has unconsciously overstated my agreement. I felt that homes should be always screened from the lake, but not certainly out of sight so that the dweller could not get a view except by leaving his premises. Cannot qualify as having an opinion of much value, but am sure I should not put them back as far as Carhart would.[33]

District Forester Peck penned and initialed the following note to Carhart:

> I fully agree that features of superlative interest belong to all the people & should be protected from selfish individual use. We have a real duty in this regard. I cannot say just how absolute we should make our rule re— Trappers' Lake as I haven't seen it, but feel we should take the safest course, & *am willing to concur in your plan tentatively* [italics supplied].[34]

The apparent reluctance to accept new ideas and to resist change on the part of some of the officials of the Forest Service is mitigated by the fact that they were obligated to carry out policy dictated by higher authority. Moreover, National Forests, though created primarily for timber and watershed protection, were contemporaneously being advertised in official Forest Service publications as ideal for locating a *waterfront* summer home. For example, the Superior National Forest extending southward from the international boundary to within a mile of Lake Superior and about one hundred and ten miles wide made this offer:

> Sites for summer homes can be leased for a term of years at an annual rental of from $10 to $25. The Superior Forest contains an unlimited number of such sites, many of them of unusual attractiveness. A few lots have already been laid out on the east shore of White Iron Lake, 5 miles east of Ely and [can be] reached by two automobile roads. The lots are 2 miles up the lake, and each one has a water frontage. The lake is large enough for fair-sized power boats, and there are a number of bathing beaches. Fishing is excellent, and trips may be made to other nearby waters where the finny tribe is plentiful.[35]

Not only were tourists with automobiles accommodated, but those who could reach the Forest by railroad were welcomed. Fine summer-home sites could be had along shores of the lakes reached by the Duluth and Northern Minnesota Railway in Cook County. The pamphlet promised that although "no lots have been laid out in this locality . . . applications will receive prompt attention." The lake region north of Grand Marais "will no doubt be a mecca for people in search of ideal summer-home sites," the pamphlet boasted, particularly since there was an "automobile road now being built into that region." Then a final commitment:

> Many other sites along the shores of the inland lakes may appeal to those who wish to get out of sight and sound of civilization, and the Forest Service will act promptly upon application for sites in any portion of the Forest.[36]

If this was the policy for the Superior National Forest, how could the White River National Forest withhold *any portion* of the Forest from summer home construction? How long could applicants be made to wait for home sites around Trappers Lake?

Additional information about the Trappers Lake area will be presented later in this study. That chapter will include highlights in the early history of the area, from the arrival of the first white man in the nineteenth century, and will trace its subsequent development to date. But now it is necessary to document some further steps taken to gain support for National Forest recreation during 1920.

CHAPTER III

JUST FOR THE FUN OF IT

This chapter will emphasize further developments in connection with National Forest recreation during 1920, and describe the official policy toward such development by the Washington office of the Forest Service. It will include excerpts from the first extensive report on recreation sent from the Denver office of the Service to Washington, and discuss the factors which were believed to have precipitated the unprecedented demand for National Forest recreation following World War I. Evidence will be presented to show that 1920 brought a somewhat ambivalent recognition of recreational development as a "major activity" of the Forest Service. In addition, there will be a review of pertinent portions of A. H. Carhart's writings in that year, including articles published in a nationally distributed magazine.

Further Developments in Forest Recreation (1920)

Carhart kept Assistant Forester Sherman in Washington apprised of developments in Forest recreation in District 2 largely through personal correspondence. In return, Sherman was a source of inspiration to Carhart. "You have every reason to feel jubilant," wrote Sherman from Washington in March 1920, "over what you have accomplished in launching the recreation associations of the San Isabel. To say that I am more than delighted is putting it mildly."[1] In another letter Sherman remarked:

> Your letter of September 28 [1920] is extremely interesting both in its showing of actual accomplishment and in its indication of the practically unlimited possibilities for recreational development in the National Forests. At present this work is in the pioneer stage and pioneer development is . . . subject to all of the disappointments and delays which you have experienced. . . . While I do not desire to add to your heavy burden of work, I will appreciate other reports from time to time as the opportunity to prepare them presents itself.[2]

Within two weeks, Sherman requested the District Forester at Denver to submit a report on recreational needs and problems in District 2. The resultant forty-eight page summary prepared by Carhart and signed by the District Forester,[3] was *the first extensive report on the subject* to be sent from District 2 to Washington; it was to be used as a means of putting at the Forester's disposal "all the information and arguments we can think of to strengthen the case which you are proposing to present to Congress."[4]

The Carhart summary, which might be called an abbreviated "ORRRC" report, maintained that ten years earlier, recreation in the Forests was a minor use incidental to other uses, but that "today it stands as the most direct and personal use made by people who utilize the Forests." An attempt was made to itemize the etiology of the sudden and unprecedented demand for development and policies to meet the recreational needs. Given among the factors contributing to the "almost phenomenal rush of a great mass of the public to the Forests" seeking recreation were the following six items:

1. The War Factor[5]

The Army introduced a large number of the male population of the country to outdoor life and physical exercise in the open. It was reasoned that once the taste for outdoor life was acquired, it would be hard to lose, and a yearning for a few days each year in camp would remain throughout life, especially with those who saw military service. They in turn would take with them friends and relatives who through direct association would acquire a taste for camping, thus increasing the number represented in this group. The war, with the intense training periods and grueling work, taught the Nation, as nothing else would, that there must be a time for play if the highest efficiency was to be attained. Obliged to remain at home rather than tour European lands, the American touring public had become acquainted with the magnificent play areas in the National Forests.

2. Disappearing Local Camping Areas[6]

With the growth of cities and the swelling of suburbia the suitable camping areas remaining were few and small. The areas in extent and type desired by the campers could be found only in the National Forests.

3. Increase of Wealth among Large Bodies of Citizens[7]

Many persons no longer found it necessary to stay with business the entire year to make ends meet and so journeyed to the National Forests on vacation.

4. The slogan "See America First" helped to generate pride in what America had to offer.[8]

5. Automobiles[9]

The total number of automobiles produced in the country by 1920 had increased beyond anything anticipated a few years earlier, and "without the universal ownership of the automobile that has come the recreational use of the National Forest would be far below its present [1920] volume."

6. Good Roads

The establishment of great trunk-line roads crossing many states and all leading to National Forest territory had been essential.

In conclusion, it was pointed out that the six factors itemized above, combined with others, resulted in the Forest Service in District 2 "now facing a great use of the Forests not present a short time ago, and which cannot be disregarded because of its importance in the National Life."[10]

Before considering further this significant first report on recreation, an attempt will be made to compare some of its observations and comments with recent literature on the subject. A summary view of the period, as seen in historical perspective by William E. Leuchtenburg in 1928, lent support to Carhart's treatise on recreation, furnished important statistical data, and illustrated the accuracy of Carhart's early grasp of the prominent position played by the automobile in the "second industrial revolution."[11] Indeed, the automobile was a prime factor in the rapidly changing economic and social structure in the United States; it had a profound effect on recreation in the National Forests.

Leuchtenburg concluded that by the year 1914 the "task of industrialization" in the United States had been essentially completed, and that "the livery stable had been torn down to make way for the filling station."[12] In 1909 Taft rode to the Capitol inauguration in a horse drawn carriage; in 1913 Wilson traveled in an automobile.[13]

A 1964 newspaper article noted that the automobile "came of age" in 1914, just half a century ago.[14] Twenty-one years earlier the Duryea brothers drove the nation's first workable gas buggy on the streets of Springfield, Massachusetts—the same year Frederick Jackson Turner pronounced his frontier thesis, namely 1893. By 1914 the gasoline-fueled internal combustion vehicle had become a highly sophisticated machine for its day, "admirably suited to the rutted dirt roads" of America's countryside. The gas buggy had reached its majority and its future seemed boundless. In 1914:

> Nearly 60,000 new cars and trucks were sold in America. . . . By 1916, this figure would be more than doubled, leading ultimately to 8 million vehicle years such as 1963 and 1964.[15]

The new automobile industry helped make the prosperity of the Roaring Twenties possible; its development in a single generation was "the greatest achievement of modern technology." Automobile production gave the whole economy a tremendous boost. In 1900, the annual output was 4,000 cars; by 1929, 4,800,000 were produced yearly; and, in the latter year, more than 26 million automobiles and trucks were using American highways.[16] Benefiting from the highest standard of living any people had ever known, the American of the post-World War I period reaped the harvest of industrial progress that followed the Civil War. Per capita income in the nation climbed from $480 in 1900 to $681 in 1929, while the number of hours of work dropped. Leuchtenburg has pointed out that:

> In 1923 United States Steel abandoned the twelve-hour day and put its Gary Plant on an eight-hour shift; in 1926 Henry Ford instituted the five-day week, while International Harvester announced the electrifying innovation of a two-week annual vacation with pay for its employees. . . .[17]

In 1914 there were almost no good roads outside of the Eastern section of the nation; a cross-country trip was a bold adventure. Conditions which may sound somewhat unreal to young Americans are graphically described by Leuchtenburg:

> . . . Automobiles sank to their hubs in gumbo muds; travelers crossing Iowa were often forced to wait sev-

> eral days until the roads dried before moving onto the next town. . . .

To stimulate road-building, the Federal-Aid Road Act of 1916 made federal funds available to states on a matching basis; as a result, ambitious road-building programs were launched all over the country.[18] Since so many Americans then owned a car, they could drive into the countryside or to the next town. "For the first time," it should be emphasized, "they saw America, taking trips to distant campsites or historic shrines. . . ."[19]

Returning now to Carhart's 1920 report, it should be mentioned that he referred again to Trappers Lake and the fact that no less than a score of people had applied for summer home sites near it. Lots laid out by the regular forest force had not been used, he pointed out, because of conflict with the District plans and policies especially established for Trappers Lake. He then gave the Chief Forester substantially the same information, previously quoted, about the need to avoid doing irreparable damage to the Trappers Lake area.[20] Carhart's report asserted "it has been necessary to withhold all areas for which applications have been made," and meanwhile, obtain an appropriation which would provide for an adequate and properly trained field force to satisfy the demand for several hundred lots without dissipating any of the beauty found there.[21] His appeal was thus clear and specific.

Later in the report, the same theme was repeated. He declared that it was easy to give the people the locations they wanted, but, he added, "it will ruin any opportunity for a complete and adequate artistic development of this lake." To hasten the work and to eliminate "the rather caustic criticism of our delay," and "as early as possible put this land into good shape for the particular use to which it is so well fitted—recreation," he suggested an allotment "for study and direction of development here of not less than $600 during the fiscal year of 1922."[22] The report then described specific proposals for the construction of trails leading to and from the Trappers Lake basin, for which amounts varying from $700 to $1,000 were requested.[23] As to the number of men needed to handle the work outlined, the report stated:

> The estimate of the number of Recreation Engineers for this District, during the fiscal year of 1922, is then five besides the present Recreation Engineer and an absolute minimum of three besides Mr. Carhart.[24]

That the report "only inadequately" covered the recreation situation in District 2 was acknowledged, as well as the fact that it was already far ahead of the developments made for implementing it. The report ended with a statement which was typical of the urgency felt by Carhart:

> There is a big National need in this caring for recreation in the National Forests, and planning should be started now on big broad lines, so the Nation may realize a just and reasonable return from this use of Forest lands. This can only be done with good plans for a foundation and the necessary funds to make those plans into functioning facts.[25]

In addition to official reports for the Forest Service, Carhart prepared articles which appeared in various publications. A few of his early illustrated writings, those dealing specifically with his beliefs in wilderness preservation and forest recreation, merit notice.[26]

The May, 1920, issue of *American Forestry*, the magazine of the American Forestry Association, contained the first of a series of such articles. The item titled "Recreation in the Forests" was accompanied by ten illustrations.[27] The theme was the necessity of recreation to human life. "An individual cannot concentrate on one thing continuously," he declared, "and do the best work." In fact, Carhart asserted:

> Recreation in the open is of the finest grade. The moral benefits are all positive. The individual with any soul cannot live long in the presence of towering mountains or sweeping plains without getting a little of the high moral standard of Nature infused into his being. . . . With eyes opened, the great story of the Earth's forming the history of a tree, the life of a flower or the activities of some small animal will all unfold themselves to the recreationist. . . .[28]

Then he mentioned the shrinking opportunities for vacationing in virgin territory:

> A few years ago by going a small distance, camping places, where nature was still supreme, could be found. But today, with man land-hungry, these places are fast disappearing. Economic use of land for the production of crops changes the face of the landscape and there remains little of the free natural country for which the vacationist longs. *This movement of subduing nature could continue to a point where there would not be left any lands where one might see nature supreme* [italics supplied]. . . .[29]

Carhart thus early recognized the problem of the vanishing wilderness—and he had a concrete solution, a constructive plan for management which he endeavored to persuade his fellows to implement. He opposed grazing, mining and power development where there would be destruction of natural beauty through what he termed misguided enterprise. Places in the forest that would not feed one hungry steer would be best left to several people to enjoy by a summer's residence. Furthermore, he believed that no one would care to build a summer home that "looks on a hillside pitted with prospect holes." And why, he asked, try to develop water power from a dainty little fall incapable of turning a wheel sufficient in size to merit destruction of the fall? Public health, he maintained, should stand before every other community consideration, not just bodily condition, but mental health as well. He predicted that,

> Recreation can become one of the greatest returns from the forests of our country. And because it is a human use, producing mental and physical health, the recreational use of forest land will always take place among the highest of all uses.[30]

Carhart was advocating the multiple use principle,[31] it should be kept in mind, and not the program of the purist who would not suffer a twig to be touched. The following remark illustrated his position on that point:

". . . And it is foolish not to realize on this great utility of the forests," he wrote, "for it is a return added to the economic uses now established without any detraction from their value." He believed that while the recreation feature could not be measured and tabulated as the other features having an established market where monetary figures were quoted,

> the recreation return from forest lands will annually amount to many million dollars and the return in good health, better, keener thinking and enjoyment of the aesthetic qualities found in the forest will add wealth to the nation that cannot be accurately estimated. . . .[32]

The article closed by pointing out that the Forest Service had recently taken a step in the right direction by employing trained landscape architects to perform the duties of a recreational engineer. No mention was made, however, of his personal role as the first and only such landscape architect. In a final optimistic word, Carhart observed that "the present is bright" and "the future holds good promise for this great forest utility."[33]

Apparently the staff at the American Forestry Association was pleased by Carhart's article, for in the issue of the following September two of his articles appeared under the heading, "The Department of Forest Recreation." It preceded an announcement set in bold type, and circumscribed with a heavy black border, too lengthy to quote in its entirety, although pertinent excerpts merit reproduction here.

> ANNOUNCING THE DEPARTMENT OF FOREST RECREATION
>
> New ideas and new methods develop to meet new or changing conditions. The first public appearance of a new publication or the premier greeting of a new department of an established magazine heralds some new situation or a condition which did not exist before or one which has grown to such size as to merit greater recognition. In this issue of "American Forestry" the department devoted to the recreational use of forest areas salutes all readers and thus signalizes a greater use of our forests as play areas and a new service for the lovers of the out-of-doors.
>
> Recreation . . . on forest lands . . is no new thing. But the universal use of forests for recreation by the people of the United States has so recently developed to national importance it may be truly said that the activity is a newcomer to the group of uses existing on American forest lands.[34]

The new department was created because information and general knowledge of the opportunity for play and outdoor life in the forest regions had not "kept pace with the new popular recreational movement," it was alleged. The editors of the magazine planned to publish information which would

> help build up the patriotic spirit of the country through directing citizens of the land to the great silent woods, the snow crowned peaks or the deep canyons where they may come to "Know America," and knowing her in all her marvelous examples of scenic beauty will come to

> love the "—rock and rills,—woods and templed hills" of their home land with a fervor which will brook no policy or movement which threatens the peace of the land or its institutions.[35]

After the introduction, prospective vacationers were furnished information in that issue upon which to plan a trip to an enticing National Forest.[36] Since the magazine was distributed nationally, the peculiar attractions of many of the nation's Forests were publicized widely. There were in 1920, scattered in twenty-four states, one hundred fifty-three National Forests containing 155 million acres of "unbeatable" vacation grounds.

In Carhart's article which immediately followed the announcement of the creation of the new department, he reminded his readers that "each person in the entire Nation owns equal share" in the National Forests:

> They are yours to use to the fullest and in any way consistent with the greatest good for all. . . . The entire system of forests is yours and mine to use. . . . There are one or two simple rules to follow . . . Be very careful with fire. . . . Be clean in camp and practice good sanitation. . . . Are not those simple enough for a child to understand?[37]

As a companion article, Carhart dealt with "Auto Camp Conveniences." He noted that with the advent of the automobile Americans "turned gypsy" and were searching for "camps."[38] Then he attempted to describe the early camps to be found in the nation, using as illustrations photographs taken on the Pueblo, Colorado, Municipal Camp Ground, located in Squirrel Creek Canyon on the San Isabel National Forest. "This area of 117 acres," Carhart said, "has been developed during the early summer of 1919 so it can comfortably accommodate about 100 people at one time."[39] Camps, he stressed, were "needed in many places now," and the need was "due to increase greatly in the future."[40]

In the October issue of *American Forestry*, Carhart pointed out that America was "recreation hungry." He dramatized the role of the automobile in American life, particularly its impact on recreation. "Ten years ago," he wrote, "a pack trip in the mountains" was a hardship "braved only by bolder spirits," but the taste for the outdoors had so developed that even girls and women clad in "sensible khaki outflts" were almost as generally present as were men in the vacation camp. A decade earlier, auto trips of a thousand miles had been material for feature stories in the newspapers, but

> Today Bill Smith packs his wife, children three, tent, dog, skillet, fishing tackle and safety razor in the family gasoline chariot and goes, not one, but several thousand miles, visiting many cities, camps and playgrounds on the way. . . .[41]

He answered the question whether the people of the United States would ever face a recreation famine, by noting that scoffers not long ago said that America's timber supply was inexhaustible and that its farm land was unlimited. He declared that there was a limit to the recreational use of certain areas especially adapted to outdoor play, though recreational resources "seem unlimited." The relatively new National Park Service was hailed as a decided step in the right direction, and of no less importance was the advancement of the recreational use of the forests by the United States Forest Service to that of a major use.[42]

Seizing on every opportunity to campaign for the dissemination of his ideas, Carhart remarked that "parks are devoted to recreation alone" and the economic resources they may contain "are not to be exploited for commercial profit." On the other hand, recreation in the Forests interfered but slightly with any of the older established economic uses and could be considered "pure profit." The movement to make commercial inroads in the Parks for private gain at the expense of the public was deplored. The Parks, "should be sanctuaries where nature will remain supreme," and should be planned to present the beauties of the park by a comprehensive scheme worked out by a competent artist.[43] Carhart argued in a cogent manner for consolidation of the Parks and Forests, noting that the "recreation found in the forest . . . just without the boundary of a park, is of as great value as that found across the imaginary line." He advocated the consolidation of administration under one executive in the same department because:

> With all of the good will possible under the circumstances, with all of the desire to co-operate that may be present, the functioning of the recreational work . . . cannot be as well correlated as though there were some central policy-making body . . . that could organize the recreation of the nation without regard to map lines, with no consideration of imaginary boundaries and which would think primarily of returning the greatest aggregate wealth to the nation and the world that is possible from our magnificent areas in the National Parks, Forests, Monuments and Reservations.[44]

Carhart suggested that the American Society of Landscape Architects be called upon to plan and develop a national recreation system on a sound basis. The Society, being professionally capable, could organize the recreation resources through a national commission. In turn, the "national commission would serve as an inspiration and model for the state organization," and the national advisory body "could be extended to aid the states." County parks were also considered in the group of public grounds "to round out what might be termed the national recreation system."[45] "Today," he stressed, "we have unexcelled material for such a system based on the great National Forests, Parks, Monuments and Reservations."[46]

Carhart's suggestions for organization and system brought some positive response.[47] The American Society of

Landscape Architects did in fact modify the duties of its standing committee on National Parks to include National Forests, so that it became known as the Committee on National Parks and National Forests. The action came about through the interest of Professor James Sturgis Pray, Chairman of the School of Landscape Architecture at Harvard University, with whom Recreation Engineer Carhart had been corresponding.[48] More will be said about Pray's role in wilderness preservation later in this study.

What was Carhart's position in live game and forest recreation in 1920? In December, 1920, he attempted to emphasize the essentiality of game to forest recreation. His writing was a mixture of poetry and exhortation:

> Purple-gray shadows crept into the lake basin. Dusk's domain was invading the land that a moment since had been gorgeous with the flash of the sun's rays the instant before he climbed down behind Marvine peak. In silence the Traveler and I sat while he smoked his pipe and dreamily watched deep black shadows come up out of the depths of the lake to hide under the overhanging spruce trees until next day's sun should drive them back to watery fastnesses behind deep reefs in the lake. . . .[49]

In such a setting the Traveler was said to have remarked that if he could only see a bunch of wild elk or one flock of mountain sheep while out there and see nothing else he would feel that every cent put in the trip was repaid. By this statement, he had placed a five hundred dollar valuation on a glimpse of a flock of bighorn in their native habitat.

Carhart also noted in the same article that the wild flowers that fell prey to unthinking recreation users, were like the lesser animals, chipmunks, squirrels and rabbits, that fell before the continual open season of the man with the rifle. In Carhart's opinion, timber squirrels and water ouzels enriched the landscape values as did a whole herd of deer.[50]

Further, he believed that "a live buck seen a dozen times a season" by a score of people has a "greater total value in the nation than a mounted head with dead eyes staring over a den full of skins, weapons and other mounted heads." He advocated that all encouragement be given to rational preservation and propagation of game animals in forest regions. Some words of praise and caution followed:

> The transplanting of large game from one forest to another where it formerly was plentiful . . . is worthy of universal commendation and the work done by the Forest Service in this field merits good support. The establishment of National and State game preserves . . . should be pushed more rapidly but only after a really thorough study of location of such areas is made.[51]

He pointed out that too often local politics played no small part in the establishment of such preserves, adding that the "game-hog" wished to strip a region of all living wild life. The value of a live animal in the recreation scheme was reiterated.[52]

While he was publishing his several articles in the *American Forestry*, Carhart revised the Recreation Plan for the San Isabel National Forest in Colorado, enlarging it significantly. His 110-page study, prepared in December, 1920, contained photographic illustrations and maps of the area.[53] He noted that there had been a report that within the last two years "a small flock of passenger pigeons, a bird believed to be extinct," had been seen on the slopes of the Spanish Peaks in the San Isabel National Forest. If this reported sighting were true, he continued, "then this area immediately around the Peaks which is also the home of the flock of turkeys is a natural bird sanctuary and should be so declared." His aim in giving "full protection" to these two rare species was, of course, to prevent their complete destruction.[54] A brief summary of this lengthy report showed the following salient points:

> 1. The forest Service to the present time has not concentrated on one large project of major importance.
>
> 2. Two forests in the district offer opportunities to produce a big development to serve many people at a reasonable immediate outlay of capital. These are the Superior and the San Isabel. . . .
>
> * * *
>
> 8. Game propagation and protection are closely related to the plan for recreational development.[55]

Carhart's concluding comments attempted to put across his little-understood idea of the "big regional planning" necessary for a forest. He cautioned against "jumping at once to the small units," which should be merely detail in the larger plan.[56]

Official Forest Service Policy toward Recreational Development (1920)

By the end of 1920, the Forest Service could no longer award a minor role to recreation. A stand of some sort had to be taken *officially* for the ineluctable purpose of furnishing guidance to the field supervisory personnel who daily coped with the problem. What, then, was the official Forest Service policy toward recreational development in 1920? Was it clear-cut? Hardly. It was no more sharply defined than the attitude of British colonists toward independence, as manifested in the Continental Congress during the pre-Revolutionary period of this nation's history.[57]

A policy statement issued in December, 1920, by the office of the Chief Forester in Washington, and sent to forest supervisors, reflected considerable ambivalence.[58] Among the subjects discussed in the memorandum, there were four questions and answers under the heading "Recreational

Development." Since these examples represented the crystallization of the rationale of the Washington office in 1920, they merit quotation:

> *Question*: What is the importance of recreational development as compared to other Forest Service activities? *Answer*: Recreational development is now recognized as a major activity . . . and as such, it may, when necessary, be given precedence over other conflicting lines of work.[59]

> *Question*: Is field supervision of recreational use an activity of major importance? *Answer*: In its protective phases, . . . yes since the large numbers of people now resotring [sic] to the National Forests for recreation would constitute a serious hazard if their use did not receive careful and continuous supervision by the field officers. In its educational phases, it is an activity of great desirability but one which at present must necessarily be subordinated to current demands of a pressing and important character.[60]

The next two propositions tend to minimize the recreational aspects of forestry and return to the basic one of providing protection. The first of these was:

> *Question*: What is the relative importance of recreational surveys, plans, and reports? *Answer*: They are of great constructive importance and should be pushed as aggressively as other circumstances and conflicting demands of work will permit, but their importance is secondary when contrasted with the big administrative and protective duties, consequently they should receive attention only when they do not interfere with the work of protecting the National Forests and regulating the use of their resources for utilitarian purposes.[61]

The final proposition was more tenuous, because in 1920 the Congress had appropriated *no* funds for the installation of recreational improvements:

> *Question*: Should the construction of recreational improvements be given precedence over any other improvement work? *Answer*: Recreational improvements are highly desirable and should be installed as rapidly as funds become available, but recognition must be given to the fact that they are not vitally indispensable for the administration and protection of the National Forests and therefore must be subordinated to protection or utilization improvements . . . to permit the proper handling of the current administrative and protective work.[62]

Though recreational development had been recognized as a major activity of the Forest Service by 1920, there remained many obstacles to such development. The next chapter will discuss the difficulties experienced by the Forest Service in the struggle to obtain federal funds for development of the recreational plans which had been proposed by the Denver District office.

CHAPTER IV

NOT SO FAST!

In the light of the validity of Arthur H. Carhart's views on the importance of proper recreational policies for the National Forests expressed in 1919 and 1920, it may be difficult for a later generation that has come to accept them to understand why they encountered opposition when first expounded. Nevertheless a description of this opposition in 1921 should prove illuminating, if only because it records a phase in the evolution of recreation policy in the United States. This chapter, therefore, will emphasize the role of countervailing forces to National Forest recreation and wilderness preservation policy in that year.

The National Park Service had openly opposed the expenditure of federal funds for the development of recreational facilities in the National Forests in 1921. Concurrently, however, there existed a greater but less obvious deterrent to such development, known as the "good roads movement." The latter, by that year, had influenced legislation so that federal funds were not only available for the construction of roads and highways into and through the National Forests, but there was an unexpended accumulation of such funds. Nevertheless, Congress had authorized the building of roads and highways to promote fire suppression, not forest recreation. The existence of millions of dollars of unexpended forest-road construction funds militated against proposals for the exclusion of such roads in favor of wilderness preservation, and helps explain why the Washington office of the Forest Service found its fire protection mission and its overall public service considerations, difficult to reconcile with the demands made by conservationists interested in wilderness protection.

Recreation in National Forests Openly Opposed by National Park Service (1921)

On January 7, 1921, Carhart spoke to the Iowa Conservation Association at Ames, Iowa, and the next day he met with a student group in landscape architecture, telling both groups of the new recreation work in the National Forests.[1] While still at Ames, Carhart also conferred with Dr. L. H. Pammel, President of the Iowa Conservation Association and Chairman of the Botany Department at Iowa State College, and with Dr. G. B. McDonald, professor of Forestry and Secretary of the Iowa Conservation Association. He told them that he planned to attend the National Park conference, scheduled to meet at Des Moines the following week, and he inquired whether its agenda was scheduled to cover only problems related to Parks or whether it would extend to those outdoor recreation problems of national scope. Carhart was assured by both Pammel and McDonald that Forest recreation was a part of the field to be considered and was urged to speak to the assembly. While Pammel and Carhart drove to Des Moines on January 9, Pammel suggested that since he was going to preside at one of the sessions, he would most assuredly call on Carhart to state the extent of recreation use in the Forests and something of the organization and extent of these lands.[2]

The conference opened the following morning, January 10, and Carhart responded to the roll call for Colorado, identifying himself as a member of the Forest Service and a representative of the Colorado Mountain Club. During the roll call it became apparent to Carhart that a "great number of State Forest men" were present, and he reasoned, therefore, that "this was certainly a conference not limited to areas particularly designated as Parks."[3] The opening speeches were delivered by Governor W. L. Harding of Iowa, Dr. Pammel, and Stephen T. Mather, Director of the National Park Service. Just before the meeting closed, Pammel called on Carhart to "say a few words" about National Forests. Since it was near the end of a long program, and not wishing to tire the audience with a long recitation, Carhart chose to speak on only "a few outstanding things." He mentioned, first, that the National Forests covered 156,000,000 acres, that they were 152 in number,[4] and that they offered a "big opportunity for recreational use." He added that during the past season Colorado had entertained 1,190,000 persons in its National Forests, and then he endeavored to show where the National Forests "fitted into a big, comprehensive, recreational scheme," using "several parables in this connection." He described the National Parks as the "big outstanding jewels of the recreation system in the Nation," and the National Forests as the "great setting for these gems of scenery." He also claimed that the National Parks were the "delicacies" in the scenic and recreation offerings, while the National Forests were the "meat and bread" of the system. Carhart finished with a reminder that the National Forests belonged to all the people and everyone was welcome to use them.[5]

Following this three or four-minute talk, several representatives of State Forest systems told Carhart that they wished there had been more time for elaboration of the recreation work in the National Forests. As it turned out, a vacancy in the afternoon program caused by the inability of one of the scheduled speakers to appear made such an elaboration possible. Unknown to Carhart, Herbert Evison of the Natural Parks agency, Seattle, handed to the presiding Chairman, Everett L. Millard, a note requesting the latter to call on Carhart. Evison then apprised Carhart of what he had done. Carhart responded, when called on, with an extempore talk which lasted about fifteen minutes, enlarging on his comments of the morning session. He noted the marked increase in the recreational use of the San Isabel in the summers of 1919 and 1920, bringing out the point that while there were no National Parks east of the Mississippi River, there were several National Forests which could be used for outdoor recreation. Re-emphasizing the fact that everyone was welcome "in these Forests," he stated that they were to be regarded as the "big reserve territory in which just ordinary outdoor recreation can be secured."[6]

Before Carhart could reach his seat, Parks Director Mather jumped to his feet, and in substance announced that he wished to dissipate any possible inference from Carhart's speech that the National Parks were not made for poor people and that they were developed only for the "aristocrats." He added that he was sure that Carhart had not meant to create such an impression. Carhart readily agreed with him that he had not intended to convey that impression at all.[7]

Then, as Carhart later reported, Mather "very evidently let his grip slip so far as his temper was concerned," and declared that it made his "blood boil" to see "a fine lithograph posted any place which said: 'The National Forests—The People's Plaground.' "[8] Mather's feelings in the matter were further reflected in the following report on his remarks:

> He then continued to state, with some heat, that the National Forests should not try to develop the recreation use; that it was not their business to do this; that they were duplicating the work of the National Park Service; that he had talked personally with Congressman [James

> William] Good, head of the House Appropriation Committee, and Mr. Good was distinctly opposed to the use of Forest Service moneys in making recreation developments.[9]

The Parks Director listed further objections to the development of the recreational resources in the National Forests. The Forest Service, he was quoted as stating, "should depend upon local support only, in this development within the National Forests," and all federal funds "should go to the National Parks for recreation development."

As Carhart reported the conference to his District Forester, "a number of people commented" that "Mr. Mather somewhat lost control of himself." And as soon as Mather finished his comments, Carhart asked for the floor and offered the following two points: first, that visitors were "already in the National Forests" in no small quantity and "must be taken care of;" and second, that

> as long as the National Forests are the people's property and the recreation use of these areas offer [sic] a greater aggregate return to these people through this use, it is the duty of the Forest Service to consider this demand and make this return to the public.[10]

The appropriateness of Carhart's observations may be judged by a prominent heading in a 1964 Colorado newspaper which boasted that visitors to that State "spent $500 million" during the last twelve months "to look at the scenery, attend conventions or visit the state's famous ski slopes."[11] Though the article did not specifically mention the National Forests, it should be noted that in addition to the scenery, two-thirds of the many ski slopes in Colorado are located in the National Forests.[12] Further, the National Forests offered "some of the best skiing in the country," according to a 1964 Forest Service pamphlet:

> In all, 166 ski areas, including more than 80 percent of the major ski areas in the West, are located entirely or partially on National Forest land. These winter playgrounds, well designed and carefully managed . . . have been built by ski clubs, civic clubs, State agencies and businessmen. All concessions operate under a forest-use permit.[13]

Returning now to the 1921 memorandum, it reported that immediately after the convention meeting had ended, Carhart encountered Mather in the entrance room to the convention hall. The two men promptly shook hands and agreed that there was "nothing personal" in the dispute. They conversed a while, although Director Mather continued to berate the Forest Service for trying to duplicate the work of the National Park Service. It was reported that "at no time" did Carhart make any sharp rejoinders to Mather's assertions. Witnesses to the dispute testified that they were glad that Carhart had spoken as he did, and asserted that his "statements and stand in the entire matter were well founded and should not have been assailed in the manner in which they were."[14] Judge A. K. Owens of Phillips, Wisconsin, complimented Carhart on his afternoon speech, and remarked that it was "one of the neatest answers to any discussion, such as had transpired," that he had ever heard from the floor of a convention. Owens observed that Carhart had refrained from argument and merely restated the two outstanding points. Dr. L. H. Miller of the University of California, and an employee of the Park Service during the summer, also "voiced his approbation" of Carhart's remarks, as did a dozen others.

But a Des Moines newspaper, possibly with an eye for sensationalism, may not have realized the somewhat embarrassing position in which it had placed the Forest Service in general, and Recreation Engineer Carhart, rather specifically. The front page of the January 11 edition[15] erroneously reported that the "Forest and Park chiefs clash." At the time, Carhart regarded the article as the writing of a rather inaccurate reporter who had a "decided thirst for bloodshed." After returning to Denver, however, Carhart found substantially the same information reported in the *Rocky Mountain News* of the same date,[16] which supported the supposition that the misstatement was deliberate and that possibly it originated from a member of the convention. In part the article reported:

> National Park Conference Marked by Clash Between Officials of 2 U. S. Bureaus
>
> Des Moines, Iowa, Jan. 10.—This afternoon's session of the national park conference being held here was marked by a controversy between the national park service and the forest service, which opened when Arthur H. Carhart of the Denver office of the Forest Service declared that national parks were unimportant in comparison with the vast area of the national forests, which were developed primarily for the poor people in contrast, he said, with the elaborate provisions made for the wealthy by the national park service.
>
> Stephen T. Mather, director of the national park service, declared in response to Mr. Carhart, that the national parks are the original recreation areas of the nation set aside specifically by congress for that purpose.
>
> The national forests were created for commercial purposes, and the recreational activities of the forest service have been a by-product, undertaken with funds appropriated by congress for other work. The forest service is duplicating and copying what the national park service has done. And entirely contrary to the assertion just made, the expenditures of the national park service in developing the parks are devoted largely to providing for the comfort and pleasure of the average man.
>
> The forest service is doing well for the local populations in its areas, while the national park service is taking care of visitors from every state.

At the conference there was yet another incident which concerned resolutions and policies germane to the proceedings and to future national conferences on state parks. During the first session, January 10, 1921, the Chairman asked that suggestions for the conference agenda be written out and given to any member of the Committee on Policy. Carhart handed a written suggestion to Harry Burhans, member of that committee, and a representative of the Denver Tourist Bureau. Burhans was a person who had "repeatedly declared his friendliness to the Forest Service and his willingness to cooperate" with it.[17] The suggestion read: "Gentlemen: May I suggest that in your deliberations, you consider the recreational use of National and State Forest lands?" Yet somewhat curiously this note did not find its way to the policy committee. On the last forenoon of the convention, Carhart was told that no one mentioned the subject of recreational use of Forest lands in the Committee on Policy, and that Burhans had not presented Carhart's note to the Committee. Harris A. Reynolds, of the Massachusetts Forestry Association, learning of this omission through Carhart, immediately declared, "By gosh, I will offer a resolution myself from the floor covering this thing. This convention ought to consider this matter and I am going to see that it does."[18]

Carhart assisted Reynolds in drafting the resolution, being careful to eliminate phraseology which he reasoned Mather would oppose. The resolution stated:

> Whereas, Forest lands, wherever located, offer an opportunity for recreation without any serious destruction [of] their economic values; and whereas, at the present time, millions of people annually receive this return from National, State, County, and municipal Forests; therefore, be it resolved that this conference, recognizing the fundamental value of Forest recreation, recommends the establishment of other publicly owned Forest lands and the correlation of the recreational use on these lands with similar activities on other publicly owned areas.[19]

Before the conference adjourned, Reynolds secured the floor and offered the resolution; several others promptly rose to their feet to second the motion. After it was seconded, Walter O. Filley of Connecticut, a State Forester, argued strongly for its adoption. This activity was followed by "rather excited conversation" between Parks Director Mather and his assistant, Horace M. Albright.[20] Albright then left the floor to speak to the chairman of the Resolution Committee. Meanwhile, W. F. Bade, President of the Sierra Club of California, who had been sitting next to and conversing with Mather a moment before, spoke in opposition to the resolution. Bade was reported to have "belittled the Forests as much as possible in a few short statements," arguing that he believed this was "no place for such a resolution," that "the recreational use of the National Forests was insignificant." After some open debate, Bade, "evidently being recoached by Mr. Mather, again tried to block its passage," but the resolution easily passed the convention.[21]

A few days after the Des Moines conference closed, Carhart prepared a special memorandum to summarize a "few observations" as a "guide to the possibility of arranging at some later date a similar conference," but one "in which the Forest Service will take active part."[22] He noted that "birds, flowers, animals and rocks" received more consideration than did "under-fed children or working people" craving outdoor recreation. The geologists at the meeting had appeared "entirely centered in geological formations," and other devotees of specialized interests were "equally self-centered."[23] As a result, Carhart observed, there had been no discussion of how to organize and present the elements of landscape in the nation's wooded areas, so that it would be suitable for human use. He felt that such planning should have been one of the objectives of the meeting. On the other hand, he praised the talks given by representatives of the Interstate Park in New York and New Jersey, the Bronx Parkway Commission of New York, and of the State Forests, Albany, New York, as outstanding exceptions, all offering "real, constructive ideas."[24]

"I am confident," wrote Carhart, "that there are features" in the forest and state parks of Connecticut, Massachusetts, New York, Pennsylvania, Michigan, Illinois, and Wisconsin, "which will aid materially in solving problems in National Forests."[25] He thought it would be desirable and instructive for landscape men in charge of recreational development in the Forests to study developments in these states, "with the greater part of the study centered in Massachusetts, Connecticut and New York." He stated that "this convention should become an annual affair," for he believed

> it proper for all Forest men interested in game and flower preservation and the human use of Forest lands, to be actively interested in the proposed convention in 1922.[26]

From Washington came an interesting reaction to Carhart's memorandum of January 17 to the Forester via a letter from a personal friend, Wallace I. Hutchinson.[27] Hutchinson had read the report of the "big doings" at the National Parks Conference in Des Moines and also "the staid and prosaic answer sent to the D. F. [District Forester] by [L. F.] Kneipp." The very personal message contained some rumor and some truth:

> I think, and Mr. Smith Riley, to whom I showed the correspondence, agrees with me that the least they could have done was to have handed you some form of meager compliment on the way you answered . . . Mather. The sentiment in this office is that . . . we have nothing to fear in the future from him; also that there will probably be a new head of the parks under the coming administration.[28]

Hutchinson corroborated other aspects of the episode at Des Moines. He endeavored to explain why Representative

Good, Chairman of the House Appropriations Committee, was "very emphatic in his statements that the Forest Service should not mingle in recreation matters" and "this business should be handled exclusively by the National Parks." He claimed:

> The reason for this may possibly be that Mr. Good spent last summer in company with the Director of the Parks on a grand vacation tour throughout the West. However, the point is that folks in this office have "laid down" completely as far as pushing the recreation game goes. It seems like the same old story of frigldity of the pedal extremities. So marked is this reaction that we are not to be allowed this year to even run a recreation picture on the front of the *Yearbook*. Under such a handicap, how can we expect to ever secure any results?[29]

Outside Support for Recognition of Forest Recreation and Wilderness Preservation (1921)

Meanwhile zealous Recreation Engineer Carhart had maintained an active correspondence, as mentioned above, with Professor James Sturgis Pray of Harvard University and a member of the Board of Trustees of the American Society of Landscape Architects (hereafter cited as ASLA). In reply to a letter he had received from Carhart, Pray wrote:

> It is indeed greatly to be regretted that the [suggested] $50,000 appropriation should have been struck out of the Forest Service Appropriation Bill, so that nothing was voted by Congress for your work this summer in the Department of the recreation areas. I did all I could from here and think still that it is barely possible that we would have succeeded through friends in Washington had not those directly associated with the Forest Service been so confident that they were going to get the clause

put back in the bill that they felt they did not need our assistance and support.[30]

With a note of finality he said that the outcome seemed to have been "somewhat of a surprise to those nearest [and directly associated with the Forest Service] . . . and nothing now can be done in the present Congress." The letter then moved to another subject:

> Your statements regarding the protection of scenic water features in the National Forests have not yet received from me all the comment they deserve, and I am moved to make. We all know, of course, that . . . *the* fundamental aspect of this situation, is that the National Forests have been set apart for most vital economic purposes and . . . any other purposes . . . are properly subordinate to these . . . as judged by the purpose of their establishment.[31]

Pray then observed that since the Forest Service had recognized that certain extensive portions of the Forests had more recreational than economic value, it would appear logical that the recreational value had become the dominant consideration. He further noted that

> if this is true, it does not seem to me unreasonable and does seem to me desirable, that all the water features within *those* areas should be protected from commercial exploitation and spoliation as they should be, in the judgment of all intelligent and appreciative people, were they in the National Parks.

That Carhart received not only the ear of Professor Pray but also his wholehearted agreement was shown in such comments as the following:

> Personally, I doubt that the public can have any adequate assurance of the protection of these features,

> if Mr. [Frederick Law] Olmsted's plan that each case should be decided on its own merits and all that is necessary be that we have reasonable assurance good judgment would be used is the only means and recourse employed for their protection. "There must," as you say, "be some structural foundation for the operation of such good judgment."[32]

Further on, Pray stated that if the general plan, which would include provisions for recreation in a Forest, could be formally adopted and made a matter of record so that all work done thereafter to develop the area "shall be in strict accordance with that plan," then "the policy which you have so ably stated . . . is clearly the only sound policy under which any development should take place in the area." The main lines of such a plan might possibly "acquire such legal status" that exemption of those areas from application of the Federal Water Power Act of 1920 could be effected.[33] Here was a clear statement looking to *de jure* delineation and protection of wilderness areas within the National Forests.

Pray's letter also reflected how Carhart solicited the support of persons not in the Forest Service to influence recognition of Forest recreation and wilderness preservation. Pray wrote:

> You suggest the possibility of my working through our A.S.L.A. Standing Committee on National Parks and National Forests to bring up with the officials of the Forest Service this whole matter of the protection of these water features. I believe that something of this sort can be done and that we probably can get a sympathetic hearing particularly through Mr. Sherman from whom I have had most friendly letters distinctly inviting the co-operation of our Committee in the determination of policies and the securing of legislation.[34]

But before acting on Carhart's proposals for assistance, Pray sought Carhart's advice. Incidentally, the following quotation from Pray's letter reflected rather conclusively Carhart's position:

> Before I bring the matter further even to our Committee, I will wait to hear from you in reply to this somewhat long . . . letter, the substance of which may, I think, be summed up as an emphasis on the importance of establishing and securing
>
> First, the formal adoption of general plans for the National Forests in which, along with other use districts, those in which recreation is the dominant function shall be clearly marked, and
>
> Second, an exemption of these recreation areas from the application of the Federal Water Power Act.[35]

The letter concluded with a comment that Pray had heard "something . . . of the stand which you took in the [First National] Conference [on State Parks], a broad stand, which particularly interests me." He then stated that he "judged that some of the views by others were anything but broad."[36]

Pray's four-page letter to Carhart brought a nine-page reply in which the latter deplored the fact that a "great opportunity for a big, broad policy-building meeting was passed by."[37]

Congress had struck down the $50,000 appropriation request for recreational development in the National Forests for the year 1921. Though grieved at the rebuff, Carhart continued his fight to gain recognition of this feature. He had apparently written to Professor Pray asking for information and statistics to help demonstrate the values of recreation, but that letter was not available. Pray's reply was such that Carhart's questions may be inferred. Pray wrote that the gathering of the "facts, judgments, and references," Carhart had requested

> to impress upon the technically trained forester, and others, something of the money-value of the returns to the public from the recreational use of those areas of the National Forests which have been set apart primarily for that use.[38]

had been delayed. "Now after all my efforts," Pray remarked, that which he was able to forward would be "not very much to your purpose." He observed that the fact was obvious that any dollar-value which might be applied to the most valuable returns in recreation, namely, returns in health, morality, efficiency, and happiness must in the very nature of things be "very arbitrary, pretty meaningless, and in fact of little value".[39] He then advanced the theory that when the science of statistics will have been applied much more extensively, the resulting figures would be more meaningful and safe compared to the figures based on small groups. It was agreed that the values spoken of "are not only intangible, they are in a practical sense priceless," and "for the four million man-days of forest recreation in one year in your own district, are beyond calculation." The true difficulty, Pray believed, was not with the impossibility of measuring those intangible values by the dollar-scale, because they were essentially "spirit-values" rather than the material-values, but the difficulty "lies with those unappreciative folk—men without vision of the higher unscalable values—who demand that these values be proved in such terms."[40]

With the letter of June 10, 1921, Pray forwarded Carhart a series of statements concerning the reduction of crime and juvenile delinquency where playgrounds and large parks had been made available to boys and girls and industrial workers. The statements, Pray understood, were to enable Carhart to "have some figures from a source which would be likely to carry weight with the minds which you are up against," and would be far "more to your purpose than any amount of defense of avowedly intangible values."[41]

One of the enclosed statements, was particularly apropos:

> Have public parks an effect on public health? Has the money expended for them brought adequate return to the people in the way of lengthened life or better health? Figures are wanting—or are inadequate . . . Tables may show who and how many people visit the parks, and how many hours are spent there . . . but the scales are yet to be made that can weigh—the influence of sunshine and pure air . . . The pharmacy of Nature has never been fully reckoned with. She never sends a bill.[42]

Another attachment showed that of the cases of juvenile delinquency brought into the Chicago Juvenile Court during the first eight years of the Court's history from July 1899 to June 1907, those living within one mile of a *large park* were 46% successful," that is, "so improved as to be qualified for release from the jurisdiction of the court—as against 39% for the whole city." Other figures were quoted, showing up to fifty percent, in some cases, of decrease in such delinquency.[43]

Still another item Pray sent to Carhart claimed:

> When the people live in the broad, open country or in a succession of villages there is not so great a need for parks; but when the population has grown in density so that one square mile in New York holds as many people as the whole of Buffalo, something must be done to stop them from dying so fast. . . . *Parks are the answer* [italics supplied]. . . . I insist then that one reason for parks is that we have a crowded working population . . . and I insist that no well maintained park is ever an expense.[44]

The above quotations were all well and good—*for parks*—but the very use of the word "park" defeated Carhart's purpose and made promotion of the recreation aspects in the National Forests even more difficult. They were not sources "which would be likely to carry weight with the minds" he sought to convert to his views. Carhart's ideas were as yet unacceptable to many officials. Indeed, his advocacy of developing the National Forests along broad lines was anathema to them.

But Carhart stayed with the task of telling all who would listen about his plan. In 1921, for instance, Carhart spoke in Minneapolis to the Minneapolis Chapter of the American Society of Landscape Architects to familiarize them with what he was "attempting to do in the National Forests."[45] He also wrote an article in that year which suggested that the City and County of Denver develop a "systematic plan for the manufacture of recreation as a commodity".[46] The "outdoor recreation system" sought to care for all classes of recreation seekers in five diversified areas. Accompanying the illustrated article were photographs, maps and diagrams outlining Denver's "Recreation Fan." The map of the "Fan" has been reproduced (Map 4). Carhart described the outdoor recreation system of Denver as "fan-shaped in its scheme." The center of the fan was the Mountain Park system behind which was the beautiful Mount Evans area. The right-hand side was made up of the Glacier Region of the Colorado National Forest and the Rocky Mountain National Park, and the southern portion was composed of the Devil's Head region in the Pike National Forest. The very top of the fan was that section of the Pike, Leadville and Arapahoe National Forests bounded on the west by the Fairplay-Kremmling Highway.[47]

With the scope of five "giant play areas, each offering distinctive play," Carhart believed it was possible to "tempt every outdoor lover" to vacation in the recreation fan. The plan definitely called for an area set aside as the "mountaineering playground of the system." Its use would be "by those on foot and should be preserved as such." In this manner, he asserted, its recreational use would stand out as "unique in the land and will be the highest possible value which can be developed here."[48] His summary paragraph deserves quotation here:

> This whole plan means that Denver can have a group of magnificent playgrounds aggregating several millions of acres in extent, each with its personal appeal, each turning out a different kind of recreation and, when combined in one system and developed for use, assuring Denver the envied position of being the "Playground City of America." Then can our Mayor and Denver's other citizens always say she "—leads in playgrounds."[49]

One final example will further demonstrate Carhart's pioneer role in Forest recreation and wilderness preservation. In November, 1921, Frank A. Waugh wrote to him concerning recreational developments in the state of Colorado:

> Your article on "Denver's Greatest Manufacturing Plant" in Municipal Facts Monthly is the best thing you have yet written. It is very practical, very much to the point and calculated to accomplish results in a field where results count most.
>
> It seems to me that the people of Denver must be rapidly waking up to a situation. . . . I believe your work in Denver and Pueblo will go a long way toward putting matters right.
>
> By the way how are conditions developing in Pueblo since the flood? I suppose the flood did interfere seriously with recreation developments on the San Isabel last summer. In particular I would like to know if it will be possible to revise in 1922 the plan for a municipal health camp in Pueblo.[50]

Because of the press of other work, Waugh's letter was not answered immediately. Carhart, in explaining his delay, claimed that he was "just starting on a regional plan for a portion of the Rio Grande [National Forest in Colorado]," and that things are booming." He then described a few of his varied activities:

> The big things on hand now are the Superior plan, a plan of the glacier area, and this section of the Rio Grande. We have organized a four recreation association at Boulder. A fifth is being talked of at Fort Collins. Both of these will operate in the Colorado National Forest.[51]

Carhart also attempted to answer Waugh's question about the health camp at Pueblo, Colorado. Though he could offer no "official dope," it was his impression that the Forest Service was not in a position to "talk real business," which he thought was "necessary when you start dealing with Pueblo." Because of past delays, the City of Pueblo had made a camp of its own on County-owned property just outside of the Forest. Continuing he remarked:

> I don't think it is good business to suggest anything to these fellows out here unless you are ready to work, for when they get a notion out in this section of the country they go. . . . But if we open up the subject again we better have definite arrangements to offer or keep still.[52]

In order to understand the references to cooperative arrangements made between the Forest Service and local communities, it may be appropriate to present here a synopsis of developments in road and highway construction during the period 1916-1930. Road building in or near the National Forests involved millions of dollars and played a determining role in the economic development of nearby communities. Proposed roads were usually built after local agreements had been formulated between the Forest Service and the affected communities.

Effect of Good Roads and Fire Suppression in the National Forests (1916-1930)

Earlier in this study an attempt was made to show the impact of increased automobile production on Forest recreation. With the automobile came the demand for better roads and highways, and between 1916 and 1921 $33,000,000 was appropriated for National Forest roads.[53] During the following decade, the "good roads movement" swept the nation.

There were compelling reasons for the construction of more and higher quality roads into and through the National Forests, and among them was the need to promote fire protection and, incidentally, recreational purposes. The Forest Service was in the unenviable position of being "damned if it did" build roads in the National Forests and "damned if it didn't"—a nightmarish dilemma.

At this juncture it is therefore necessary to present a brief survey of the key developments in behalf of good roads and fire protection in our National Forests during the period 1916-1930. This survey should at least partially clarify related points made elsewhere in this study regarding the effect of the demand for good roads on wilderness preservation policies in those years.

In his report on the Forest Service for the fiscal year ended June 30, 1916, Forester Henry S. Graves noted that material progress had been made in development work during the year. Outstanding features included: an increased "use of the resources," a "larger volume of business," and the advancement of the interests of the local communities. In addition, the building of roads in "regions hitherto inaccessible" was given as "one of the largest factors" in work.[54]

There were only two federal appropriations available in 1916 for the construction and maintenance of roads, trails, and other improvements in the National Forests. They were referred to jointly as the "Ten Per Cent Fund." One of them amounted to $400,000 and was provided by the regular appropriation bill for the primary purpose of construction and maintenance of improvements necessary in the "protection and administration of the Forests." The other was an amount equal to ten percent of the receipts from the National Forests, which Congress had authorized for the construction of roads and trails primarily to aid in the "general development of the local communities." Most of the road building in fiscal year 1916 had been from the latter source which amounted to $278,216.56 plus "cooperative funds from the local communities."[55] For the purpose of this study, the ten percent fund will be designated as category one.

On June 11, 1916, Congress passed the Federal-Aid Road Act which furnished a second category of revenue for road construction in the National Forests. By Section 8 of that Act, $10,000,000 was authorized for roads and trails "within or partly within the National Forests" when necessary for the "use and development of resources upon which communities in and near the Forests are dependent." The new law opened the way for undertaking road development greatly needed by such communities and desired by the public in general. By September 1, 1916, the Secretary of Agriculture approved regulations consistent with that legislation.[56] That Act made available, "until expended," $1,000,000 for the fiscal year 1917, with the same amount for the nine succeeding years, but because of the scarcity of experienced engineers who had left for military service, little construction work was accomplished in 1917.[57]

Forester Graves noted in his report for the fiscal year ended June 30, 1918, that the war had profoundly affected the Forest Service, opened new opportunities, and made some old problems more pressing.[58] Graves stated that ever since the administration of the National Forests began, their "protection against fire" had been "the greatest single problem confronted." Effective procedures of preventing, detecting, and suppressing fires had been developed, "but where the country is still an utter wilderness," with scanty means of communication, no local population, and supply centers far away, "quick action to put out fires before they gain headway" was very difficult and the fighting of large fires very expensive.[59] Where fires reached so great a size that "scores or hundreds of men must be gathered, transported, equipped, and maintained for days and even weeks on the fire lines, far within the Forests," expenditures became disproportionately high. In some cases, equipment and supplies had to be packed in on horseback or on foot to the vicinity of the fire, sometimes taking from five to seven days to arrive at the fire scene. By that time, he observed, the fire may have spread to such proportions that "second and third calls for help" became necessary, under adverse conditions. Graves called attention to how the "incomplete systems of roads and trails" had greatly increased the difficulty of quick movement when changes in the point of attack became necessary, and how the lack of such facilities was "often mainly responsible for inability to extinguish fires quickly and for a consequent large property loss."[60] Concerning construction of improvements of various kinds, the report reflected that it was the general policy to make no demands upon the country's supplies of labor and materials needed "for bringing the war to a successful issue," and that moneys available would be "allowed to accumulate in the Treasury until the end of the war."[61]

The Forester's Report for 1919, saw the inclusion *for the first time* of a section entitled "RECREATION AND GAME."[62] It mentioned that "plans for the management of the National Forests must aim to provide for an orderly development of all their resources," and for the use and benefit of the public, because they would be "incomplete if they failed to take into account the wild life and recreation resources.[63] The expanding use of the Western National Forests "must be handled with full recognition of their recreation values, present and future." Graves wrote, for recreation required "careful and forward looking plans" providing both for its protection and its development. Then he declared:

> Of particular importance for the increase of use is the systematic and progressive development of roads and trails by which the Forests are being made more generally accessible. Every road and trail, whether it is built primarily for protection or for the development of some material resource, opens up new features of scenic interest. In a variety of other ways also development to meet the increased demand for recreation use is being undertaken. A number of recreation centers are being made ready for the public under plans carefully worked out by recreation engineers.[64]

Actual road construction carried out during calendar year 1918 had been restricted, as in 1917, so as not to interfere with the prosecution of the war. The high price of labor and materials forced postponement or reduction of the work from that which had been planned, but large amounts of investigative and survey work were carried out in anticipation of "an increased construction program following the end of the war."[65] To make up for the almost entire work stoppage during those two years and to provide employment opportunities for those released from war activities immediately upon the cessation of hostilities, plans were laid for utilizing "as far as practicable all funds available for road survey and construction." Labor became difficult to obtain during World War I in quantity and quality, and as a rule, the wage rate had not decreased, while the cost of materials had on the whole increased. The accumulation of "almost 4 years' appropriations" proved sufficient for "hardly more work than could be financed in 1917."

The situation was greatly relieved, however, on February 27, 1919, when the Post Office appropriation act was passed. By Section 8 of that act, a third category of funds was made available for the National Forests. $3,000,000 was authorized for each of the fiscal years 1919, 1920, and 1921, as a *cooperative fund* for construction and maintenance of roads and trails within or partly within National Forests, "when necessary for the use and development of resources or desirable for the proper administration, protection, and improvement of any Forest;" the fund was to remain available until expended.[6] Thus on June 30, 1919, there was an accumulated unexpended balance of $5,637,728.10 in funds available for road and trail construction derived from the three appropriations categories thus far discussed: the Ten Per Cent Fund, Section 8 of the Federal-Aid Road Act Fund, and Section 8 of the Post Office Act.[67]

The year 1920 brought with it a change in forestry leadership in Washington. Secretary of Agriculture D. F. Houston was replaced by E. T. Meredith, and Henry S. Graves resigned as Forester on April 15, 1920, in favor of William B. Greeley. Greeley stated in his report of the work in the Forest Service for the fiscal year ended June 30, 1920, that he was continuing the program laid down by Graves, one which "set forth the urgency of a national forestry policy." The program, he stated, was based on the conviction that the problem of "halting forest devastation" was "fundamentally a national, not a local, problem, and must be faced and handled as such." Greeley urged that the

> speediest, surest, and most equitable action can be secured through dependence on the police powers of the States for the enforcement of such reasonable requirements as should be made of private owners and on the State governments for providing organized protection of private lands against fire.[68]

Under the caption "RECREATION AND GAME," Greeley noted that recreation "bids fair to rank third" among the major services performed by the National Forests, with only "timber production and stream-flow regulation taking precedence." The appeal for local recreational facilities and the demand for summer-home sites had grown so rapidly that there was "need for men of special training to direct and plan for the most effective development of this service." He then pointed to the need for a "special fund of $50,000 for recreational development" to bring about the fullest use of the National Forests, and to contribute "their proper quota to the Nation's health." An appropriation of that amount would permit the employment of "several trained landscape engineers" and "more rapid and at the same time more careful development" of public facilities and conveniences, in cooperation with local communities.[69] Greeley reported that the mileage of road and trail construction during the year 1919 had "eclipsed all previous figures." Special effort had been made to complete as quickly as possible the roads and trails "essential to an effective system of fire protection," and accessibility of the forests for recreation had been greatly increased by completion of many of the projects.[70]

On January 1, 1920, there was an unexpended balance of $7,253,736.45 in the road and trail construction fund from the three previously identified sources. Additional installments of these appropriations, which became available for expenditure on July 1, 1920, totaled $4,472,025.25. It was noted that "the last installment" of the third source for National Forest road funds, Section 8 of the Post Office appropriation act of February 20, 1919, had been received on July 1, 1920.[71] This fact brought a note of concern. Greeley remarked:

> The total expenditure, approved from Federal funds for the calendar year 1920, is $8,127,323, which will leave a balance on January 1, 1921, of only about $3,600,000 in all appropriations. After January 1, 1921, there will be no further appropriation from the Federal Forest road-construction fund [Category Three], and only $1,000,000 will be available annually from the section 8 fund [Category Two]. It is clearly evident that the program of development on which so excellent a start has been made the last two years must be sharply curtailed unless additional funds are provided at once.[72]

The Forester's Report, dated October 6, 1921, stated that the plans for the calendar year 1921 contemplated work on about 700 miles of road and 1,800 miles of trail. That construction, according to the Forester, together with related plans and commitments, would exhaust the unexpended balance of all road and trail appropriations already made, "with the exception of the 10 per cent fund [Category One]," which would be used largely for trail maintenance work.[73] Lack of funds threatened to interfere with plans for completion of work on 13,640 miles of road and 39,280 miles of trail that had been planned. Fire-fighting roads were called for, especially in the sections "entirely without roads," or "served by roads which are simply wagon tracks through the woods, and are narrow, dangerous, steep, and entirely unsuited to travel." An adequate system of roads and trails was deemed necessary to lessen the "destruction of resources essential to local prosperity."[74]

The Forester's plea was favorably acted upon and the plans for completion of the Forest roads and trails suffered no interruption, for on November 9, 1921, Congress passed the Federal Highway Act. By Section 23 of the act, $5,000,000 was made immediately available for Forest roads and trails, and $10,000,000 was to be made available on July 1, 1922.[75] In the meantime, the interest in the construction of "better roads throughout the nation had become widespread," the Forester reported in 1922, and the "general demand for Federal aid on roads traversing the national forests, which form links in State and county highway systems," had been met. The Congressional appropriation of November, 1921, had "met the requirements very satisfactorily" and the "present legislation" would probably answer the needs for many years to come.[76] Funds under the act were separated into two classes of roads. For the purpose of this study the classes will be referred to as the fourth and fifth categories of forest road funds. The appropriations in the fourth category, the "Forest Highway Fund," were intended for aid to the States and counties in the construction of roads which are essential links in the public highway system, while the appropriation in the fifth category, the "Forest Development Fund," was intended for the administration, protection, and development of the Government's own properties in order that they may not only be safeguarded, but also made of maximum service to the public.[77]

It may be helpful to summarize the foregoing discussion concerning forest-road appropriations for the period 1921-1930 in the form of a table. The upper portion of Table 1 shows the total forest-road appropriations to December 31, 1921, as reflected in the Forester's report of September 30, 1922.[78] The lower portion of the Figure, listing forest-road appropriations and expenditures from July 1, 1922, through June 30, 1930, was compiled in the interest of clarity and simplicity.[79] It should be noted that the five separate funds were combined and presented by fiscal year, to coincide with the Forest Service reporting system which was apparently changed in 1922 or 1923. At any rate, the report of the Forester for the fiscal year ended June 30, 1923, stated that for the previous eighteen months, "greater progress was made in road and trail work than in any preceding period of the same length."[80] A pronouncement which succinctly stated one of the objectives of the material here presented.

United States Good Roads Association (1921-1923)

When Congress passed the generous Federal Highway Act of November 9, 1921, did it do so spontaneously? Or was there, perhaps, a concerted movement by interested parties? A review of some of the activities of the United States Good Roads Association, Inc., may suggest an answer. That association was organized and chartered on April 25, 1913, with permanent headquarters in Birmingham, Alabama. Present at the first meeting of the association were "four U.S. Senators, ten Congressmen, and a number of the most prominent good roads men in the country." The first president was Senator

TABLE 1
CONDITION OF FOREST-ROAD FUNDS (1921-1930)

Fund	Total appropriations to Dec. 31, 1921	Total expenditures	Unexpended balance on Jan. 1, 1922
10 per cent	$ 3,042,248.40	$ 2,678,226.43	$ 364,021.97
Section 8	6,000,000.00	4,515,539.80	1,484,469.20
Federal forest-road construction	9,000,000.00	7,611,429.74	1,388,570.26
Forest highway	2,500,000.00	———	2,500,000.00
Forest development	2,500,000.00	———	2,500,000.00
Total	$23,042,248.40	$14,805,195.97	$ 8,237,052.43
Year	**Total appropriations to June 30**	**Total expenditures**	**Unexpended balance on July 1**
1923	$34,541,840.00	$23,203,867.00	$11,337,973.00
1924	42,570,409.68	32,597,949.70	9,972,459.98
1925	50,591,148.97	43,013,055.93	7,578,093.04
1926	59,588,330.54	53,033,405.46	6,554,925.08
1927	67,602,539.92	62,583,372.80	5,019,167.12
1928	75,616,626.70	71,153,778.25	4,462,848.45
1929	83,656,998.28	80,653,467.79	3,003,530.49
1930	91,783,011.09	89,122,195.25	2,660,815.84

John H. Bankhead, who served eight years until his death, when Governor C. H. Brough of Arkansas succeeded him. It had for its object "the uniting of all state and county Good Roads Associations and individuals to promote state and Federal Legislation and build Inter-State and National Highways." By 1921, an Association invitational letter[81] to the Governor of New Mexico stated:

> The Association . . . has members in every state in the union. Your state is well represented on the roster. The founders and incorporators of this Association wrote in the Constitution that the Governors of each state in the union should be elected and invited to become Vice-President during their term of office. . . . We shall be pleased to have your acceptance and cooperation for the advancement of good roads throughout the Nation.[82]

States in 1921, two of whom became Presidents of the United

The list of names on the letterhead, about one hundred in all, included the names of all the Governors in the United States, namely, Governors Calvin E. Coolidge and W. P. G. Harding. Senator Oscar W. Underwood of Birmingham, Alabama, was also listed as a State Vice-President.[83]

Contemporaneously, the year 1921 also saw an increased emphasis on forest fire prevention, which furthered the interests of the good roads movement. A letter signed by the then Secretary of Agriculture Henry C. Wallace and addressed to Governor M. C. Mechem of New Mexico, noted that President Harding had issued a proclamation designating May 22-28 as Forest Protection Week, and urged that the Governors of the various States set apart that week for the purpose of such educational and instructive exercises "as shall bring before the people the serious effects of the present unnecessary waste by forest fires."[84] The Total loss from forest fires for the five years ending 1920 was estimated at more than $85,000,000, and the magnitude of the area burned over during that period a "startling" 56,488,000 acres. Worst of all was the statistic

Wallace furnished, that of the 160,000 fires which had occurred, "over 60% were due to human agencies." Moreover, loss of life was not infrequent, as in the Minnesota disaster of 1918, where nearly a thousand persons were either burned to death or suffocated.[85]

The Good Roads Association met for its tenth annual meeting in Phoenix, Arizona, during the period April 24-29, 1922, at which time delegations were expected from the forty-eight states of the union. "In fact," President Brough boasted, "we expect to hold the largest and most enthusiastic convention of good roads boosters that has ever been held in America." The meeting was to be "fraught with great importance" because of the start of a movement to urge the Federal Government to make a continuing appropriation of one hundred million dollars annually for the succeeding five years, and also to make appropriations for the building of national highways.[86]

What evidence is there that the Association worked to secure such Legislation? Its official organ for 1923 described the Association's accomplishments for the previous decade.[87] It pointed out that ten years before, 2,500 enthusiastic good roads boosters representing twenty-seven states throughout the union had met to organize the Association, and that since that time it had worked "in season and out of season for the cause of good roads." The Association was the first in the country to advocate and help to secure the passage of federal aid in congress. It was the backbone in the fight for federal aid and was the "prime mover in winning public sentiment, which forced Congress to place on the state books" federal aid bills for road construction. Since the first appropriation in 1916, Federal aid has proven a most important factor in encouraging and stimulating road building, the Association *Bulletin* reported. It declared:

> It was the United States Good Roads Association, . . . which started the propaganda throughout the nation, which won the support of the general public and the

> various officials of civic organizations and members of the senate and congress to enact in a law the principles of federal aid. . . . It has accomplished more good in promoting good roads and in creating federal legislation than any other association in existence. It has been the leader in the movement. . . . It had a mission, a work to perform, it has demonstrated its usefulness. Its work must continue as the road building progress in this country is only in its infancy.[88]

The *Bulletin* also included an account on the annual meeting in Greenville, South Carolina, in April, 1923, and plans for the 1924, or twelfth annual, convention in Albuquerque, New Mexico. The plans embraced a "United States Good Roads Show" in conjunction with that convention, at which time manufacturers and dealers of road machinery and material would be afforded "a splendid opportunity of exhibiting their machinery and material to the men directly responsible for road construction."[89]

While the Good Roads Show may have been a splendid opportunity for the manufacturers and dealers concerned, the Forest Service had to cope with the mounting problems caused by the good roads and the automobiles which travelled over them. In 1923, Chief Forester Greeley claimed that the extension of excellent roads into regions "hitherto almost inaccessible save on horseback or on foot" was bringing people into the forests by thousands from increasing distances. He summed up the situation with a note of finality: "The automobile and good roads are, of course, here to stay."[90] Further on he said:

> Special problems are constantly arising in connection with the recreational and wild-life resources of the national forests. . . . A plea is not made for the reservation of certain national forests, or parts of them, from the commercial use of timber and forage, or even from customary forms of recreation, like public camp grounds, summer homes, and hotels—indeed, from the

> very building of roads which would make these areas accessible to considerable numbers of visitors. What these people want is not parks but stretches of untrammeled wilderness, deliberately reserved as such. . . . This plea has been made particularly with reference to the Kaibab National Forest in Arizona and the Superior National Forest in Minnesota, or parts of them. . . . It is a wholesome reaction from the multiplication of the improved roads and automobiles.[91]

The foregoing summary account of the push for good roads and the need for fire protection has carried the story past the beginning of the second *de facto* application of the wilderness principle, so that it is now necessary to return to an earlier period to describe that development.

CHAPTER V

TAKE ANOTHER STEP

The second *de facto* application of the wilderness concept in the United States took place in the Superior National Forest in Minnesota. Its origin could be traced to Recreation Engineer Arthur H. Carhart's "Preliminary Report" of 1919.[1] It advanced a step further when in 1921 Carhart paid a second visit to that Forest,[2] and drafted a second, or revised, report.[3] Out of this plan came the first major dispute over road building in National Forests, and the dispute concerned what became known as the Boundary Waters Canoe Area.

Before proceeding to the details of that dispute, and those which followed it during the decade, it may be advisable to include a brief history and description of the Forest under consideration.[4] Such coverage should provide the perspective and background useful to a clearer understanding of the problem that arose.

Brief History of the Superior National Forest, Minnesota, to 1920

An examination of the map (Map 5) will reveal that the Superior National Forest is located in the extreme upper right hand corner of the State of Minnesota, adjacent to the northwestern shore of Lake Superior. For the purpose of this study only passing reference need be made to the Sioux, Chippewa and other tribes of Indians who occupied this region prior to the coming of the first white men in the seventeenth century. It was in 1634 that French civilization met the stone age in the western great lakes region with a flash of gunpowder. The Jesuit Priest Jean Nicolet, a representative of Samuel de Champlain, coasted down Lake Michigan in a canoe to the shores of Green Bay. There Nicolet encountered a group of Winnebagos. Armed with two long pistols, the Frenchman, with a love for dramatic effect, pointed his pistols skyward and "shot thunder" from his hands. The initial terror of the Indians, who thus encountered a white man for the first time, turned to panic, but Nicolet assured them his mission was one of peace and they soon recovered from their fright. This event occurred fourteen years after the Pilgrims landed at Plymouth Rock.[5]

Even though there is some tenuous evidence that Nicolet continued his journey until he had discovered Lake Superior, the date of its unquestioned discovery was 1641, when two enterprising Jesuit missionaries, Charles Raymbault and Isaac Jogues, made their way to Sault de Ste. Marie and saw the lake. Hence, that year, the French had acquired a knowledge of the whole system of the Great Lakes.[6]

Medard Chouart and Pierre d'Esprit, better known respectively, as the Sieur des Groseilliers and the Sieur de Radisson, were probably the first two white men to tread the soil of Minnesota in the spring or summer of 1660.[7] From that time until 1763, the French *voyageurs* and *coureurs de bois* exploited the area. With the signing of the Treaty of Paris on February 10, 1763, the Seven Years' War was concluded, France ceded to England all the territory east of the Mississippi river, save two islands in the St. Lawrence Bay and the city of New Orleans, and Spain received from France the Louisiana Territory lying west of the Mississippi. Thus, the French had been driven from North America, and the great valley of the Mississippi was opened to eager Anglo-American frontiersmen.[8]

From February to October, 1763, the "Northwest Territory" was presumed open to settlement by the colonists. By the Proclamation of King George III on October 7, 1763, colonists were strictly forbidden to purchase or settle on Indian lands, and squatters who had already crossed beyond the Line of Proclamation were ordered "forthwith to remove themselves from such settlements."[9] Then, the act of Parliment of 1774, the Quebec Act, extended the government of Quebec's boundaries to the Ohio and Mississippi rivers. That poorly-timed act helped to trigger the War for American Independence.[10]

The Treaty of Paris, consummated on September 3, 1783, provided among other things for American independence with the boundaries extending north to the 45th parallel and the Great Lakes, westward to the Mississippi, and southward to the 31st parallel. The area of Minnesota east of the great river, therefore, remained a part of the British Empire for only about twenty years. Title to the land did not, however, at once vest in the United States. The colony of Virginia had long asserted a claim to the area by her charter of 1609, and by subsequent actions taken by the Virginia legislature.[11] Virginia's claim was ceded to the United States in 1784; Minnesota East became the property of the United States, and was later merged into the Northwest Territory.[12]

Under the terms of the Northwest Ordinance of 1787, lands north of the Ohio and east of the Mississippi were to be divided for eventual admission into the Union as states.[13] In addition, that ordinance contained a Bill of Rights which guaranteed, in part, that "the legislatures of those districts or new States, shall never interfere with the primary disposal of the Soil by the United States." and more importantly, that:

> The navigable waters leading into the Mississippi and St. Lawrence, and the carrying places between the same

> shall be common highways and forever free, as well to inhabitants of the said territory as to the Citizens of the United States.[14]

The Louisiana Purchase in 1803 and the Convention of 1818 enabled the United States to acquire part of what is now Minnesota;[15] and the Webster-Ashburton Treaty of 1842 defined the zigzag boundary in the disputed area between Lake Superior and the Lake of the Woods, that is, the border between Canada and Minnesota.[16]

With the international boundary problem solved, the United States faced an internal one in Minnesota, for it had to deal with Indian removal before white settlement could progress. Prior to 1837, there was no land in the area of Minnesota open to settlement. The first pioneers in the wilderness of Minnesota's lakes and forests were traders whose cabins were built beneath the walls of Ft. Snelling.[17] That famous fort was established in 1819 at the fork of the Mississippi and Minnesota Rivers, and was built on a site selected in 1805 by Lieutenant Zebulon Pike as part of a general plan for frontier defense.[18]

Growth was slow, for all settlers were illegal squatters on either Indian lands or the federal military reservation about the fort. A new Indian cession was needed before the Minnesota country was ready to welcome a sizable migration.[19] That cession came in 1837 with the ratification of treaties with the Sioux and Chippewa which gave the United States the triangle between the Mississippi and the St. Croix rivers, as well as a chunk of northern Wisconsin. The first arrivals in the triangle were lumbermen, attracted by the towering stands of virgin pine and hardwood that covered all the wild country west of Lake Superior.[20] As growth of settlement went on, the thoughts of pioneers turned to self-government. They had been for a time a neglected part of Wisconsin Territory, but after May 29, 1848, when Wisconsin became a state, their isolated triangle was without any government whatsoever.[21] A memorial praying for territorial status was carried to Washington and pushed through Congress in the spring of 1849. The new territory contained only 4,000 inhabitants, and an increase in population could not be expected without another Indian cession. In 1851 the leading Sioux chieftains were brought together and were persuaded to sign away their claims to most of western Minnesota. The new cession was quickly engrossed, and by 1852 there were twenty thousand settlers living there. Loggers cut off the virgin timber and farmers grubbed out their clearings from the wilderness.[22]

The next major happening took place on September 30, 1854, when a treaty was negotiated at La Pointe, Wisconsin, with the Chippewa of Lake Superior, via which those bands ceded to the United States the "triangle" north of Lake Superior.[23] Five months later a second treaty was negotiated by which they surrendered another immense area in northern Minnesota.[24] The acquisition of 1854 was spoken of as a "miners' proposition," that is, having been made in the interests of miners, while the treaty of 1855 was regarded as one for the benefit of the lumbermen. Folwell reported: "About the headwaters of the Mississippi and the Crow Wing were the best stands of pine timber in the territory. The two treaties were indeed part of one scheme."[25] There were other early Indian cessions of land, but because of their inferior importance need not be detailed here.

On May 11, 1858, Minnesota became a state, with a population that, according to the 1860 census, totalled 172,023.[26] But before Minnesotans could concentrate on their development as a state, there was one last chapter to be written about the Indians. On August 18, 1862, a large party of Sioux Indians rose in protest to the treatment they had received at the hands of the whites.[27] They killed 447 to 450 settlers and soldiers in the massacre,[28] but were decisively defeated on September 23, 1862.[29] The white settlers were in full possession of the land called Minnesota, "the mother of three seas."[30]

In 1862, President Abraham Lincoln signed the Homestead Act, and under its provisions, settlers took up a million and a quarter acres of public land in Minnesota from 1863 to 1865.[31] Following the Civil War the people of Minnesota were concerned with booming and exploitation.[32] That spirit of exploitation took and used the pine forests following the standards of their own time and place in history. But a first step was taken by the state of Minnesota to preserve a part of its natural heritage which came about in a manner worth repeating. That action came when the Minnesota legislature established Itasca State Park on thirty-five sections of land, granted by Congress and, for the most part, still public. On May 4, 1891, the Governor of Minnesota appointed Jacob Vradenberg Brower Commissioner of the new park.[33]

Brower's claim to fame arose partly from having fully confirmed the location of the utmost sources of the Mississippi River at Lake Itasca. In the autumn of 1888, Brower spent thirty days in the Itasca basin and made a careful examination of its topography; in the summer of 1889, he worked there for another fifty-eight days. His crowning labor, seconded by the Minnesota Historical Society, forever put to rest the question of the source of the Mississippi, which had interested geographers for more than a century.[34] He proved the essential correctness of Henry R. Schoolcraft's observations on or about July 13, 1832, concerning that lake. Schoolcraft served in the office of Indian Affairs of the War Department and was the first explorer to look upon its waters. He had asserted the right to give it its name, which was composed of two Latin words: *veritas,* for truth, and *caput* for head. Schoolcraft struck out the first syllable of *veritas* and the latter syllable of *caput,* and merging those remaining, declared, "I-tas-ca shall be the name."[35] The Mississippi was too majestic for one man or one group to have the glory of its full discovery; it took nearly three centuries to unlock the mystery of its source. Blegen remarked that "not until that long task was completed did the land truly lie open."[36] Paradoxically, the following year, 1890, was the year cited by Frederick Jackson Turner as the one in which the historic westward movement closed.[37]

One mark of Minnesota's having come of age was the tide of population which soared from 200,000 in 1865 to 1,-300,000 in 1890.[38] To accomodate such a population, Minnesota, following the Civil War and for the remainder of the nineteenth century, began to build its great cities. The region was mined for its precious ores and forests of white pine and other hardwoods fell to the ax, the saw, and fire.[39] As early as 1872 the American landscape architect Horace William Shaler Cleveland had seen the need for city planning which looked to the future. But he had spoken to a generation that did not see with his vision what great cities Minneapolis and St. Paul would become, and what a boon parks, wide and beautiful avenues, and convenient playgrounds would eventually prove.[40] His outstanding contribution in this period was his advocacy and designing of connecting parkways and riverside boulevards between the "United Cities" along the Mississippi.[41]

By 1894, however a movement for the conservation of Minnesota's forests gained momentum as the result of a calamity. In that year, a disastrous fire of hurricane force roared down upon the village of Hinckley and burned to death 197 persons there.[42] That holocaust re-enforced the preaching of another pioneer, a former Civil War officer, Christopher Columbus Andrews. For the previous two decades he had advocated using and saving the forests in a reforestation plan, and preached about the danger of fires.[43] The need for fire prevention led to the appointment of a chief fire warden, then a forestry board, a forestry service, and ultimately a conservation commission.[44] Crisis brought reform.[45]

At the turn of the century significant change lay on the horizon—the Federal government was about to enter the picture in Minnesota forestry in a substantial way. Forestry Commissioner, C. C. Andrews had endeavored, but failed, to obtain approval of the Minnesota Legislature for his plan to dedicate permanently certain land for forestry purposes. The wheat farmers and other special interest groups had not been sufficiently inclined toward forest preservation proposals in that era of boom and build.[46] Nevertheless, by 1902, Andrews and some interested citizens of the Twin Cities had created a 200,000-acre forest reserve near Lake Winnibigoshish in the Upper Mississippi Valley.[47] Andrews then turned to the Federal government for support. His overtures were successful, for between 1902 and 1908 the Commissioner of the General Land Office withdrew from entry some 518,700 acres of forested land in Cook and Lake Counties,[48] and in the following year steps were taken by the Secretary of Agriculture to have the President designate the area as the Superior National Forest.[49]

When President Theodore Roosevelt proclaimed the formation of that new National Forest on February 13, 1909, it contained approximately 1,018,638 acres, somewhat less than the acreage in the withdrawals mentioned above.[50] The President's Proclamation did not include, however, the central strip of the choice lake country on the international border between Basswood Lake and Saganaga Lake. That strip was not added until 1936. The ownership status in the latter area produced controversy and management problems not yet solved.[51] Additions to the Superior National Forest, authorized by the Weeks Act of March 1, 1911,[52] have been made through the years since its establishment in 1909, but need not be detailed here. It should be noted, however, that from its inception until the rush to the National Forests for recreation after World War I, it did not suffer from neglect. An estimated 12,750 recreationists visited the Superior National Forest in 1919.[53] The stage was set for the conflicts which arose after 1920.

Second De Facto Application of the Wilderness Concept in the Superior National Forest, Minnesota (1921)

According to the findings of the Boundary Waters Canoe Area Review Committee, little was heard about the Superior

National Forest during the period 1909-1920, but the two decades following 1920 constituted a story of successive controversies, at times extremely bitter. The disputes were carried on, of course, between preservation-minded recreationists and those interested in the production of timber and water power. While there were ample precedents for the development of the land and its natural resources above and below the ground, there were "neither precedents nor policies upon which to base programs for the recreationists."[54] In 1964 the Committee noted:

> The first attempt to indicate and to develop guiding principles was made in 1919 when Arthur H. Carhart was employed as a landscape architect for the Forest Service. His appointment meant (1) recognition of the necessity of recreation planning in the national forests, (2) production of the first plan of management of what was later to become the Boundary Waters Canoe Area of the Superior National Forest, and (3) the first actual studied application of protected wilderness as an integral part of national forest management.[55]

Continuing, the report stated that the following paragraph was basic to Carhart's general thought:

> It is evident, if Minnesota wishes to retain the scenic beauty which is hers, there must be some immediate action toward general preservation of good timber stands bordering lakes and streams. This does not mean that cutting shall be excluded from these locations but that the aesthetic qualities shall, where of high merit, take precedence over the commercialization of such timber stands.[56]

The Review Committee emphasized that in Carhart's final report as a member of the Forest Service, he had reiterated the same idea, but in more specific terms:

> I again state that this area can be developed as a timber-producing agent, as a commercial factor, if proper consideration is given the timber stands on shorelines, but in particular points, such as Saganaga, Sea Gull, Otter Track, Little Saganaga, Insula, Alice, LaCroix, and similar lakes, the scenic and recreational values are so precious to the nation that, so far as the lake unit itself is concerned, they should take precedence over all other possible uses of the lakes.[57]

When Carhart resigned from the Forest Service at the end of 1922, he made a comment which "is as true today as it was then," the committee stated: "The recreation work needs more funds and organization to work with in order to approach the needed recreation progress."[58]

What else did Carhart do to promote preservation of Superior National Forest lands before resigning from the Forest Service on December 31, 1922? It has been pointed out that he had made a return trip to the Superior National Forest in May, 1921, to outline a comprehensive recreational plan for that Forest. That same year he drafted a plan, a revision of the one presented in 1919, in a report of 144 pages, complete with photographic illustrations and maps of the area, carefully identified.[59] This revision might warrant complete reproduction here because it also stated so well Carhart's position, but limitation of space permits reference to only the salient points not covered above. Though his rationale remained consistent with his other writings, the 1921 report was keyed to the Superior National Forest area and its uniqueness. He wrote:

> If we are to have broad-thinking men and women of high mentality; of good physique, and with a true perspective on life we must allow our populace a communion with nature in areas of more or less wilderness conditions.[60]

Under a heading entitled, "National Recreation," he asserted:

> The various areas of outdoor territory offering the opportunity for touch with nature must be so handled that this necessity will not be impaired but rather will be protected and developed in a proper manner. All governmentally owned lands, capable of offering the needed association with nature, must be considered in this system.[61]

Carhart believed that the Superior National Forest had greater importance in the scheme of national recreation than perhaps any other publicly owned area. Under the heading, "The National Forest," he declared:

> The Superior is the only nationally owned plot of ground of any magnitude in which there are not now any man-made utilities which savor of urban conditions and in which the principal attraction is the timber-bordered water surfaces. Other nationally owned areas are for the most part in mountainous territory where the majestic sweep of mountain ranges constitutes the appeal producing elements . . . . There is as much a demand inherent in the body of citizenry for association with forested lakes and streams as with mountains, but whereas we have approximately 160 million acres of various types of mountainland, we have only about 1¼ million acres of forest lakeland, and this property is in the two National Forests within Minnesota.[62]

Then he stressed the point that whereas there were many millions of acres of other types of forest land to meet the demand for recreation of various kinds, there was only that one lake country, nationally reserved, and suited for water recreation.[63] Carhart clearly advocated wilderness preservation as a part of his 1921 report, for he used the word wilderness on numerous occasions. Among his unambiguous statements were the following:

> Twelfth, that urban type, man-made developments, either in service as represented by traffic lines or residence units, detract from this one area in which a wilderness lakeland type predominates, and thus imperil the high values, present in our national property, which may at some future time, and are now to no small extent, needed by our people to meet their desire for this sort of contact with the outdoors.
>
> Thirteen, that in excluding these modernized, man-made developments we are protecting from extinction the things of high sentimental and historical value which lie in the typical canoe travel within the area.[64]

The plan was

> dedicated to the ideal of human service and to the purpose of making Americans of greater mind, body and soul, and through them preserve our national life from disintegration because of its oppressing association with man-made, artificial life.[65]

He reiterated under a heading which has direct bearing on this study, "Wilderness Spirit," that there was "so little wilderness left where natural conditions are supreme that the Superior stands somewhat by itself in this type."[66] One final quotation should suffice: "The whole place should be kept as near wilderness as possible, the wilderness feature being developed rather than any urban conditions."[67]

Now that Carhart's recreation plan for the Superior National Forest has been reviewed, the question of formal acceptance and application of the wilderness principle can be explored. It should be noted that Carhart's carbon copy of the plan discussed immediately above was clearly marked "1921," but that Region 9 of the Forest Service in Milwaukee, Wisconsin, and the Washington office, referred to that report as Carhart's "1922" report. A letter from the Washington office to Region 9, written in 1955, stated:

> We have the original copy of Mr. Arthur Carhart's report entitled "Recreation Plan, Superior National Forest" submitted May, 1922 and approved by District Forester Peck on November 8, 1922.[68]

That statement, in itself, constituted *irrevocable evidence that Carhart's plan was formally approved two years before the one proposed by Aldo Leopold.* Leopold's plan for the Gila National Forest was not formally approved until June 3, 1924.[69] The Gila National Forest will be discussed in a separate chapter later in this study.

In a book written by Carhart in 1955, *Timber in Your Life,* he stated that at the time he was making the study of the Superior forest "it was all just a job to be done." He added,

> Looking back and referring to the report containing my recommendations for public use of this lakeland, I have a feeling of having had guidance of some sort beyond my actual abilities and perceptions.[70]

The guiding policy he suggested was set forth in the report by such statements as the following:

> The Superior National Forest stands today 1921 the refuge of the canoe and the sanctuary for the American seeking a typical lakeland region to satisfy his inherent longing for the communion there afforded with nature in her moods.[71]

He then observed that the Superior plan embraced a far greater area than the Trappers Lake unit, and that many acres of existing and future "commercial" forest lands were involved. The latter fact was certain to be a major consideration when the plan was first presented for approval of Carhart's immediate supervisor, Assistant Forester Carl J. Stahl. Although Stahl knew and loved the Superior forest country, Carhart later wrote, "I wasn't sure he would approve the plan I presented." But, he added:

> When he withdrew the $53,000 already allotted to start the Supervisor's ambitious road scheme, there was an upheaval. The Supervisor of the Superior National Forest, Calvin A. Dahlgren, I learned, was scared stiff of the water. He wanted roads; he demanded them. So did local "boosters" who had been "sold" the road plan. Not all of the forest personnel were in accord with my proposals and Stahl's actions. Some of them were determined to "develop" the Superior by building many roads. Being inside the Forest Service, my hands were tied.[72]

Carhart also explained that Will O. Doolittle, then Secretary of the American Institute of Park Executives and Editor of the Institute's publication, *Parks and Recreation,* and Paul B. Riis, Chairman of the Institute's National Park, Forest and Wildlife committee, had kept the "road boosters" of the early 1920's from destroying the wilderness values in the Superior National Forest. While Carhart did not minimize the valiant work of many Minnesotans, the Izaak Walton League, and later the Quetico-Superior Council, who labored to protect the recreational wealth of the Superior, he singled out for special praise Riis and Doolittle, "two warriors at the head of a small group fighting their heart out to prevent the debasement of that supreme lake country."[73] How that fight began and gained momentum will be detailed in a later portion of this study. For now it should be emphasized that the withdrawal of the $53,000 in 1921 by Assistant Forester Stahl, as a result of Carhart's report and recommendation, was the second *de facto* application of the wilderness concept. That action was confirmed on November 8, 1922, when Carhart's report was formally approved by District Forester Allen S. Peck.

CHAPTER VI

WHAT'S IT ALL ABOUT?

This chapter will examine the attitudes of foresters and conservationists toward forests in general, and recreation in the National Forests in particular, during 1922. The survey will endeavor to show that while there were some positive changes in the air regarding recreational development, the Forest Service still continued to tread rather traditional paths, adhering closely to its primary mission of timber production. Despite earlier statements that recreation was a "major activity" of the Service, the facts were otherwise.

Attitudes Toward Forests and Forest Recreation (1922)

Earlier in this study it was shown that A. H. Carhart was instrumental in the modification of the National Parks committee of the American Society of Landscape Architects, so that in 1920 it became known as the Committee on National Forests.[1] Also, a year later at the First National Conference on State Parks, he participated in the introduction and passage of a resolution supporting recreational use of the National Forests.[2] Following that step, he became involved in planning improvements for State Parks. In February, 1922, Everett L. Millard of Chicago requested Carhart to assist him in drafting recommendations for the Second National Conference on State Parks.[3] Millard wrote that he had been requested, as Chairman of the Committee on Legislation for the American Society of Landscape Architects, to submit a report there. The Conference, he added,

> opens May 22 in the Palisades Park, New York, and we shall want to prepare a set of recommendations, although probably not a proposed uniform state park act. The material you hope for from Prof. J. S. Pray and Prof. Frank Culley would be very helpful in this, and I am sure your own will be still more valuable, if you can send it to me. Won't you write them again, and then see if all this material can be given me as soon as possible. I am really relying on you more than anyone else to help produce something worthy of permanent record.[4]

Unfortunately, Carhart's reply to this request is not available, so his contributions to the planning for State Parks cannot now be documented.

As in 1921, so in 1922, there were a series of letters between J. S. Pray and A. H. Carhart dealing with the "whole movement of outdoor life" as they termed it. In March, 1922, Carhart informed Pray that there was a movement on foot to call a meeting at St. Louis during the last week in April, for the purpose of forming a federation of outdoor clubs. The federation would act as a "clearing house" for all outdoor societies, forestry clubs, park societies, audubon societies, mountain and prairie clubs, and all other organizations having contact with the outdoors. Carhart believed it was "an excellent movement and if you have any way to support it it will be well worthwhile doing."[5]

Apparently the outdoor groups met in St. Louis, but failed to form a Federation. However, in Washington, two years later there was a meeting, attended by 309 delegates from 128 national organizations interested in federal recreation policy, which was called the National Conference on Outdoor Recreation. On April 14, 1924, President Calvin Coolidge issued a statement related to the meeting, which read, in part:

> Our aim in this country must be to try to put the chance for out-of-doors pleasure, with all that it means, within the grasp of the rank and file of our people, the poor man as well as the rich man. Country recreation for as many of our people as possible should be our objective.[6]

Writing in 1922, Frank A. Waugh attempted to show that forestry and outdoor recreation in the National Forests were compatible.[7] He aimed at enlarging the arbitrary and narrowly limited meaning that the word forest had come to have in America—that of a tract of woodland where trees were grown exclusively for economic uses. In order to illustrate his point, Waugh traced the history of forest recreation from the earliest times. He asserted that forests had been reserved for the recreation of royal hunters, and that such recreation was "historically the oldest purpose of a forest." He expressed concern over the popular misconception about the National Forests. Few people seemed to believe that they were valuable for grazing cattle and sheep, for protecting municipal water supplies, and for enjoying other utilities promoted by the Forest Service, so that proposals for forest legislation and administration had been handicapped. Such ignorance, Waugh wrote, had caused many practical difficulties in drafting adequate plans for dealing with the exceedingly valuable recreation utilities in the National Forests. He noted that the erroneous definition of forestry "has no historical foundation, either in law, in forest practice nor in common usage."[8] Though

Waugh may not have been entirely accurate, his article reflected the rationale of the period and illuminated his rationale as a landscape architect *vis-a-vis* that of a forester. Referring to the royal hunting forests established by the ancient rulers of Persia and Babylon, he asserted that "certainly whenever the first of these protected hunting grounds was proclaimed there the first national forest was established."[9]

Turning to English common law and in the usage of the mother tongue in respect to forests, Waugh gave a legal definition of a forest according to John Manwood's *Laws of the Forest,* first published in 1598.[10] He then quoted the following interesting extract:

> In those days it was a matter of little ceremony either to make or to enlarge a forest. Thus saith the law:
>
> 'It is allowed to our sovereign lord the king, in respect of his continual care and labour for the preservation of the whole realm, among other privileges, this prerogative, —to have his places of recreation and pastime wheresoever he will appoint. For as it is at the liberty and pleasure of his grace to reserve the wild beasts and the game to himself for his only delight and pleasure, so he may also, at his will and pleasure, make a forest for them to abide in.'[11]

While it was the stated purpose of Waugh's article to erase certain misconceptions about the definition of a forest, it is presented here for two other purposes: it shows that in 1922 recreational development in the National Forests suffered at the expense of the production of marketable timber; and it documented the fact that even in the time of William the Conqueror forests had been managed on a multiple-use principle. Waugh quoted further, but from another writer:

> (William) the Conqueror acquired, by the right of conquest, not only the demesne lands of the Confessor and of the nobles who had opposed him, but also all the rights of the chase over great woodland or open stretch-

> es . . . where royal hunting rights had previously been exercised by Saxon or Danish kings. The Conqueror took advantage of his autocratic position . . . to carry out 'afforestation' not only over the restricted areas that had been the hunting grounds . . . but over almost all the old folkland that remained unenclosed. The term 'forest,' that had been long in like use on parts of the Continent, was then introduced into England. . . . Within these afforested tracts, he decreed that the right of hunting was vested solely in the Crown. . . . The feudal idea about all wild animals, however monstrous and harsh in operation, possessed a rough logical basis. It was argued that all such animals were *bona vacantia, or* ownerless property, and hence pertained to the king; . . . and that therefore the right of exercising the chase, or taking all kinds of beasts of venery, belonged solely to the king.[12]

The explanation continued with more quotations, and dealt with "permanent forges of some size, belonging to the crown, within the forest bounds" in Duffield Frith. It also dealt with coal mining, procuring of peat, and quarrying of stone for building purposes, all of which were regulated, and were confined to sites on the fringes of the forest, where possible. Trades, such as tanning of hides, detrimental to the deer, "through odour or otherwise," were "rigorously prohibited within forest bounds."[13]

Waugh found "without exception" that examination of the records showed that the early idea of a forest was to harbor wild game for the recreation of royal hunters. In fine, he concluded that recreation was the very oldest forest utility and historically the only one. He asserted that attempts to draw a distinction between forests and parks by lay members in America had been futile, and that the "common newspaper mind" thought of a forest as "a tract used for recreation." The fallacy in that reasoning lay in the fact that enormous areas of woodland were used for both purposes. His own definition of of forest was "any tract of land, usually characterized by a predominant growth of trees, maintained and managed for various human utilities."[14]

The foregoing attitude toward forests as just so much lumber, was one which Recreation Engineer Carhart had attempted to change during the previous three-year period. His efforts to gain outside support were redoubled in 1922, and since he could not openly oppose official Service policy, the correspondence between Carhart and Pray in that year bore the caption *"CONFIDENTIAL,"* at the head of each page. One such letter, dated May 27, 1922, from Pray to Carhart reflected, in part:

> I have been interested in your confidential letter of April 29. . . . The letter went to Colonel W. B. Greeley with the changes you suggested. I also sent copies to Mr. E. A. Sherman and to Professor F. A. Waugh. As yet I have heard from none of these. . . . It goes without saying that I respect your confidences and will not let any of these statements of your confidential letter escape me. I would be very much interested to receive the copies of letters which you have and which outline the "whole deal," if you care to send them to me.[15]

The "whole deal" referred to the proposed road construction in the Superior National Forest which the Forest Supervisor, C. A. Dahlgren, was planning to put through, notwithstanding the opposition of Assistant Forester Carl J. Stahl, previously mentioned.[16] The next chapter will outline that episode.

In the May 27 letter, Pray also indicated discouragement at a statement by Associate Forester Sherman. The statement had included:

> The field districts are now beginning to realize that, while most of their work in recreational development will be done by foresters, most of the districts now look forward to the time when they will have at least one man whose basic training will be that of a landscape en-

> gineer or its substantial equivalent. . . . In short all of the foregoing words merely mean that in the Forest Service we will need a lot of foresters who will have some training in recreational engineering, and we will need a few recreational engineers who will in turn have to become foresters in fact and view-point, in order to best serve our Forests.[17]

Pray believed that it was not necessary that the recreational engineers should be foresters in fact, and that it was "a fatal mistake for them to be foresters in view-point." Moreover, he declared:

> For most of the work in recreational engineering to be carried by foresters who know a little of landscape, but are not thoroughly trained in our art is very, very bad. I do not see how you can forecast it otherwise. I admit that the statement goes far for a forester, but I am personally disappointed to find Mr. Sherman is not prepared to go much farther, in fact to go the whole way to Landscape Architecture, . . . in the Forests . . ., and to see that it is only necessary for the landscape architect or recreational engineer to know enough forestry to appreciate the point of view of the foresters with whom he must cooperate, which is very different from saying that he must himself be a forester.[18]

By June, 1922, a certain disenchantment with the Forest Service was discernible in Carhart's personal correspondence. Pray's opinion of Sherman's attitude toward landscape architecture seemed to augment that disillusionment. Carhart confided to J. S. Pray that:

> The recreation situation in the National Forests is rapidly nearing a showdown. I have felt it since last fall more acutely than ever. When I came out here I thought that there was a magnificent opportunity to do a work that would be of national importance and of magnificent scope. The opportunity still exists but until there is a

> very definite change in conditions the opportunity might as well be buried at the bottom of the sea.[19]

Moreover, he declared that he had definitely decided that "unless things change very materially by the first of the year in the way of support of recreational development in the National Forests," that he would leave the Service, and the "foothold that landscape architecture has in this work will either have to be held by some other man or it will be lost." Carhart remarked that "the reply that Mr. Sherman made to you I think gives you a very clear insight into the attitude of the Forest Service with regard to this work." The seven-page letter deplored Sherman's statement that

> under present financial conditions the employment of additional recreation engineers necessarily would require a further reduction in the personnel engaged upon these other lines.[20]

There seems little doubt that Carhart's efforts had been frustrated, and that he felt rejected and ignored. It was his feeling that "the people in Washington" did not have what constituted the "recreation landscape design that is needed on every Forest." He noted that whenever he had met with them they had "lectured" him on what he "should and should not do." There were, however, three persons who were credited with appreciating "just what the regional planning of a forest for human use means," namely, District Forester A. S. Peck, Assistant Forester Carl J. Stahl, and Supervisor A. G. Hamel of the San Isabel National Forest. But, he asserted, "the conversion of three or four men" was but a "drop in the bucket," because

> so long as your superior officer calls you in and simply tells you what you can and cannot do and does not try to get ideas from you, one can hardly break in and demand that he be heard.[21]

In the midst of that letter, Carhart suggested the desirability of creating an organization on the order of the recently established (1964) Bureau of Outdoor Recreation:

> I am frankly wondering if the recreational development of the forests will ever reach the importance and degree of consideration needed under the Forest Service. I have been thinking of the possibility of a distinct recreation planning and development service.[22]

Carhart was not unaware of the fact that Congress had "not given the Forests to the Service for recreation," that the law specifically stated that the Service was to administer them "for the production of timber," but he believed that "Congress cannot justly thus tie up some of the best scenic recreational territory in the United States and lose to us the value of such territory through human use." He described the greatest need in the National Forests as "functional, regional basic planning." He then emphasized that if that was not done "WE ARE GOING TO LOSE NATURAL BEAUTY THROUGH ILL-ADVISED PLANNING," which he estimated in the aggregate "WILL FAR SURPASS IN TOTAL QUALITY AND QUANTITY WHAT WE NOW HAVE IN THE NATIONAL PARKS."[23]

After mentioning his intention to leave the Forest Service by the end of the year, Carhart included a promise which he later fulfilled:

> I am not done with recreation in National Forests when I leave. I will not be muzzled by censorship . . . and while I am not going to do any "muckraking" I will be free to tell my ideas and views without restriction. . . . Before the scenic, aesthetic and other human use values are ruined, I want to do what I may to aid.[24]

Meanwhile in a personal letter to Associate Forester Sherman, dated June 29, 1922, Carhart expressed concern over the "apparent sidetracking" of adequate recreational design in the National Forests, the lack of appointment of permanent, trained men to handle the recreation planning in other districts, and the "readiness of many of the field and other men to point to recreation as a horrible example of the wandering of the forester from forestry."[25] He pointed to the "disposition on the part of the Service to ask for funds for sanitation and fire protection," instead of "frankly going after needed money to handle the entire field of recreational development" as one of many indications that the recreation was "not being squarely faced."[26] He urged that the needs in recreation be considered sufficiently early in order to "present them properly to Congress next winter," that "we cannot expect to convince Congress . . . unless we possess the courage of our convictions," and that the "evident partial shelving of this activity of national importance does not show a very strong conviction on our part."[27] Carhart was aware that he was considered "hog wild" on recreation by "some eminently practical men" whose views differed from his, but, he affirmed, "there are several thousands of people before me that were considered crazy by their associates that afterwards were given revised ratings."[28]

First Appropriation of Federal Funds Expressly for Forest Recreation (1922)

It would appear from the tone of the letter cited above that Carhart had become a sort of "Frankenstein" to Sherman. Although he did not become "dangerous" to his creator, he had become at least an irritant. Carhart, it should be noted here, recently stated that he continues to admire and respect Sherman, whom he described as "a very dedicated man," and one with whom he had "never had a falling out."[29] True to his reputation as a gentleman, Sherman replied to Carhart's letter, which had pointed an admonitory finger at the Forest Service, in polite but firm language. The position of the Forest Service at that time is best told in Sherman's own words:

> I am not at all surprised at your concern over the apparent sidetracking of adequate recreational landscape design in the National Forests. . . . I am not unmindful of the proper position of recreation in the use of the National Forests . . . [but] we must save our National Forests first if they are to be of any value for recreation or for any other purpose. . . . The Forest Service is not the Government by a long shot, but is only a part of the Government, and . . . it must work as a coordinating part. We cannot do all the coordinating ourselves. Congress insists upon doing some of it. As a matter of fact, Congress is the boss.[30]

Sherman continued by pointing out that recreational development in the National Forests had been greatly hindered as a result of matters "entirely beyond our control." Congressman J. W. Good, Chairman of the House Appropriations Committee, had become "sold" on the idea that

> the Forest Service was entering into competition with the National Parks in furnishing public recreation grounds. Mr. Good reached this conviction during a trip which he took in the Western National Parks in company with Park Director Stephen T. Mather. He conceived the idea that it was bad business for the Government to compete with itself. He had the wrong idea of the basis upon which our activities rested, but his convictions upon this point were very firm. He was one of the most influential men in the lower House of Congress, and although I feel he was wrong in this case, nevertheless I have great admiration for his tremendous business ability, and feel that his presence as Chairman . . . was easily worth fifty million dollars a year to the nation.[31]

Sherman explained that when the appropriation request of "$40,000 for recreation" was turned down "it was useless for us to butt our heads against a stone wall." In its place was substituted the idea of "construction projects valuable for recreation purposes as incidental to necessary sanitation and fire protection," upon which basis Forest Service received "an item for $10,000 in its last appropriation bill." The significance of that amount, though admittedly small, was spelled out.

> In the first place it does recognize (1) the use of the National Forests for recreation purposes; (2) the necessity for regulating that use, and (3) the responsibility of the Government for providing funds for such regulation. The $10,000 is merely incidental. The important point is that Congress has recognized the work and it is merely a question of time and proper presentation of the case to secure adequate funds.[32]

With what may be termed fatherly patience, Sherman justified the seeming inconsistency of not having "squarely faced" the recreational situation, by stating that it had always been his policy to "accept a compromise" which gave him half the victory whenever refusal to do so was "certain to result in complete defeat." He admitted in a two-word sentence, "We compromised."[33]

Sherman's letter of July 5, 1922, pinpoints the birth of the expenditure of federal funds for recreational purposes in the National Forests, albeit under the guise of "necessary sanitation and fire protection." Sherman emphasized:

> The result is that we have secured the recognition by Congress of three of the four important points necessary to secure the development of our recreational resources. The only legal instrumentality that we lack is authority to expend money for the primary purpose of recreational development. Thus far it has been made secondary.[34]

In the same letter, Sherman discussed the efforts of Chief Forester W. B. Greeley during the preceding two years to obtain increased appropriations for more ranger and forest guard positions to aid in fire protection and control, the results of which had been fruitless. But the letter closed in a spirit of optimism. It pointed out that considering the obstacles during the previous three or four years, both political and financial, the Forest Service had made much greater progress than under the circumstances they had any right to expect. The drive against the National Forests in favor of the National Parks had largely "spent itself" and "left us in a stronger position than ever before," Sherman averred.[35]

Sherman's explanations, however, did not assuage Carhart's fear that irrevocable damage was being done to the landscape in the National Forests as a result of the unplanned development of recreational resources. He, therefore, answered the Associate Forester in a six-page letter in which he asked pointed questions about recreation and fire protection. He reiterated that improperly executed recreation design had "dissipated recreation values almost as thoroughly as fire ruins them."[36]

It might be helpful at this juncture to note that when Carhart used the word recreation it had a connotation which transcended the usual dictionary meaning. Webster, for example, defined *recreation* as refreshment in body or mind, as after work, by some form of play, amusement, or relaxation. Carhart, on the other hand, had in mind the unique ability of the natural landscape or wilderness features, unmarred by man-made "improvements," to *re-create* the human mind, body, and spirit. The improvements he would make would be calculated to preserve the wilderness features of certain zones by furnishing less spectacular areas with basic camping and trail facilities in a graduated regional plan. By substituting the word *wilderness* for *recreation,* employed in the quotation in the paragraph immediately above, the point Carhart stressed may be more readily grasped, namely, that improperly executed recreation design had "dissipated *wilderness* values almost as thoroughly as fire ruins them." In that context, the terms may be considered synonymous.

Carhart also remarked to Sherman that some day, not far distant, the Forest Service would be held as strictly accountable for "blundering methods" in recreation as it would "if we did not fight fire or allowed old time slash cutting of timber." He believed that it would be far better to exclude recreation development altogether, than to do it in a "patchy, poorly planned manner."[37]

The remainder of the letter recapitulated the thousands of words which had been written before on recreation, with an occasional look into the future. Carhart wrote that he was "not a bit convinced" that "we are through with the Park drive on forest lands. One group, the commercial interests, have been pitted against the recreation-hungry majority." He warned that the whole outdoor recreation movement could not be smothered permanently—that it was based on a demand "as primal, as fundamental as the demand for wood or wool," and that the demand could be satisfied by the Forests.[38]

Earlier that month, Carhart had written many of the same thoughts to District Forester A. S. Peck in Denver.[39] He expressed his conviction that the Forest Service was not managing efficiently "this resource belonging to the nation." That Carhart had the strength of his convictions and the courage to present them to his superiors was again demonstrated in the following sentences:

> The one efficient line of action is administration according to the rules of the Forest Service manual of regulations. The fact that this is so is repeatedly presented to one who will make an intelligent study of this work and must indicate some laxness on the part of our organization.[40]

He urged Peck "to impress these needs on the men who are more nearly the heads in forest work," in order that the "Congress this coming session" could be vigorously presented with the situation in the National Forests. Fundamentally, what was needed was "a well outlined program . . . of properly and adequately planning, protecting, developing and administering a resource which is a part of the wealth of the nation." He feared for "our scenic heritage" which he described as "nothing less than a priceless treasure," and recommended as a minimum action, that the Forest Service "at least let the people know that we have it, and the things we need to properly take care of it."[41]

District Forester Peck's reply came a month later.[42] His letter was a terse summary and exposition of the weak position held by recreation in the over-all Forest Service picture in 1922. Some excerpts are illuminating:

> My suggestion would be that you do not worry too much about the future of the recreational development in general. . . . It took a great many decades for the forestry movement to gain the momentum which is now carrying it forward with considerable strength, and it will probably take a decade or so more to accomplish the general widespread recognition of recreation as a resource, which you believe in. While I would not wish to discourage your efforts in the least, I want to help you direct them to the best advantage. We must not expect to accomplish everything in three or four years.[43]

Time was running out for Recreation Engineer Carhart. When he wrote a memorandum on November 27, 1922, about his much beloved Trappers Lake, he knew that at the end of the following month he would be leaving the Forest Service.[44] Rather resignedly he wrote:

> It seems hardly necessary to say anything further regarding the road situation around Trappers Lake. The general approval of the majority of people has endorsed our stand with regard to the exclusion of an auto highway around the lake shore. . . . A highway reaching to the edge of Trappers Lake at any point is definitely and greatly detrimental to the scenic values found here, which are genuinely of national importance.[45]

Final Efforts of the First Forest Service Recreation Engineer (1922)

In the last few days of November, 1922, Carhart produced two additional memoranda dealing with matters that were weighing heavily on his mind. The first one concerned "the needs with reference to administrative and technical organization" in the National Forest recreation field, which he "offered in memorandum form as a matter of record." It was a criticism of the Forest Service for "not handling recreation in the Forests, either as it should be handled or as thoroughly" as it was handling other lines of work.[46] If Carhart was the original "broken record," endlessly repeating the same phrases, he was also progressive in his thought. His five-page message was replete with details for re-organization of the Forest Service by districts or by "Grand Regions"; it was another clear indication of his dedication to the Service he was about to leave.

That memorandum was followed by a three-page statement of the "functions of a landscape architect acting as Recreation Engineer for the Forest Service," which included his obligations and relations, as well.[47] The statement might properly be called the first "job description" for the position he had occupied. He outlined the duties necessary for planning a region. The duties were separated into two divisions of human use: travel and residence. All recreation, he noted, came from "travel through a country, either from landscape or scene," or from a stay in "residence" at some local point, or both.[48]

Then he turned to a discussion of zoning in the National Forests which would result in the preservation of wilderness values:

> All residence planning . . . is strictly in the field of work of the Recreation Engineer. . . . This means designation of areas where all possible residential use is allow-

able, areas where it is allowable under some restrictions . . . and zones where general residence is strictly subordinated to other recreation uses. . . . The proper preservation and presentation of all scenic features in a just and reasonable balance with other forest functions, and planning all phases of human use, is the sum total of the duty of the landscape architect in this work.[49]

There can be no doubt of Arthur H. Carhart's sincerity and dedication to the ideals for which he fought while a member of the Forest Service. Frank A. Waugh wrote to Carhart in December, 1922, that he felt some of the difficulties about which Carhart had written, but had been inclined to take a more hopeful view of the situation as it existed in the Forest Service.[50] He felt that some of the men in the Service were very much alive to recreational needs, but that Congress's reluctance to make appropriations for recreation was one of the greatst problems they faced. "I have not been able to see any way of educating Congress to an intelligent view," Waugh confided, "inside the next few years," thereby confirming Carhart's conclusions.[51]

One of the last official acts performed by Carhart was the reading of a paper before the Denver Section of the Society of American Foresters on December 16, 1922, which was subsequently published in the *Journal of Forestry*.[52] His presentation was a reiteration of the fact that recreation was a necessity not a luxury, that the demand would increase, that it was a value present in every forested area regardless of status, name or administration, and that it was an annual "crop" of the forest.[53]

But that was by no means Carhart's swan song, because far from being a dying swan, he was a dynamic personality in the wilderness preservation world, and was heard from again and again.

The Personnel office of the Forest Service in Denver officially commented on the resignation of its only Recreation Engineer in the following manner:

Arthur H. Carhart, on January 1, became an official subscriber and correspondent of the Review as a member of the firm of McCrary, Culley and Carhart of Denver. In the Service, Mr. Carhart filled a unique place as Recreation Engineer in District Two, and by his efforts did much to put D-2 in a distinct and forward place in recreational development. We wish him all success in his new work.[54]

CHAPTER VII

O.K., ALL YOU CATS, KEEP OUT!

This chapter will illustrate how the first major dispute was instigated over the proposed construction of certain roads in the Superior National Forest of Minnesota. The portion of that Forest specifically under consideration is now known as the Boundary Waters Canoe Area. It is worth re-emphasizing that that border lake country has remained a national problem despite numerous attempts during and since the 1920's to resolve the perennial controversy.

The Forester and the Recreation Engineer Express Honest Differences of Opinion Regarding Forest Policies

In his letter of resignation to the Forester, which became effective December 31, 1922, Recreation Engineer Carhart asserted that the compensation for his work had been deficient on two counts: salary and accomplishment.[1] He felt that there had not been adequate development of the plans he had prepared, and that:

> The recreation work needs more funds and organization to work with to approach the needs. A constant statement that the Forest Service cannot supply either prevents much needed recreation development progress.[2]

His next observation explained why he resigned from the Forest Service. He wrote:

> A certain cycle of accomplishment has been finished in recreation work of this District. It is the strictly pioneer work. Principles, methods and plans on which this work can progress for several decades have been demonstrated and proven sound. The next cycle is the development and application of principles now established. This will take much more support than the Forest Service seems now able to give. If I were to start this second cycle of recreation planning and direction I would rush to finish it. That would probably take ten to twenty years. In the face of present conditions with the needed forces of men and money in this work lacking, I do not desire to enter this next phase of recreation planning and direction in this District.[3]

The closing paragraph of the resignation assured the Forester that "my interest in human service from forest lands will not diminish with my withdrawal from the Service. My heart is too much with the work for that."[4]

Carhart's letter of resignation brought a reply from E. A. Sherman, then Acting Forester, in which the latter stated:

> I cannot question your decision to leave the Service . . . but, considering it from the Service's point of view, I can and do regret it. You have done so much to establish the recreation use of the National Forests on a high

> plane of public service that I cannot help but wish you would stay to do a little more.[5]

Sherman regretted that Carhart's work in the Service had not taken him farther afield and into the Districts, so that it would have become more apparent why the resources placed at his disposal for recreation work had fallen short of the reasonable requirements and importance of that work. The Acting Forester suggested that:

> Perhaps if you had learned more intimately of our fire problems in Districts One, Five and Six; of the pressing demand for increased timber-sale work and research work; of the need for more intensive range management and of the numerous other major activities now suspended or, at best, slighted through lack of funds, you might perhaps have felt less impatient at the slowness with which Congress, in the first instance, and the Forester, in the second, made available money with which to work in your chosen line.[6]

Sherman's closing statement seemed to recognize that Carhart's plans for recreational development in the National Forests would stand the test of time, and reflected sympathy for but not agreement with all of Carhart's views:

> However, I feel sure that the severance of your relations with the Service will not diminish your interest in its work, and that with each passing year we will approach more closely to the exacting standards which you set yourself and which I am free to admit should govern the entire Service.[7]

On February 13, 1923, Carhart addressed a letter marked *"PERSONAL"* to Sherman in which he again stated his position regarding Forest Service policies in general, and the handling of recreation in particular.[8] That letter evoked a reply from Sherman which tersely demonstrated the seeming irreconcilability of their views:

> While I do not entirely agree with you either as to your facts or conclusions, I am nevertheless very glad to get your viewpoint and believe that I can appreciate it in some degree. While I do not feel it would be desirable to publish the letter, as it is rather too much of a family matter for that, at the same time I would like to have your permission to send a copy of it to each of the District Foresters, so that they may know how our recreation work appears to a specialist.[9]

Carhart replied to Sherman by candidly stating that he did not expect any Forest Service men to agree with his ideas, and that he was not surprised that Sherman did not agree with him.[10] Concerning the request to make distribution of Carhart's letter to the various District Foresters, Carhart believed that it would "only thicken the passive resistance to constructive recreation planning." Instead, he suggested that if there were anything of value to Sherman in the letter, that it be passed on "in some manner through you without there being a copy of the letter sent to the District Foresters."[11] To that suggestion, Sherman replied that he had dismissed the idea of such a distribution, particularly since the letter had been intended for his personal information.[12]

That the aims of the two professional disciplines, namely, forestry and landscape architecture, were difficult to achieve in the Forest Service has been demonstrated in the foregoing chapters. Carhart felt that by leaving the Service he could be free to help overcome what seemed to be a losing battle for recreational development and wilderness preservation.

Setting in Motion the First Controversy in the Boundary Waters Canoe Area (1922)

Even before leaving the Forest Service, Arthur H. Carhart had carefully laid the ground work for the crusade which he was to carry on following his resignation. The first hint at organizing a movement to protest Service policy appeared in a letter from Carhart to Pray in June, 1922.[13] He noted that while there was not a "written promise" made to him, when he accepted employment with the Forest Service, that there would be "adequate backing of my plans, there was every such thing implied." He remarked that it was "put up" that the Forest Service recognized that recreation was "one of the greatest uses of forest lands . . . and that it would most certainly receive attention from the Service." While there had not been a "real breach of contract" nor a "genuine reversal of this stated attitude," there had been a "real breaking of faith with me and with this work in not giving it the real support it merits." He asserted:

> The F. S. [Forest Service] executives still state to the world that they recognize recreation as a major utility and they continue to say so to people in the Service, but they have not put action behind these words. Further they are breaking faith with the people of the United States if they turn to simply timber production without regard to the protection and enhancement of the scenic wealth, for they are just as ruthlessly destroying wealth of this nature as the piggish lumberman would destroy wealth in wood if the Service were not in charge of these forests.[14]

Carhart observed that there was in the Forest Service at that time "a definite move" to accomplish two things. First, to sell the forest idea to the people "whether they want it or not," and second, to obtain additional appropriations of money from Congress to "HIRE MORE FOREST TRAINED MEN." He believed that other things would stand "little chance of consideration until these two things are put over."[15]

The letter to Pray continued:

> I found that there has gone out a letter which expressly states that there will be little or no considera-

> tion given [to] asking for recreation improvements this year. I have repeatedly got this from the Supervisors. When I talk [about] recreation work they say that when they asked even for the most rudimentary, even life preserving, needs they "had their fingers rapped" most mercilessly. This is according to law too for there is no money which can rightfully be allotted to forest recreation.[16]

Carhart explained further that three years before there had been a tendency to "stretch a point" and give a little attention to recreation, but under the "present strictly foresters' regime," the field men had been led to believe that it was time to "pull away from recreation because it is taboo." The fault lay not with the field men, but with the "counter current" that the "return to forestry" had set up. At this point in his letter, Carhart commented on the need to start a protest movement to aid in molding Forest Service policy toward greater recognition of the necessity to plan recreational development in the Forests. His own words were:

> I am thoroughly convinced that it is time to get right into the firing line and open up with the people who love America, and get them thoroughly aroused over the matter. If we can get only enough money to secure two landscape men in every district it may save from despoliation some of the most beautiful areas that are in our country today. We will then be strong enough to make our ideas felt and can stand more of a chance in the Forest Organization.[17]

Carrying his idea further, he suggested:

> Better yet, if a planning committee or commission were to make a reconnaissance of recreation and scenic territory in the U.S. backed by all interested organizations, it might be even more effective. I'll pledge all my knowledge to that commission whether I am officially connected with it or not. I don't care to be associated

> with the work particularly but DO WANT TO SEE SOMETHING OF THE KIND STARTED.[18]

Unfortunately, Carhart's letter of June 17, 1922, to J. S. Pray, failed to rally the desired vigorous support of the American Society of Landscape Architects. As a member of that Society's National Parks and National Forests Committee, Carhart's best help had come through Pray's direct correspondence with the Forester and Associate Forester, W. B. Greeley and E. A. Sherman, respectively.

But Carhart had another affiliation which was to prove more responsive. As a "senior fellow" in the American Institute of Park Executives he was acquainted with Paul B. Riis, the Institute's Chairman of the Department of Wild Life Preservation.[19] Carhart saw that it would be extremely difficult to achieve his program of recreational development and wilderness preservation in the Superior National Forest without an additional source of influence. Accordingly, in a letter dated December 6, 1922, he outlined what he referred to as "the Superior situation."[20] By that message, he informed Riis about the "road scheme" for the Superior National Forest. Though no prior letters to Riis were among the Carhart Papers examined, by implication Carhart had already furnished him with some information about the Superior National Forest road program. Carhart remarked:

> I'll outline more of the Superior situation. Take your map. Here is the road scheme that is being talked [sic]. A road from Grand Marais to Gunflint already built and usable for autos. A road from Ely to Gunflint to make one of the damnable "circle trips" that are good things but not when they become a disease. A road on this line would leave Ely, pass White Iron, follow the general line of the Kawishiwi [river] to Snowbank, from there to little Saganaga and thence to Gunflint. This is the most untouched portion of the Superior that I saw. Little Saganaga is a jewel. And the two roads I spoke of [are] in connection with the western section of

> the forest that are proposed this year. The one that is almost certain to go through is from Ely to Buyck. It leaves Ely passing by Big Lake, and crosses the Stewart and Sioux rivers. I do not think that this road is so harmful but it is planned to run a stub from the general location of Big Lake to a bay of Lac La Croix, one of the most beautiful lakes in America.[21]

Carhart argued that the road from Ely to Buyck would go through the heart of "all kinds of moose territory." The administrative argument for such a road was that fire crews could get into the center of the forest quickly. He then declared that the "entire Forest Service is fire mad. They are giving it more attention than any other single feature." Carhart doubted that the Ely-Buyck road plan could be stopped, but he considered even more serious the proposed road going north from Big Lake to La Croix, because it opened up the whole territory. The Ely-Buyck road would not touch the water routes, but the Big Lake-La Croix road would tap the heart of them. Then he proposed the strategy they might employ:

> We must concentrate on the stub road to la Croix in preference to all others. . . . I would say that it is a very diplomatic move to oppose both. Then when it comes to a show down, do a little needed trading, so there will be a giving in on the Ely-Buyck and stop opposition to that on the grounds of an iron-clad promise that there will be no road built to la Croix.[22]

The Ely-Gunfiint road proposal was deemed an even more serious problem, because it lay outside the Forest. Carhart suggested arousing the sentiment of the people in Ely against construction of that road, by convincing them that "the world thinks that they have a much more desirable recreation ground without that road than with it." Carhart declared that "Don Hough is the man on that if he is with us. I have not heard from him yet." Hough would hopefully "fill the local papers up there with the right sort of propaganda," but since he was planning to put in a canoe service in that part of the country, his cooperation was not assured.[23]

A solution to the problem of blocking the construction of roads into and through the Superior National Forest needed an appropriate start. Carhart could not openly precipitate the formation of such a protest movement, but he could, through Riis, accomplish his aim. He suggested the subterfuge which Riis would use in order to launch the opposition from the outside, while actually the movement would start with Carhart from within the Forest Service. These precautions were taken so that Carhart and his future source of information would not be compromised. To obtain data about the proposed road construction, Carhart offered to Riis the following pretext:

> It might be that if you get [Will H.] Dilg[24] to write the Forest Supervisor Calvin A. Dahlgren at Ely and ask him if there was any road development planned for the forest for the future, he could get the information which can be the basis of action. Just write him a casual letter as though interested in the development of the country by roads and the whole scheme will be spilled then. If we get the information back that I expect, then there will be sufficient basis for action all along the line. I can get the inside of the thing here at all times.[25]

Continuing, Carhart wrote:

> There is no reason why you should not write everyone you can rely on getting things lined up. If we can get an organization already to move, instead of having to build it after things are starting up there, we will be in an infinitely stronger position than we would be otherwise. Why not write every one of the men you can rely on, outline the value of the Superior National Forest and point out the probable menace in the road program up there, and what the real outdoor people will lose through it. Get them all ready to put up the proper line of argu-

> ment in an article, and get each ready to move at short notice to get articles in every outdoor paper in the country if necessary.[26]

The lengthy letter of "instructions" included the hope that the Superior National Forest could be held "without the manicuring process applied there that has gone on in other wilderness places." He believed that

> it is right now of more importance because of type and situation than any other single public property except the Yellowstone, Glacier, and Grand Canon [sic]. Maybe position with reference to population makes it more so. It is the equal of those at any rate.[27]

He then turned to a discussion of what could be done in the Parks and Forests generally, adding that he believed that the development of the Superior National Forest "should be decided on the basis of just service to the people of the country."[28]

Further on, Carhart declared:

> By all means place all our correspondence with [Will O.] Doolittle.[29] He should be informed to the last letter. I think I will send you about ten maps of the Superior today so you can outline on them the proposed roads through this Forest when you start lining up the working team.[30]

Until Carhart's severance from government service, his activities in promoting this protest movement were necessarily conducted *sub rosa*, for as he put it, "there is a very strict censorship of all writings and speeches that prevents any out and out statement of personal findings and ideas." But after his resignation, he would continue to be informed of happenings in the Forest Service:

> Now as to source of information. . . . Knowing the inside workings of this Service as well as I do I think I

> will be in a position to keep thoroughly informed as to where to hit and when, so we need not worry. Just remember that my resignation to this government bureau is no surrender in any way, but merely a transfer to another regiment.[31]

He assured Riis that they would "know what is going on all of the time" through the man who had been his chief, Carl J. Stahl.[32] He was not so sure what would happen when Riis approached the Forest Service personnel of the Superior National Forest at Ely, Minnesota.

> There may be a surprise for you in Ely . . . when the question of the road is brought up. I have been trying to educate that bunch up there to the fact that they have in the Superior without roads one of the most unique areas in America. . . . I think the leaders see it. But there is this road fever that is running riot . . . and it may put the thing through without any chance of breaking up the plans.[33]

While it was not going to be a victory without effort, Carhart believed that the attitude of the public in the vicinity of Ely was more favorable than was generally the case, because he had already done some spade work:

> They have had the fact that the Superior is unique without roads pointed out to them time after time, and they at least partly believe it. But I have so far been the one to do the pointing out. If the big men of the community were to get the same expression from say a dozen or more of the big men in outdoor fields, they would probably be won over for the most part.[34]

Toward the end of the seven-page "battle plan," he remarked that he wished he could "make the next statement unusually emphatic." It related to the future of game and the sport of hunting in the United States, which he believed was "more concerned with the National Forests and the game inside of them than any other areas in the whole Nation."[35] In his characteristic enthusiasm for the outdoors, and for the movement to save the Superior, Carhart added:

> Talk of public shooting grounds——156,000,000 acres of them in the Forests if they but be handled so the game has a fighting chance. I am going to uncork some articles for the magazine [*Parks and Recreation*] soon on this. . . . Now this has gone on long enough. There may be some food for thought and some reasonable lines of action. Hope so. . . . I'll be willing to write every day if necessary and hope that it will not bore you.[36]

The campaign to preserve the border lake country was fought on many fronts, and understandably, involved many thousands of persons whose activities cannot be reported here. There were, however, certain initial steps which had to be taken to arouse nationwide protest. In P. B. Riis, Carhart indeed found a kindred spirit. He not only accepted his assignment, but gave it all his time and effort. From December, 1922, through March, 1923, Riis addressed letters of appeal to various persons and organizations[37] throughout the country, requesting them to write to the Forester in Washington to ask for an audience to discuss the road program in the Superior National Forest. The response was gratifying.

Acting Forester Sherman did not ignore the request for audience. Moreover, the "Father of the Forest Service," Gifford Pinchot, then Governor of Pennsylvania, had been brought into the picture. By a letter dated February 13, 1923, Sherman wrote to Riis, in part:

> Mr. R. Y. Stuart, Commissioner of Forestry, Pennsylvania, has sent to this office a copy of your letter of Jan. 24 to Governor Pinchot concerning proposed road construction in the Superior National Forest, Minnesota.

> *The question of the position which the Forest Service should take regarding road construction within the Superior National Forest first arose about two years ago when Mr. Carhart, then Recreation Engineer of the Forest Service, submitted his plan for the development of the recreational resources of that Forest. In this plan Mr. Carhart very strongly recommended that the Superior National Forest be regarded and developed exclusively as a canoe forest or, in other words, that transportation by canoe should be relied upon to the exclusion of all other methods. This idea made a strong appeal to many members of the Forest Service who had the pleasure of reviewing Mr. Carhart's report and there was a strong sentiment favorable to the adoption of his recommendations. Continued study made it evident, however, that the Forest Service would be unable to rigidly maintain this form of development and the principle underlying Mr. Carhart's entire report was with some reluctance abandoned* [*emphasis added*].[38]

The remainder of the letter detailed the position of the Forest Service regarding the canoe country in the Superior National Forest, and the considerations which led to the three road projects, previously discussed.[39]

When Riis received Sherman's letter, he immediately communicated with Carhart, sending him a copy with the following handwritten note attached:

> February 16, 1923. Received today. Will not reply until I hear from you. May be construed as basis for negotiations. [William T.] Hornaday[40] will run for year, is nearly blind & will see what good if any he can do in that time. Is much interested. Theodore Wirth[41] well pleased with our efforts & wants us to go. A short reply to Sherman should answer unless his communication is official. Copy sent to Wirth, Doolittle & Hornaday. [Signed] Riis.

There was much simultaneous activity and unavoidable crossing of letters in the mails, especially during February, 1923. The wheels were beginning to gain speed. On February 7th, for example, Riis, located at the "command post" in Rockford, Illinois, heard from L. H. Pammel of Iowa State College.[42] Pammel informed that he had received a letter from Governor J. A. O. Preus of Minnesota who had declared:

> Permit me to thank you for your letter of February first.
>
> I am greatly pleased to know of your interest in the Lake Superior Forest. It is my hope that the Lake Superior Forest will be reserved for future generations in as near a state of wilderness as is possible. There can be no excuse for the state retaining the land which was there and spending any money for forests and game protection unless the forest is available to a considerable number of people of the state. In order to do this there must be some roads which reach some portions of the forest. The Superior National Forest, however, is so large that there is no danger that enough roads will be built in there to destroy its wilderness for a great many years to come.[43]

A week later, Governor Preus felt the pressure of the correspondence which he began to receive. When he received a letter from Le Roy Jeffers of New York City, he asked in reply:

> May I ask from whom you learned that there is a movement on foot to establish an automobile highway through the Superior National Forest? I know nothing about the matter.[44]

That letter found its way from Jeffers to Riis, who wrote to the Governor explaining that the Committee for the Preser-

Arthur Carhart at Saganaga Lake, Minnesota, June 20, 1921, now in the Boundary Waters Canoe Area he helped to save—Photo Courtesy U.S. Forest Service.

Fig. 1

Arthur Carhart, 1962

Fig. 2

Travelling through Lake Superior *Fig. 3*

Motoring through San Isabel *Fig. 4*

Fig. 5
Coureurs de bois—Voyageurs

Trappers Lake, Colorado—Photo Courtesy of Denver Public Library Western Collection. *Fig. 6*

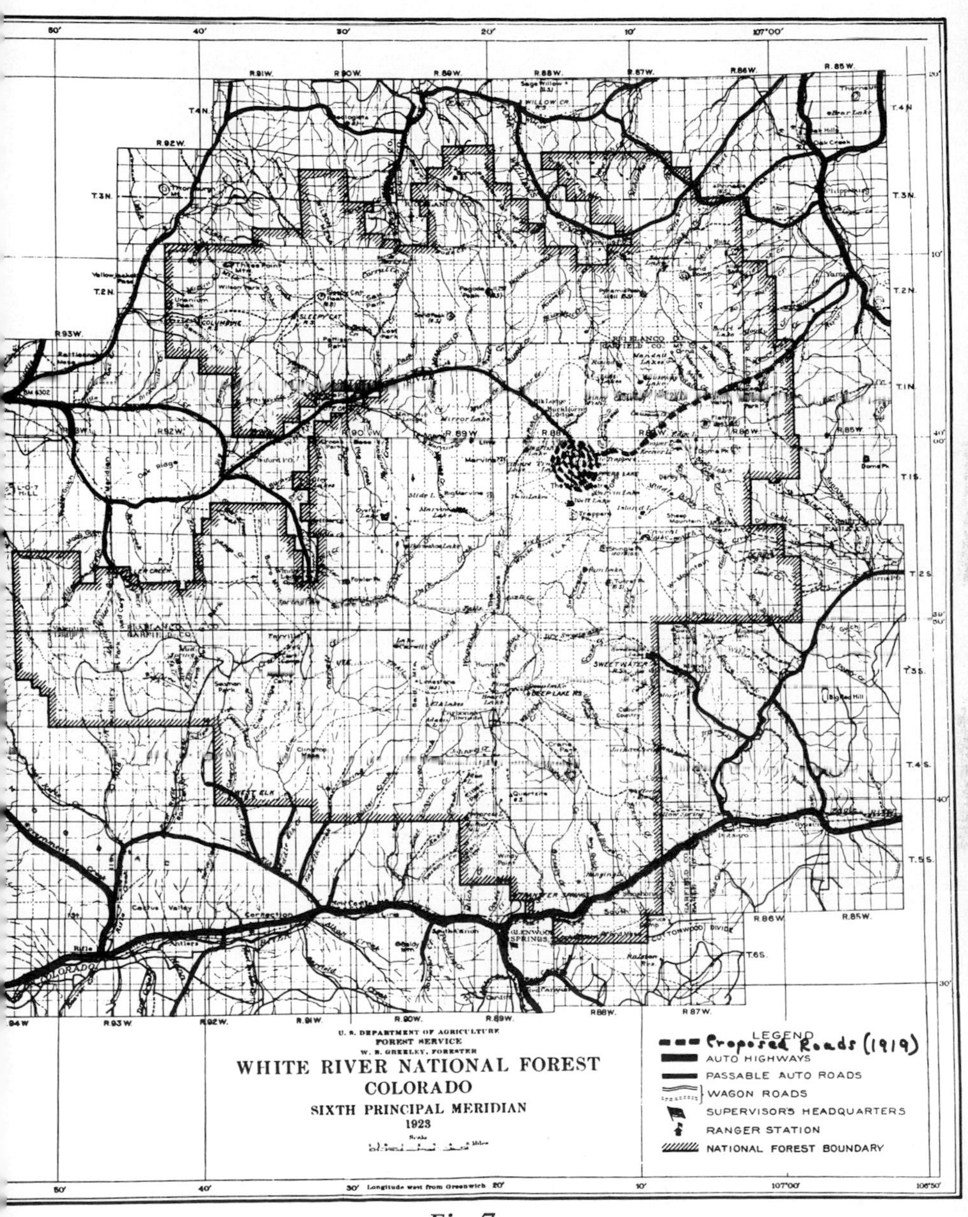
U. S. DEPARTMENT OF AGRICULTURE
FOREST SERVICE
W. B. GREELEY, FORESTER
WHITE RIVER NATIONAL FOREST
COLORADO
SIXTH PRINCIPAL MERIDIAN
1923
LEGEND
Proposed Roads (1919)
AUTO HIGHWAYS
PASSABLE AUTO ROADS
WAGON ROADS
SUPERVISOR'S HEADQUARTERS
RANGER STATION
NATIONAL FOREST BOUNDARY
Longitude west from Greenwich
GLENWOOD SPRINGS
COLORADO

Fig. 7

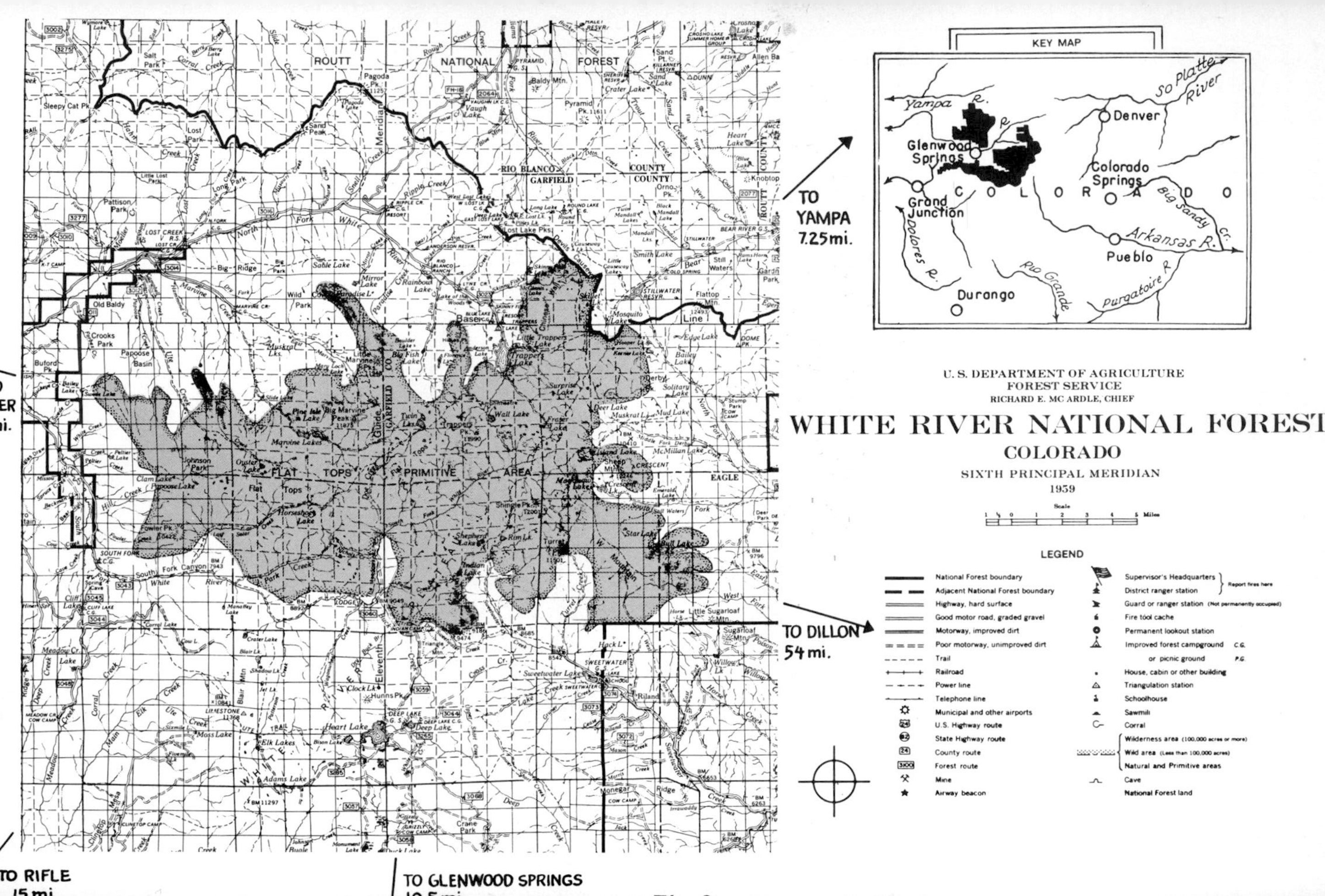
KEY MAP
Denver
Colorado Springs
Pueblo
Durango
Grand Junction
Glenwood Springs
COLORADO
So Platte River
Yampa R.
Dolores R.
Rio Grande
Arkansas R.
Big Sandy Cr.
Purgatoire R
TO YAMPA 7.25 mi.
TO MEEKER 18 mi.
TO DILLON 54 mi.
TO RIFLE 15 mi.
TO GLENWOOD SPRINGS 10.5 mi.
U. S. DEPARTMENT OF AGRICULTURE
FOREST SERVICE
RICHARD E. MC ARDLE, CHIEF
WHITE RIVER NATIONAL FOREST
COLORADO
SIXTH PRINCIPAL MERIDIAN
1959
Scale
Miles
LEGEND
National Forest boundary
Adjacent National Forest boundary
Highway, hard surface
Good motor road, graded gravel
Motorway, improved dirt
Poor motorway, unimproved dirt
Trail
Railroad
Power line
Telephone line
Municipal and other airports
U.S. Highway route
State Highway route
County route
Forest route
Mine
Airway beacon
Supervisor's Headquarters
District ranger station
Report fires here
Guard or ranger station (Not permanently occupied)
Fire tool cache
Permanent lookout station
Improved forest campground C.G.
or picnic ground P.G.
House, cabin or other building
Triangulation station
Schoolhouse
Sawmill
Corral
Wilderness area (100,000 acres or more)
Wild area (Less than 100,000 acres)
Natural and Primitive areas
Cave
National Forest land
ROUTT NATIONAL FOREST
FLAT TOPS PRIMITIVE AREA
RIO BLANCO
GARFIELD
COUNTY
EAGLE
Meridian
White River

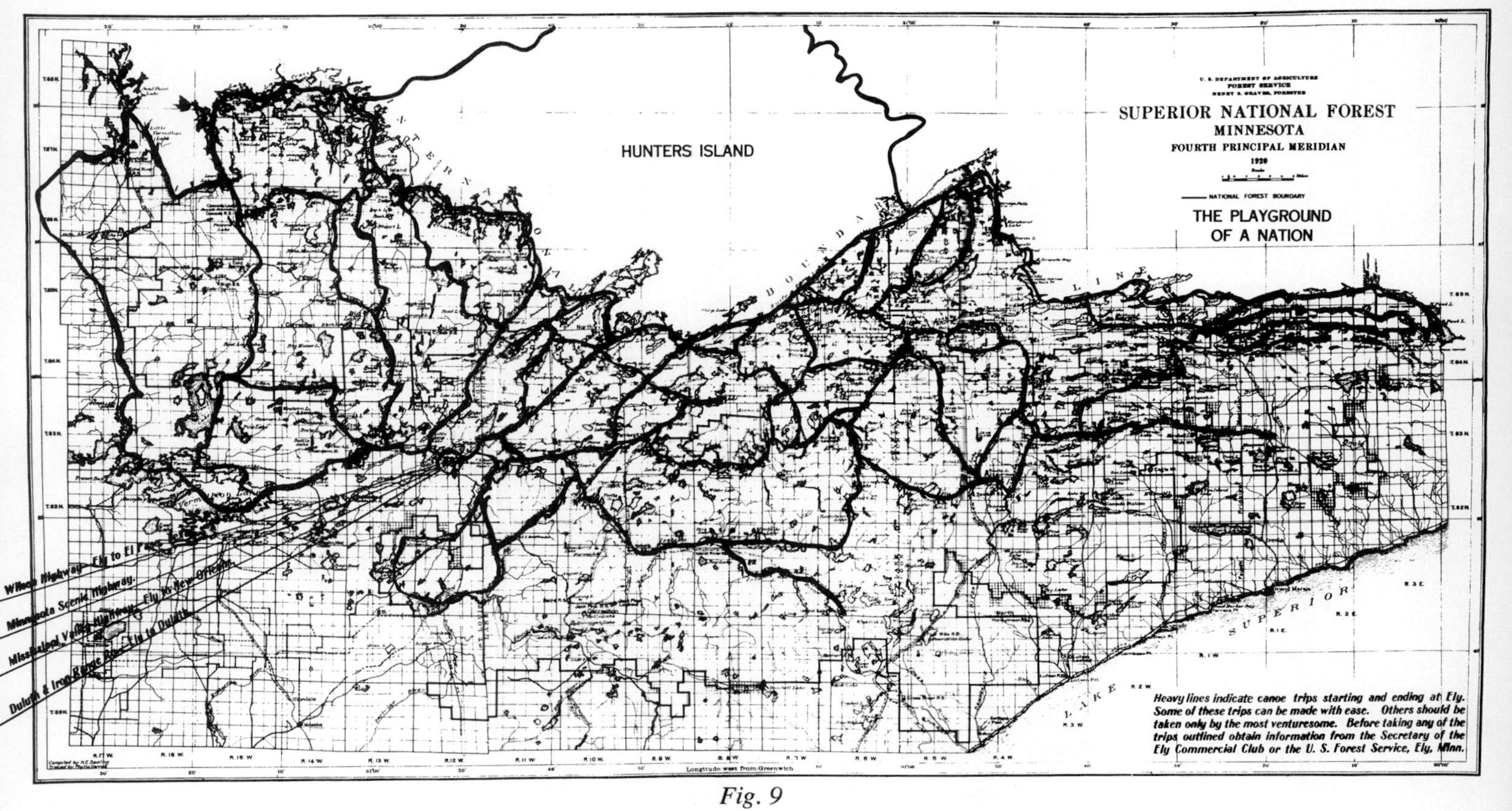
U. S. DEPARTMENT OF AGRICULTURE
FOREST SERVICE
HENRY S. GRAVES, FORESTER
SUPERIOR NATIONAL FOREST
MINNESOTA
FOURTH PRINCIPAL MERIDIAN
1920
NATIONAL FOREST BOUNDARY
THE PLAYGROUND OF A NATION
HUNTERS ISLAND
BOUNDARY LINE
LAKE SUPERIOR
Minnesota Scenic Highway.
Heavy lines indicate canoe trips starting and ending at Ely. Some of these trips can be made with ease. Others should be taken only by the most venturesome. Before taking any of the trips outlined obtain information from the Secretary of the Ely Commercial Club or the U. S. Forest Service, Ely, Minn.
Longitude west from Greenwich

Fig. 9

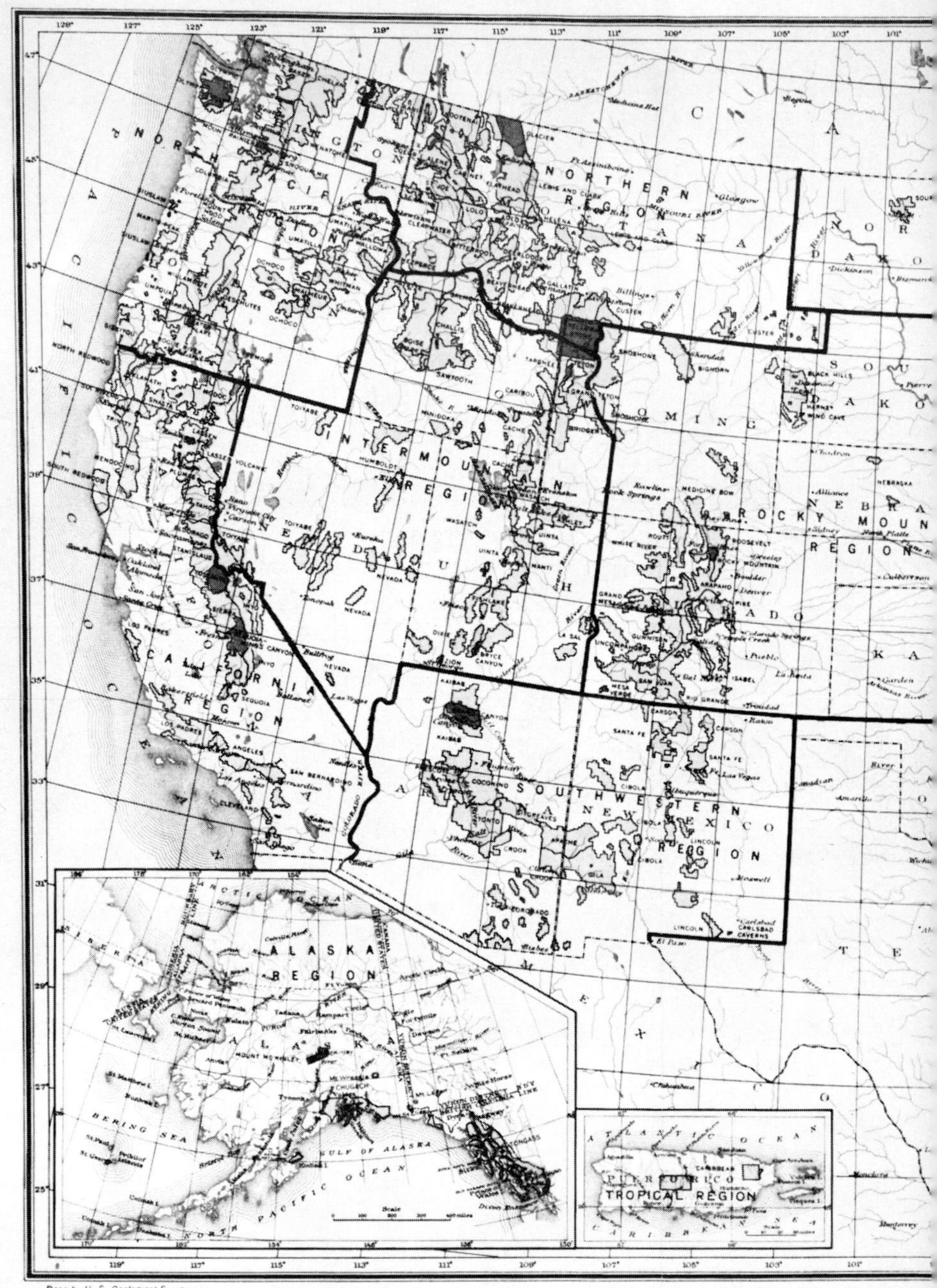

Base by U. S. Geological Survey

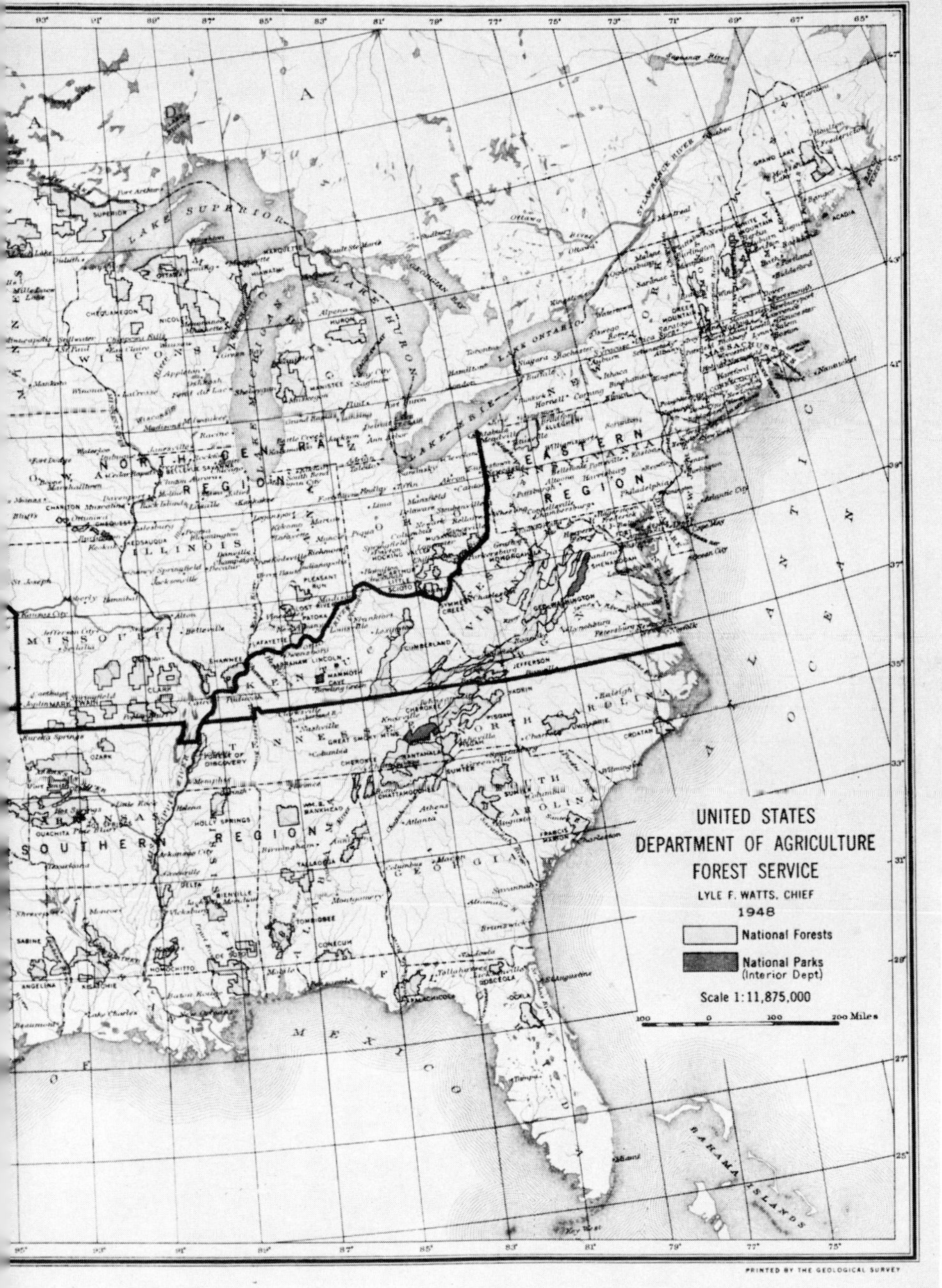
UNITED STATES
DEPARTMENT OF AGRICULTURE
FOREST SERVICE
LYLE F. WATTS, CHIEF
1948
National Forests
National Parks
(Interior Dept)
Scale 1:11,875,000
100 0 100 200 Miles
NORTH CENTRAL REGION
EASTERN REGION
SOUTHERN REGION
PRINTED BY THE GEOLOGICAL SURVEY

Fig. 10

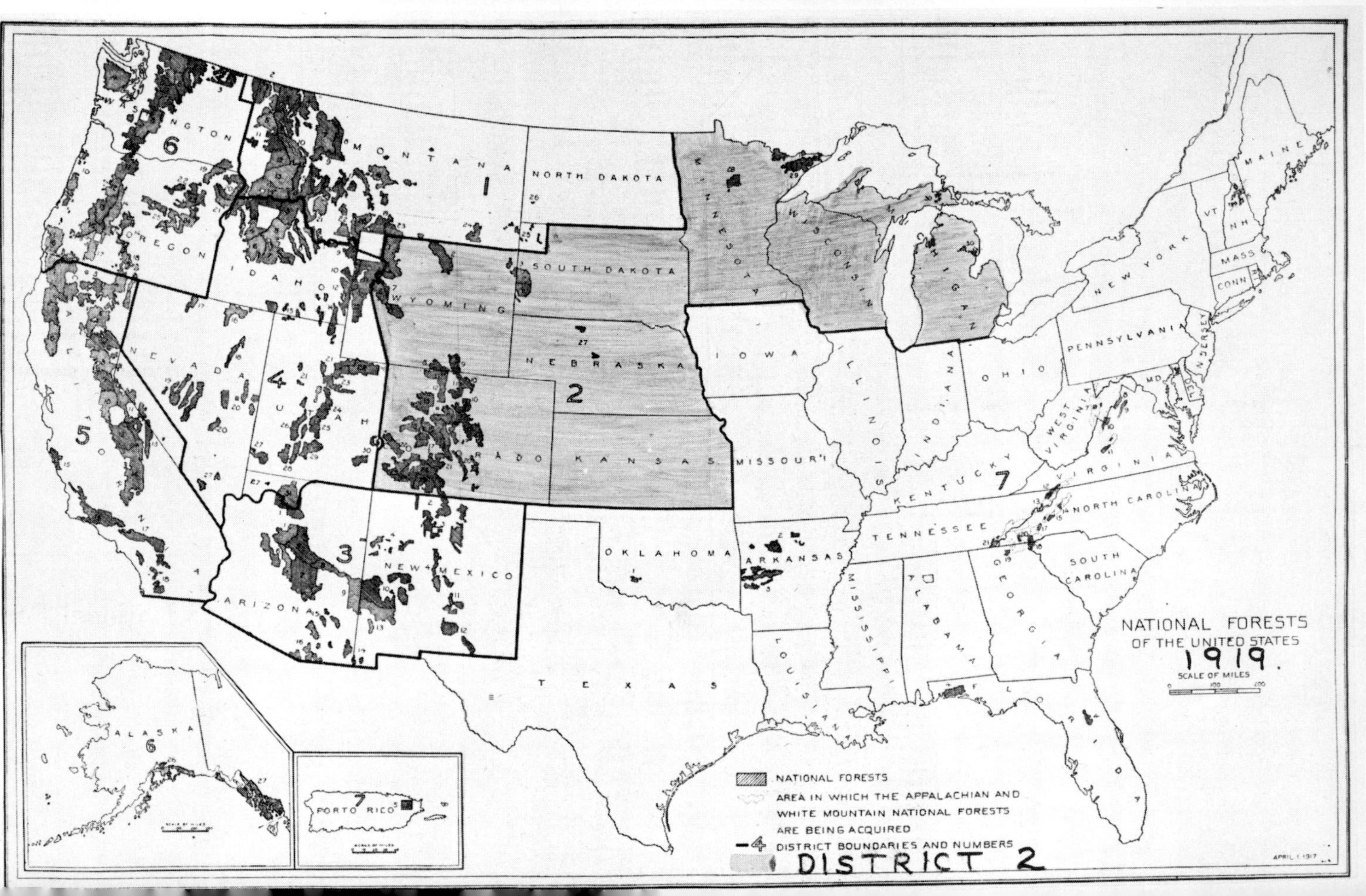
NATIONAL FORESTS
OF THE UNITED STATES
1919.
SCALE OF MILES
NATIONAL FORESTS
AREA IN WHICH THE APPALACHIAN AND
WHITE MOUNTAIN NATIONAL FORESTS
ARE BEING ACQUIRED
—4 DISTRICT BOUNDARIES AND NUMBERS
DISTRICT 2
APRIL 1 1917
WASHINGTON
OREGON
CALIFORNIA
NEVADA
IDAHO
MONTANA
NORTH DAKOTA
SOUTH DAKOTA
WYOMING
UTAH
COLORADO
NEBRASKA
KANSAS
ARIZONA
NEW MEXICO
OKLAHOMA
TEXAS
MINNESOTA
IOWA
MISSOURI
ARKANSAS
LOUISIANA
WISCONSIN
MICHIGAN
ILLINOIS
INDIANA
OHIO
KENTUCKY
TENNESSEE
MISSISSIPPI
ALABAMA
GEORGIA
FLORIDA
SOUTH CAROLINA
NORTH CAROLINA
VIRGINIA
WEST VIRGINIA
PENNSYLVANIA
NEW YORK
N. JERSEY
DEL
MD
MAINE
VT
NH
MASS
CONN
RI
ALASKA
PORTO RICO

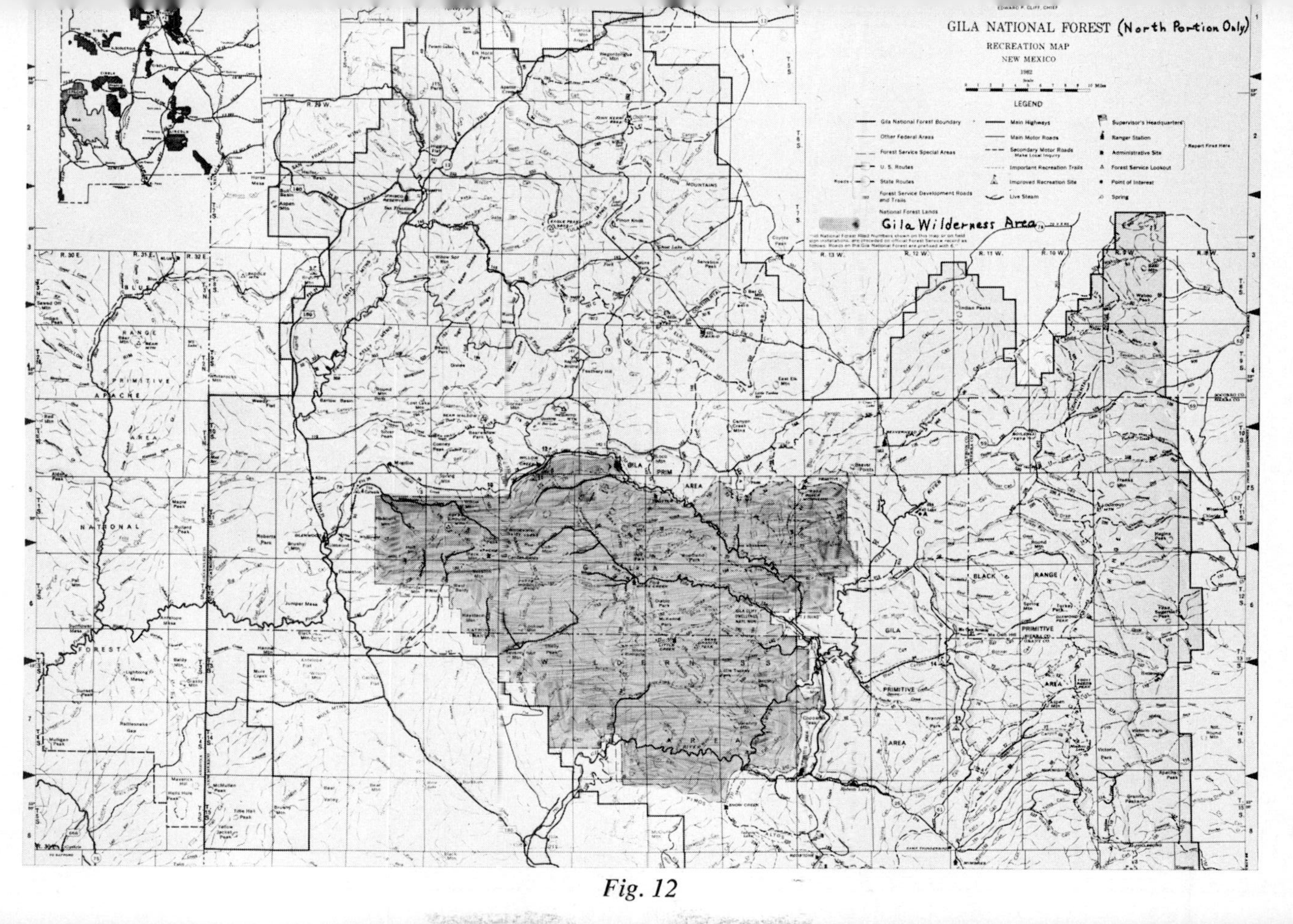

EDWARD P. CLIFF, CHIEF
GILA NATIONAL FOREST (North Portion Only)
RECREATION MAP
NEW MEXICO
1962
LEGEND
Gila National Forest Boundary
Other Federal Areas
Forest Service Special Areas
U.S. Routes
State Routes
Forest Service Development Roads and Trails
National Forest Lands
Main Highways
Main Motor Roads
Secondary Motor Roads
Important Recreation Trails
Improved Recreation Site
Live Steam
Supervisor's Headquarters
Ranger Station
Administrative Site
Forest Service Lookout
Point of Interest
Spring
Report Fires Here
Gila Wilderness Area
BLACK RANGE
GILA PRIMITIVE AREA
GILA WILDERNESS AREA
BLUE RANGE PRIMITIVE AREA
APACHE NATIONAL FOREST

Fig. 12

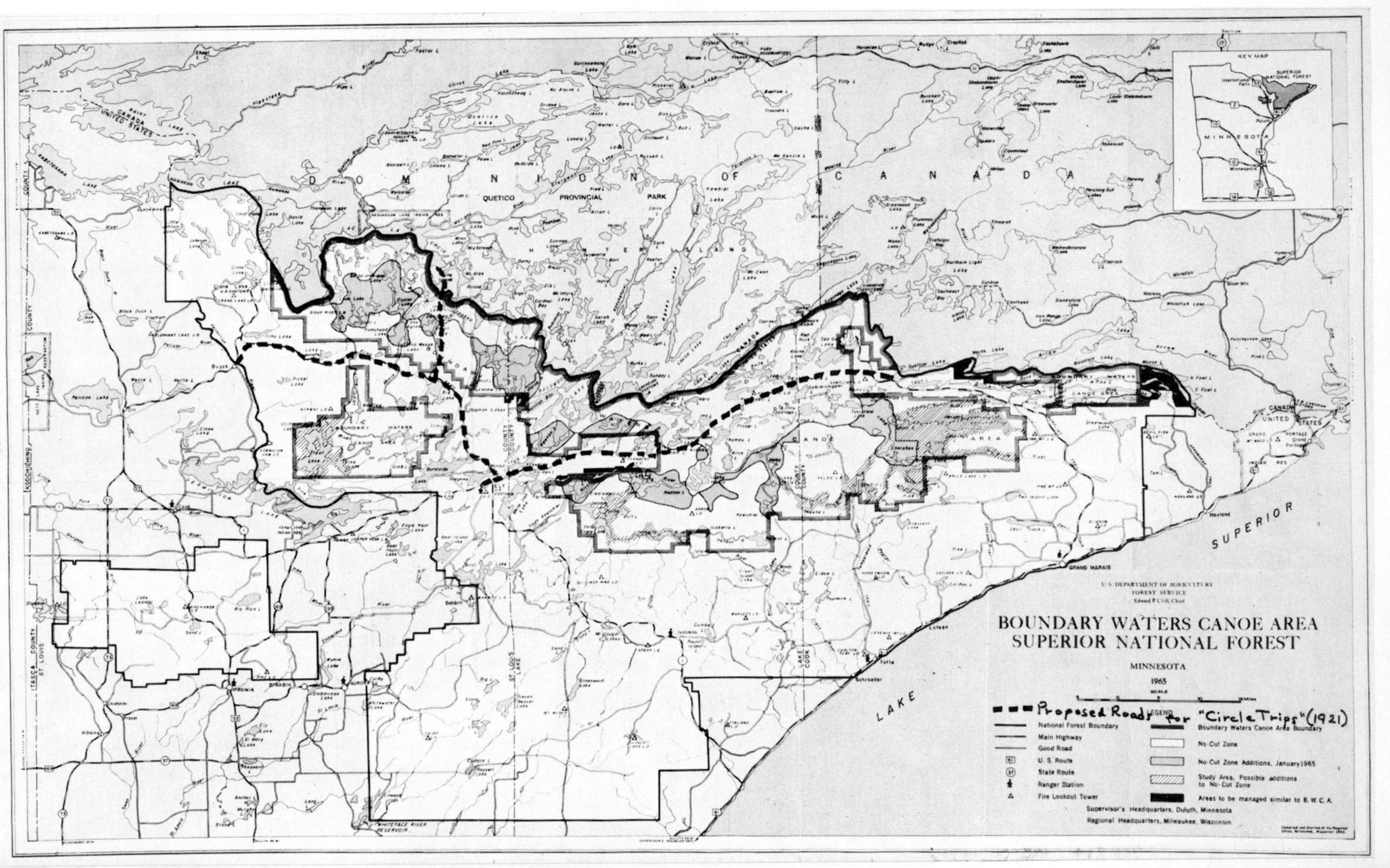

U.S. DEPARTMENT OF AGRICULTURE
FOREST SERVICE
Edward P. Cliff, Chief
BOUNDARY WATERS CANOE AREA
SUPERIOR NATIONAL FOREST
MINNESOTA
1965
SCALE
LEGEND
Proposed Roads for "Circle Trips" (1921)
National Forest Boundary
Main Highway
Good Road
U. S. Route
State Route
Ranger Station
Fire Lookout Tower
Boundary Waters Canoe Area Boundary
No-Cut Zone
No-Cut Zone Additions, January 1965
Study Area, Possible additions to No-Cut Zone
Areas to be managed similar to B.W.C.A.
Supervisor's Headquarters, Duluth, Minnesota
Regional Headquarters, Milwaukee, Wisconsin
KEY MAP
SUPERIOR NATIONAL FOREST
MINNESOTA
DOMINION OF CANADA
QUETICO PROVINCIAL PARK
HUNTER ISLAND
BOUNDARY WATERS CANOE AREA
LAKE SUPERIOR
GRAND MARAIS
CANADA
UNITED STATES
KOOCHICHING COUNTY
ITASCA COUNTY
ST LOUIS COUNTY
LAKE COUNTY
COOK COUNTY
WHITEFACE RIVER RESERVOIR

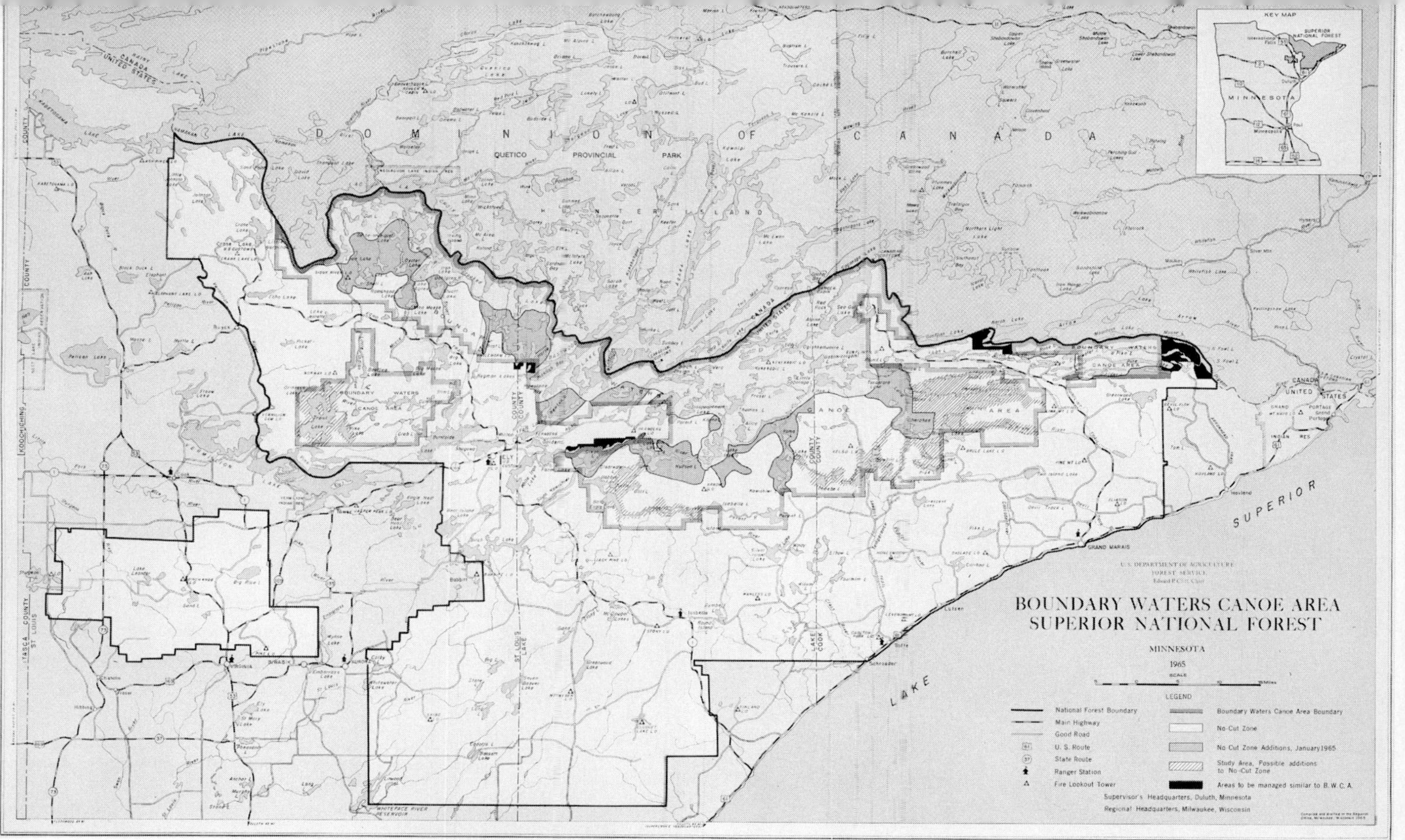
BOUNDARY WATERS CANOE AREA
SUPERIOR NATIONAL FOREST
MINNESOTA
1965
U.S. DEPARTMENT OF AGRICULTURE
FOREST SERVICE
LEGEND
National Forest Boundary
Main Highway
Good Road
U.S. Route
State Route
Ranger Station
Fire Lookout Tower
Boundary Waters Canoe Area Boundary
No-Cut Zone
No Cut Zone Additions, January 1965
Study Area, Possible additions to No-Cut Zone
Areas to be managed similar to B.W.C.A.
Supervisor's Headquarters, Duluth, Minnesota
Regional Headquarters, Milwaukee, Wisconsin
KEY MAP
SUPERIOR NATIONAL FOREST
MINNESOTA
DOMINION OF CANADA
QUETICO PROVINCIAL PARK
HUNTER ISLAND
LAKE SUPERIOR
GRAND MARAIS
VIRGINIA
ELY
COOK COUNTY
LAKE COUNTY
ST LOUIS COUNTY
KOOCHICHING COUNTY
ITASCA COUNTY
CANADA
UNITED STATES

Fig. 14

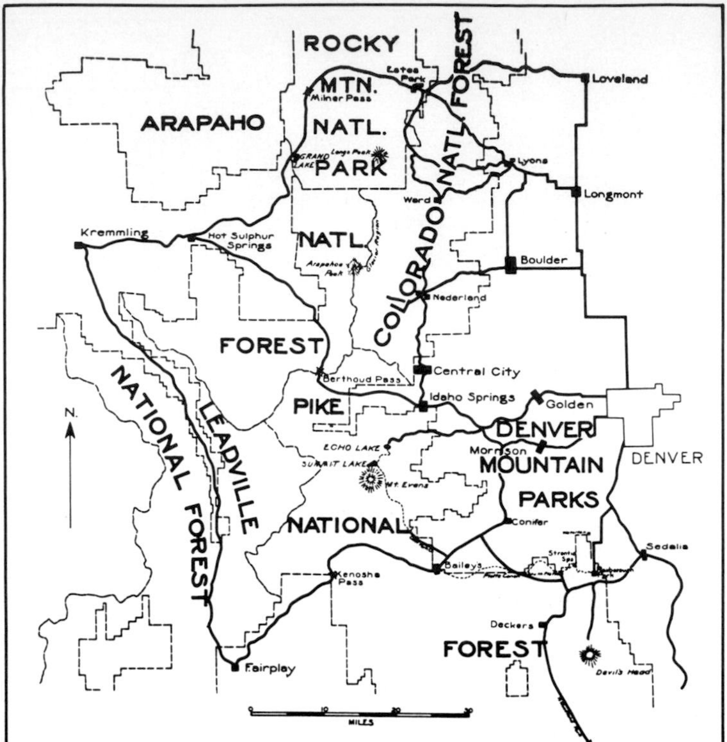

DENVER'S "RECREATION FAN"

HOW IT REALLY IS

This map shows how near realization is Denver's Recreation Fan. The main developments to be made are the construction of a return drive from Mount Evans and the construction of a road from Roxborough Park to South Platte by way of Strontia Springs.

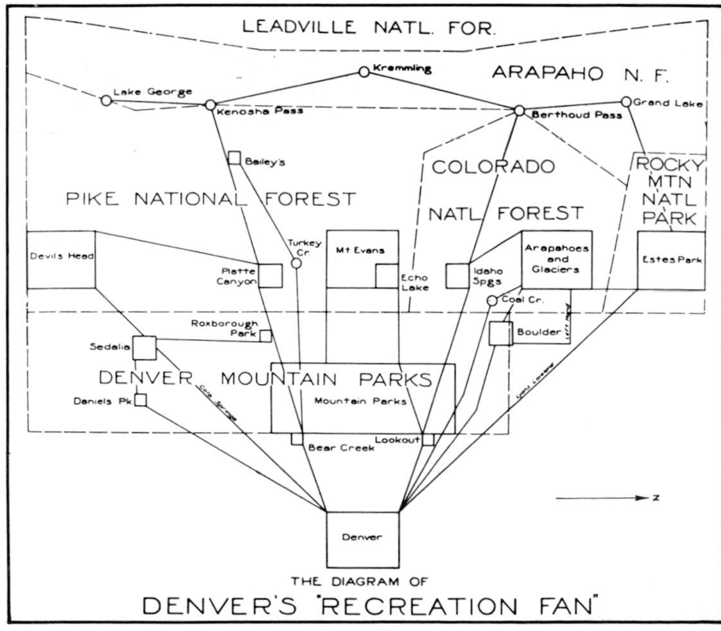

THE DIAGRAM OF

DENVER'S "RECREATION FAN"

Fig. 15

In the Denver Public Library's Special Collections Room, the Conservation Library Center takes form under the guidance of Arthur H. Carhart, Consultant (left), and City Librarian, John T. Eastlick (right). Important materials arriving daily are sorted and stored preparatory to complete cataloging. (1962) *Fig. 16*

As initial efforts to gather materials produce rapid results, the objectives of the Conservation Library Center are being interpreted continually to conservation leaders such as C. R. Gutermuth, vice president, Wildlife Management Institute (left) and Dr. Ira N. Gabrielson, president, Wildlife Management Institute (right) shown conferring with Arthur H. Carhart at the Denver Public Library, 1962. *Fig. 17*

At a special reception in March, 1962, coinciding with two national conservation conventions held in Denver, many distinguished guests were introduced to the Conservation Library Center. Here, the valued contents of a trunk donated by Katherine Seymour are viewed by (left to right) Arthur H. Carhart; Dave Brower, Sierra Club; Seth Myers, secretary, Outdoor Writers' Association of America; E. Budd Marter, III, Outdoor Writers' Association of America; and Carl O. Gustafson, American Conservation Association. *Fig. 18*

vation of Wild Life, American Institute of Park Executives, had had considerable correspondence with parties interested in the program. He asked Preus to "aid us to preserve in its present condition . . . this heritage."[45]

Meanwhile, Riis heard again from Washington, but this time from Henry C. Wallace, Secretary of Agriculture.[46] Wallace wrote that he had been advised that the Forester had already written at some length in explanation of the approval by that Department of three road projects partly within the Superior National Forest in Minnesota. He reaffirmed the Forester's decision to construct the roads, adding that he felt "rather unable to withdraw my approval of Federal cooperation in the construction of the three road projects." He declared his willingness to give further consideration to that decision upon presentation of features warranting the same.

Within a few days, Carhart was in possession of Wallace's letter, which was sent to him by Riis. His reply to Riis was on the order of a "pep talk" by an athletic coach to his players.[47] The letter closed with these comments:

> Does this give you some thunder? Hope so.
>
> It looks like we might have to give someone hell before this stops. But I'm ready to include high water with the order of hell if necessary. Go to it Riis.[48]

A second letter from the Acting Forester to Riis on February 20, 1923, told of the "wide-spread objection now being expressed" against any step which might possibly impair the value of the Superior National Forest as a game sanctuary, or as an area within which "natural conditions are scrupulously preserved for the lover of wild life."[49] Those who objected, and particularly the canoeist, made it apparent that they and the organization responsible for protection, maintenance and development of that area, had need for a "fuller understanding of mutual ideals and wishes than now appears to exist." Sherman wondered if it would be possible to arrive at an understanding as to some "middle ground" preventing wholesale exploitation but preserving a large share of all economic values, both material and spiritual.[50] He proposed a conference where representatives of the wild life organizations who advocated the wilderness type of management could meet with commercial interests and officers of the Forest Service. Such a meeting would "harmonize the views of the different elements." The conference, if held, would be "rather well attended by intelligent representatives of various interests which may have a stake in the future of the region." The meeting was to be held either at Ely, Duluth or St. Paul, not much later than March first.[51]

Riis acknowledged receipt of that letter, thanked Sherman for consenting to the conference, and stated that he had taken steps to get interested parties to participate. He also believed that nothing could be arranged much sooner than the middle of March, since the representatives would need a little time to arrange their affairs in order to attend.[52]

In the meantime, Carhart had considered Sherman's letter of February 20th forwarded to him in Denver by Riis. Riis had apparently drafted a reply to Sherman which Carhart edited. Carhart wrote:

> Here goes for just as snappy a set of answers to your many recent contributions as I can give you. . . . Have corrected letter to Sherman. It is mighty good. Re Sherman's latest letter. We have them where I knew they would get. That is they are going to get all interested together, pow-wow and then do pretty much as the majority consider right. I knew that as much of a protest as has gone in would move them. . . . You can see how Sherman has swung in the latest letter. He is now ready to talk some sort of a compromise. In other words we have very near [*sic*] gained our point *IF* we stick for it. There is a tendency to let up if we think we have put it over, and then a rebound on the part of the economic and local interests will bum up the whole deal again.[53]

That Carhart was directing the movement from Denver may be seen clearly throughout his letter to Riis. He analyzed the Forester's letter of February 20th, pointing out that:

> His second paragraph of letter Feb. 20th, opens way for us to get back of an exchange program there to secure private lands in ownership of government. BUT we will not do this if the recreation values are not to be considered. Do you get the point? Now go him one better and propose as it is desirable to have some lake country of this type accessible by auto, and also from a purely economic standpoint, it is good business we propose that Superior be EXTENDED to take in considerable land now outside the boundaries, so it will go all the way to the Canadian line at all points, and probably extend it southward, if it is possible to do it.[54]

It was Carhart's belief at that time that the Forest Service would "support pretty strongly" the "whole deal" if "we can propose and endorse it." In his opinion, both the consolidation and the extension were "sane and worthy projects."[55] Subsequent developments have shown him to be correct.

The letter of instructions from Carhart to Riis touched upon many topics which need not be detailed here. Of importance was his advice that the meeting be postponed until after Will H. Dilg and Will O. Doolittle "come up with their articles if possible, and then your position is strengthened." The letter then shifted to Carhart's desire to continue to remain in a position of anonymity:

> Your whole list of people who should be at the meeting is good. *But I better not be there. You can use my lines of argument to a much better advantage than I can myself.* [emphasis added] Cannot you get Dilg? . . . And what of the outcome of such a conference? What is our objective? Seems to me this: A study of the area by Will O, you and one other (not me) to suggest a policy for following throughout the coming years. That study to

> be made this summer, and the road building help up for the season until the study is finished. It will take about 6 weeks to make the study. . . . *But keep me out of it.: I think my influence is best when not apparent* [emphasis added]. Washington and Minn[esota] have both heard my views. They should now hear yours.[56]

There were other letters of a similar nature and content which outlined the preliminary steps that led to agreement to a conference held at Duluth, Minnesota, on April 3, 1923. But while those letters were being written, and before that conference was held, there were articles published about the Superior National Forest which merit attention. At least a few of them should be reviewed, for they were a definite part of the protest movement.

First Article Seeking to Preserve the Superior National Forest (1922)

The historian, George E. Mowry, has pointed out that it was probably more accurate to state that the reform spirit of the early 20th century created the muckrakers and the muckrake magazines, and that movement for reform was well under way before their first articles appeared.[57] On the other hand, in the 1920's a host of outdoor writers had aroused a general feeling of concern for the "vanishing" natural areas by repeatedly extolling the wonders of nature and wilderness. However, the first article drawing attention to the threatened exploitation of the Superior National Forest appeared in the November-December, 1922, issue of *Parks & Recreation.*[58] That pilot article commented on one previously published by Emerson Hough, who had expressed concern over the early extinction of the remaining original fauna in America's National Parks. Hough had asserted that of all the Parks only three "retain any notable portion of their original wild fauna

—Glacier Park of Montana; Yellowstone Park of Wyoming and Grand Canyon of Arizona."[59]

Some pertinent excerpts from the pilot article follow:

> Mr. Hough has not mentioned one of the most likely game and wilderness refuges left in the United States. He is probably not familiar with it or he would have included it in his list of places where there is still a chance for the game. Furthermore it is far nearer to the center of population than any he mentions and more valuable. It is the Superior National Forest of Northern Minnesota.
>
> The Superior Forest is just south of the Canadian line. It contains a million and a quarter acres of which a fifth is water. Just across the border is the Quetico Forest Reserve of Canada similarly dotted with innumerable lakes and streams. They are both game preserves. The total game area in this section that is governmentally owned or controlled is twice the size of the Yellowstone and unlike the Yellowstone there is not one road or hotel in it. There are about four million acres of genuine game refuge there.[60]

Continuing the article declared:

> This international area is relatively more important than any of our nationally owned areas as a wilderness preserve. The conditions in the Yellowstone, Glacier and Grand Canyon are similar. If one were lost the other would still be with us. But if we lose the Superior National Forest and if it were to be profaned and mangled by claptrap developments we would have lost the only nationally owned lake country reserve we now have.[61]

A discussion of the game in the Forest then followed. Game population was estimated at 1,500 moose, 2,500 whitetail deer and some 20,000 beaver. The Superior was said to be "strictly a canoe country," and "it should be retained as the one place where that sort of travel is typical." Conservationists and lovers of the wilderness in the outdoors "should add the Superior National Forests to the places needing the most active safeguarding," set their face "firmly against any 'hurdy-gurdy' development or a commercial exploitation which would ruin the wilderness loveliness of this Forest."[62] So ended the clarion call to oppose the road projects.

In keeping with the strategy considered essential by Carhart, articles timed so as to meet the public eye just prior to and during the conference with the Forest Service officials and the commercial interests, were in a state of readiness. Accordingly, when definite word was received that the conference was to be held, *Parks & Recreation* published a series of illustrated articles in the March-April issue concerning the Superior National Forest.[63] One such article reported that "just prior to going to press," word had been received from C. H. Squire, Acting Assistant U.S. Forester, that a conference respecting the building of roads within the Superior National Forest would be held on April 3rd, at Duluth.[64]

The lead article in the March-April issue of *Parks and Recreation* was entitled, "Birth of a Wilderness."[65] That article gave an over-all view of the Superior National Forest's charms and attributes. It told of the extensive lumbering operations which had wrought little perceptible and no permanent damage to the Forest. But that was the story of yesterday. Another day had dawned and the people faced parting with that canoe sanctuary, where Nature had struck a seemingly perfect balance, because the state of Minnesota might convert the sylvan lakeland into an auto playground. Then in italics:

> *Shades of Radisson, du Lhut, Hennepin, Verendrye and brave companies of rovers, have you blazed, battled and bled that others may follow your arduous trail in the sombre forest in luxurious ease, by no effort of their own, fouling the sweet fragrance of the woodland, hushing the sacred strains of its cathedrals with screaming claxon and discord, piecemeal tearing asunder and destroying the elements of wilderness beauty?*[66]

The foregoing article and those that accompanied it were published before the participants met in conference.[67]

The Conference at Duluth (April 3, 1923)

An article published in May-June, 1923, reported that President Theodore Wirth of the American Institute of Park Executives opened the discussion at Duluth for the opponents of roads in the Superior National Forest by pointing out that the Institute had become interested in the matter because it sensed a national problem in the recreational development. The article claimed that it became apparent at once that the protest against the roads was well justified because their construction had been considered from a purely local standpoint and no consideration whatever had been given the interest of the people at large.[68]

Thereafter those who favored and those who opposed the roads were given equal opportunity to present their views and then the conference went on record almost unanimously as opposed to any roads in the Superior National Forest.[69]

The conference had accomplished much. Secretary of Agriculture Henry C. Wallace, with whom "friendly protest" had been lodged to hold up the road program for a year so that the entire situation could be gone over and considered from every angle, withdrew his approval of federal aid for the proposed construction.[70] The Secretary decided to cancel "for the present" the entire Ely-Buyck road and part of the Ely-Gunflint and Grand Marais-Gunflint roads. By so doing, the Forest Service was obliged to forego $160,000 of state and county funds, pledged for auto highways in the Superior National Forest. The latter roads were originally planned to form the auto tourists' circle roads via Duluth-Ely-Gunflint-Grand Marais-Duluth.[71]

In lieu of the proposed auto highways, the Forest Service then contemplated the building of a low grade, forest administration road, "badly needed from a fire protection standpoint," from Ely to the Fernberg Lookout Tower.[72] That low grade road conformed to mutually acceptable policy for forest administrative roads, and did not touch upon lakes and waterways then serving as regular canoe routes, nor did it otherwise impair recreational values. As to the proposed Grand Marais-Gunflint Road, for the eastern part of the Superior National Forest, a "serviceable" auto road would be built to Gunflint Lake, the first of the boundary waters encountered west of Grand Marais. At Gunflint, a traveler could then choose his trail over the boundary waters or branch off over canoe trails into the interior of the Forest. Other administrative trunk line roads were tentatively considered for later construction to serve "lateral pack horse trails that will put every part of the Forest within reach of fire crews in a few hours travel."[73]

In addition to the immediate gains for exponents of wilderness concepts, there were several others which were to mold the future of the Superior National Forest and the wilderness preservation movement. At the Duluth conference a resolution was adopted recommending the outright purchase of all private lands within the Forest, and also an extension of it to embrace all lands between the three parts of the Forest and the Canadian boundary. Another approved resolution stipulated a restudy of that Forest so as to take into account "every possible feature of development, economic, recreational, scenic and aesthetic," aimed at giving the highest possible service to all the people of the United States.[74]

Formation of the Superior National Forest Recreation Association (April 3, 1923)

Organization and propagandizing had brought certain results for those favoring the wilderness concept, but it was believed that to implement the call for the consolidation and extension of the Superior National Forest, a special organization would be needed. Accordingly, a permanent organization was formed on the floor of the conference, and named the Superior National Forest Recreation Association (hereafter cited as SNFRA), to continue the work of the *ad hoc* group led by P. B. Riis. Riis was chosen as its President, and Donald Hough its Secretary. Annual dues were set at one dollar.[75]

Among the names of those chosen as Association Directors were: Will H. Dilg, Editor, *Izaak Walton League Monthly*, Chicago, Illinois; Will O. Doolittle, Editor, *Parks & Recreation*, Minot, North Dakota; and Arthur H. Carhart, Denver, Colorado. The newly-formed Association was to function primarlly as a guardian of thc Forest. As a service feature to its members, it would publish a monthly bulletin, acquainting them with new canoe routes and trails, fishing, where game might be seen, and so on. That service, however, would be enlarged to engage actively in implementing the recommendations made to the Forest Service at the recent conference. The SNFRA chose as its official organ the *Izaak Walton League Monthly*.[76]

The Izaak Walton League of America

In retrospect, it might be said that one of the most significant results of the Duluth Conference was the designation of the *Izaak Walton League Monthly* as the official organ for the SNFRA. That selection, however, carried both strengths and weaknesses. For the long range wilderness preservation movement, it was good to have included the Izaak Walton League of America, the founding and purpose of which will be noted shortly, in the struggle to carry out the aims of the Association. The Waltonians were to develop into one of the most powerful of all national conservation organizations, particularly in the subsequent controversies over the Boundary Waters Canoe Area. On the other hand, it was a drawback for Paul B. Riis, personally, because the more powerful Izaak Walton League, by 1927, had easily eclipsed the SNFRA and exercised hegemony over it. Riis lost his key position in the movement to save the Superior National Forest, and that loss culminated in the gradual dissolution of the scantily financed SNFRA.[77]

The Izaak Walton League had been founded by Will H. Dilg on January 22, 1922. At that time it had a grand total of fifty-four members, and but one chapter. From that beginning, and with little funds, it grew because it represented a great hope—a hope which burned in the breast of sportsmen and lovers of the outdoors throughout the nation. An enthusiastic Waltonian wrote in 1928, when there were more than 3,000 chapters throughout North America, that it had grown because "it had to grow":

> It was like the dog that climbed the tree. A dog (skip this if you've heard it) according to its owner, once climbed a tree when chased by an angry bull. "But," objected a friend, "you must be mistaken—dogs can't climb trees." "This dog did," said the owner. "He climbed the tree all right. He had to!"[78]

Indeed, the League had climbed the tree, especially so during its first six years of existence. Though organized in January, it was not until August, 1922, that the first issue of the *Izaak Walton League Monthly* was published.[79] The front page of the *Monthly's* first issue carried an editoral by Emerson Hough, "Time to Call a Halt," in which he deplored the sinful waste of America's resources, and the taint of greed and commercialism that had been laid upon them. He wrote:

> Can this weak, new, little journal, openly established as a pulpit of heresy to the orthodox selfishness and commercialism in sport, work that great miracle [of giving the ages a part of the America that was ours]? I do not know. I dare not predict. But may we not all at least join in that clean hope?[80]

Hough's editorial was followed in the September issue by one written by Zane Grey, entitled, "Vanishing America," in which he echoed the same plea:

> My one hope for the conservation of American forests and waters is to plant into every American father these queries. Do you want to preserve something of America for your son? Do you want him to inherit something of the love of outdoors that made our pioneers such great men? . . . Do you want him, when he grows to manhood, to scorn his father and his nation for permitting the wanton destruction of our forests and the depletion of our waters?[81]

The League championed the causes which needed to be brought to the attention of the American public regarding the great outdoors. Theirs was a platform for more forests, more clean streams, more fish and game, more outdoor life. But the cause which seems to have fired their imagination was the one pertaining to road construction in the Superior National Forest. That became their *cause celebre*—the cause they cut their teeth on. In a letter to J. S. Pray, dated May 12, 1923, Carhart wrote:

> The Superior deal was most trying, illuminating and finally gratifying. I am certainly happy to see it turn out as it has. Now there is to be formed an association [SNFRA] to stand guard over it as you probably have heard from Mr. Riis. I am sorry to say that other organizations [such as the Izaak Walton League] have better standing with him than the ASLA [American Society of Landscape Architects].[82]

The IWLA had supported Riis prior to the Duluth conference of April 3, 1923, and following that conference articles appeared in the *Monthly* which directly concerned the Superior National Forest road situation.[83] From that time, the League's activities in the struggle for the Superior National

Forest have been ceaseless. Distinguished men have always been among its followers; Herbert Hoover, while serving as Secretary of Commerce, was one of its National Officers, and in 1929, after he had become President of the United States, he was the League's Honorary President as well. His affiliation with the IWLA was to aid immeasurably in the successful passage of the Shipstead-Newton-Nolan Act of 1930, an act which provided for protection of recreation values in the Boundary Waters Canoe Area.[84] President Hoover signed that Act on July 10, 1930.

Following the Duluth Conference and for the remainder of 1923, A. H. Carhart continued to write articles concerning the Superior National Forest and the need for Congress to allot adequate funds for the Forest Service to handle the aesthetic values of recreation. He believed that what Congress would do depended largely on the amount of real knowledge it had or might get of the needs in recreation within the National Forests, and to no small extent on what the "folks back home" had to say about those needs.[85]

By December 1923, SNFRA had asked Senator Medill McCormick to introduce a bill in the Senate, and Congressman Charles E. Fuller one in the House, authorizing the Secretary of Agriculture to examine and locate for acquirement any lands in private ownership within or adjoining the Superior National Forest which, in his judgment, were chiefly valuable for the production of timber or for production of stream flow. The area to be included covered upward of two million acres. To make possible that purchase, Congress was asked to make an appropriation of up to thirty million dollars. That proposal was in redemption of the pledge made on the floor of the Duluth Conference the previous April to assist the Forest Service. Considerable impetus had been given to the movement for extension of the Forest at a meeting in Cloquet, Minnesota, May 12, 1923, where such outstanding figures as Governor J. A. O. Preus of Minnesota, Chief Forester W. B. Greeley, and a number of Senators and forestry experts seriously discussed a program looking toward reforestation and a perpetual supply of lumber.[86]

The year 1923 had been an eventful one in National Forest history. It is worth emphasizing that when the Secretary of Agriculture withdrew federal aid for road construction in the Superior National Forest, he reaffirmed the second *de facto* application of the wilderness principle.[87] Moreover, that was the first time the Department Secretary had made a decision respecting the exclusion of roads in the National Forests in favor of wilderness preservation. As such, Secretary Henry C. Wallace's decision in April, 1923, may be considered the forerunner of what was to be nationwide regulation and protection of wilderness values in all the National Forests by 1929.

The spade work had been done at Trappers Lake in 1919, and the issue of roads versus wilderness had been contested intramurally during the period 1921-1922, and given a public hearing by 1923. At that point, it might be said that "the action stage" had indeed been reached, and Washington had added its approval to the elements of the wilderness concept. The next chapter will detail additional developments in the drive for wilderness preservation during 1924.

CHAPTER VIII

TAKE A THIRD STEP

Between the summers of 1919 and 1929 the wilderness concept was born and received official acceptance at the national level. It has been explained above that the idea was first expounded in mid-1919 at Trappers Lake, Colorado, and the principle applied in that year. A second application occurred during mid-1921 in the Superior National Forest; that application was approved by the District Forester in 1922, and confirmed by the Secretary of the Department of Agriculture early in 1923. There was a third application of that principle in June, 1924, a point in time midway between the genesis of the idea and promulgation of the first Forest Service regulation having nationwide applicability. This chapter will describe that *third action* in connection with the Gila National Forest in New Mexico.

Third De Facto Application of the Wilderness Concept (1924)

The movement to establish wilderness areas which began in District 2 during mid-1919, had come to the attention of

Assistant District Forester Aldo Leopold of District 3 when he discussed the wilderness concept with Arthur Carhart as described in an earlier chapter.[1] Yet it was not until late 1921 that he began writing on the subject. His first article dealing with the wilderness concept was published in November, 1921, and entitled, "The Wilderness and its Place in Forest Recreational Policy."[2]

Though *not first*, Leopold's 1921 article merits attention because it was quite a "radical" view for a Forest Service officer to have expressed publicly at that time. Leopold noted that when National Forests began to be selected, the first argument of those opposing them had been that they would remain an unused wilderness. To that argument, Gifford Pinchot had replied that on the contrary they would be opened up and developed as producing forests. Pinchot at that time also enunciated the doctrine of "highest use," and its criterion, "the greatest good to the greatest number," which Leopold believed "must remain the guiding principle by which democracies handle their natural resources."[3]

Leopold asserted that Pinchot's promise of development had been made good, but that the process had

> already gone far enough to raise the question of whether the policy of development (construed in the narrower sense of industrial development) should continue to govern in absolutely every instance, or whether the principle of highest use does not itself demand that representative portions of some forests be preserved as wilderness.[4]

In a most tactful manner, Leopold then proceeded to question the Forest Service policies to that time concerning forest development. He wrote:

> That some such question exists, both in the minds of some foresters and a part of the public, seems to me to be plainly implied in the recent trend of recreational use policies and in the tone of sporting and outdoor mag-

> azines. Recreation plans[5] are leaning toward the segregation of certain areas from certain developments, so that having been led into the wilderness, the people may have some wilderness left to enjoy. Sporting magazines are groping toward some logical reconciliation between getting back to nature and preserving a little nature to get back to. Lamentations over this or that favorite vacation ground being "spoiled by tourists" are becoming more and more frequent. Very evidently we have here the old conflict between preservation and use, long since an issue with respect to timber, water power, and other purely economic resources, but just now coming to be an issue with respect to recreation.[6]

The purpose of Leopold's paper was declared to be to give definite form to the issue of wilderness conservation, and to suggest "certain policies for meeting it, especially in the Southwest." Leopold was, like Carhart before him, aware that he was "rocking the boat," as it were, for he remarked that it was quite possible that the serious discussion of that question would seem "a far cry in some unsettled regions [of the nation], and rank heresy to some minds." He added that similarly timber conservation had seemed a far cry in some regions, and rank heresy to some minds, a generation before.[7]

Leopold defined "wilderness" as

> a continuous stretch of country preserved in its natural state, open to lawful hunting and fishing, big enough to absorb a two weeks' pack trip, and kept devoid of roads, artificial trails, cottages, or other works of man.[8]

Then he branched off into speculative proposals which are difficult to paraphrase, for they stated:

> First, such wilderness areas should occupy only a small fraction of the total National Forest area—probably not to exceed one in each State. Second, only areas naturally difficult of ordinary industrial development

should be chosen. Third, each area should be representative of some type of country of distinctive recreational value, or afford some distinctive type of outdoor life, opportunity for which might disappear on other forest lands open to industrial development.[9]

Leopold observed that previously the Forest Service had been inclined to assume that recreational policy had to be based on the desires and needs of the majority only. He believed that inasmuch as there was "plenty of room and plenty of time," it was their duty to vary the recreational development policy, in some places, to meet the needs and desires of the minority also. A somewhat familiar refrain followed:

> The majority undoubtedly want all the automobile roads, summer hotels, graded trails, and other modern conveniences that we can give them. It is already decided, and wisely, that they shall have these things as rapidly as brains and money can provide them. But a very substantial minority, I think, want just the opposite. . . . It will be much easier to keep wilderness areas than to create them. In fact, the latter alternative may be dismissed as impossible. Right here is the whole reason for forehandedness in the proposed wilderness area policy.[10]

He stressed the fact that the public demands for camp sites and wilderness trips, respectively, were both legitimate and both strong, but nevertheless distinct. He declared further that:

> The man who wants a wilderness trip wants not only scenery, hunting, fishing, isolation, etc.—all of which can often be found within a mile of a paved auto highway—but also the horses, packing, riding, daily movement and variety found only in a trip through a big stretch of wild country. It would be pretty lame to forcibly import these features into a country from which the real need for them had disappeared.[11]

In order to describe the workings of the proposed wilderness area policy he offered this example:

> The Southwest (meaning New Mexico and Arizona) is a distinct region. . . . It has a high and varied recreational value. Under the policy advocated in this paper, a good big sample of it should be preserved. This could easily be done by selecting such an area as the headwaters of the Gila River on the Gila National Forest. This is an area of nearly half a million acres, topographically isolated by mountain ranges and box canyons. It has not yet been penetrated by railroads and to only a very limited extent by roads.[12]

He reasoned that because of the natural obstacles to transportation and the absence of any considerable areas of agricultural land, there would be no net economic loss, should the policy of withholding further industrial development be adopted. The only exception would be that the timber in that area would remain inaccessible and available only for limited local consumption. He noted that the entire area was grazed by cattle, but that the cattle ranches would be an asset from the recreational standpoint because of the interest which attached to cattle grazing operations under frontier conditions. If preserved in its "semi-virgin state," it could absorb a hundred pack trains yearly without overcrowding, Leopold asserted, and "highest use" demanded its preservation.[13]

In the introductory chapter of this study, Aldo Leopold was quoted as having written that the earliest action he could find in his files was a letter dated September 21, 1922, notifying the District Forester that two local Game Protective Associations had endorsed the establishment of a wilderness area on the headwaters of the Gila River, in the Gila National Forest.[14] The map (Figure 12) delineates that area. Though that specific letter, or copy of it, was not found among the official Forest Service files, one dated September 1, 1922, was available.[15]

This letter disclosed that Forest Supervisor A. H. Douglas of the Datil National Forest, Magdalena, New Mexico (now Gila National Forest with headquarters at Silver City, New Mexico),[16] was less than enthusiastic about Leopold's plans for that Forest. Supervisor Douglas wrote to the District Forester, Frank C. W. Pooler, to acknowledge receipt of his letter of July 31, "together with Section 1, 'Lands' of Mr. Leopold's inspection report of the Gila." He returned the map showing the area that could be placed in the proposed wilderness area, and explained that he had changed Leopold's line slightly because of a "number of mining companies having property" in the area, and because of a road "used by automobiles."[17] The actual changes made by Douglas need not be detailed here.

Douglas believed that the proposed area would interfere with a road which "should be built some day" to shorten the distance from Silver City to Magdalena by 100 miles" and also "open up a good body of timber on the western slope." His closing comment merits reproduction:

> The wilderness idea is allright [*sic*] but I believe that we should not allow it to stand in the way of development of a country in which we have a great deal of timber which is ready for sale.[18]

That letter was received in the District office on September 5, 1922; a pencilled note for District Forester Pooler was added to it and initialed by Aldo Leopold. The note asked Pooler: "Do you care to have me complete the proposal for your consideration? AL" The reply came in the form, "AL—Yes Pls. FCWP [Pooler] 9/18." With that preliminary approval to "complete the proposal," Leopold prepared a three-page report on the proposed wilderness area, an outline, dated October 2, 1922, with a map delineating the boundaries.[19]

In that, the first *written proposal* for wilderness preservation in District 3 of the Forest Service, Leopold outlined his plan under a number of headings, which were to be expanded in the next report concerning wilderness, in 1924, but their initial consideration is pertinent here.[20] Under "Object," Leopold wrote:

> To preserve at least one place in the Southwest where pack trips shall be the "Dominant play". See article attached: "The Wilderness and Its Place in Forest Recreational Policy".[21]

Under "Need," he observed that because other areas had been opened to auto travel, they were no longer suitable for pack trips. The "Function" of the plan was to provide a "National Hunting Ground," a form of recreation which had not been provided for or recognized by the federal government. As to "Suitability of the Gila Area," the points in favor of the plan were:

> The area is non-mineral, non-agricultural, and I know of no power possibilities of any consequence. The surrounding areas amply provide for summer homes and the usual forms of recreation. The area has, in my opinion, been cut down to allow for all necessary through routes of travel. After a personal examination of the fire situation, I believe that more roads would add as much or more fire risk than they would help combat. The only question is the timber. It cannot come out without very expensive investments. Some timber will probably have to be sacrificed wherever this policy is carried out. Is it not possible that an untouched reserve of stumpage for a possible National emergency might be a good thing?[22]

The section headed "Public Opinion" reported that the local citizens were "entirely favorable," according to inquiries made by Leopold. He added a note of realism when he declared, "I expect some opposition, however."[23]

The section entitled "Policy for Administration" was further subdivided into the headings: Roads, Trails & Phones,

Uses, Grazing, Lands, Game & Fish. The only entries which need to be emphasized here were these:

1.	*Roads:*	Road & Trail Plan to omit any further extensions of the existing road system.
2.	*Trails & Phones:*	Continue development same as on any other area. Necessary for fire protection.
3.	*Uses:*	No additional permits for any but grazing uses to be given. This excludes permanent improvements like summer homes, hunting lodges, hotels, etc. Existing permits within the area not to be renewed if relinquished.[24]

Like the memorandum Arthur Carhart prepared for Leopold December 10, 1919,[25] Leopold's proposal of 1922 was brief but significant. The expected opposition to it was not long in coming, nor was it from any great distance. One of the Assistant District Foresters, R. E. Marsh, Forest Management Division, District 3, soon took exception to the proposal.[26] Marsh, in his memorandum of November 28, 1922, referred to a "recent discussion" in District Forester Pooler's office regarding the proposed Wilderness area on the Gila in which it was suggested that "more accurate information be secured as to the amount of timber involved" in that area. Marsh remarked that as he understood the "Wilderness idea, it would mean a policy of withdrawing all timber within the area certainly from general market development," and possibly from development for local use. He had some doubt as to "just what the policy as to timber for small mills cutting for local use might be." It appeared to Marsh that "to properly fulfill the functions of a real Wilderness, road and other developments should be kept at a minimum." Under the foregoing assumption, the proposed Wilderness area would be in "direct contravention of the existing timber use policy statement."[27] He concluded that the only "big chances available for new big development in the state [of New Mexico] are involved in this proposed Wilderness area and the nearby areas of the Datil Forest."[28] Then came the "forester's view" which has been mentioned in various contexts earlier in this study:

> This Gila area, if and when it becomes accessible, could support on a permanent basis a single band mill cutting 15 million feet per year, which at $2.00 per M is $30,000 annually in revenue to the government. Figuring the overturn at $20.00 per M would mean an annual circulation of at least $300,000 directly based on this industry. Following the project farther back, the indirect returns to the community are still greater. The time may come when economically this timber will be greatly in demand.[29]

His concluding paragraph reflected Marsh's awareness that a change in timber policy would be called for if the proposal were to be approved:

> This area is at the present time very inaccessible and we have even heard reference to the fact that it will remain so for an almost indefinite period. My own opinion is that we have been over-pessimistic as to the rapidity with which our present inaccessible areas will be removed from the inaccessible class. As I have stated before look for a real change in the demand in the southwest in the period from 1927 to 1932. If the Wilderness area is to be approved and if it involves, as I assume it would, its elimination at least from general market and lumber production, it is not too early to draw a timber use policy statement which will definitely indicate this.[30]

That Leopold's proposal was not a "burning issue" in District 3 may be seen by the casual handling it received as reflected in the following memorandum. A memorandum, dated March 1, 1923, from Assistant District Forester John D. Jones to District Forester Pooler contained this opening sentence:

> Mr. Leopold's report of October 2 on the proposed Wilderness Area was inadvertently routed to the L files without either Mr. [M. M.] Cheney or I [J. D. Jones] seeing it, therefore, I did not read the report until February 5.[31]

Jones then discussed the "billion and a half feet of sawtimber in this area," mentioned in Marsh's memorandum of November 28. In Jones' judgment, "in a region like the Southwest where the Forest resources are already far below the local needs," it would be unwise to eliminate "15% of the National Forest sawtimber of the State from permanent use."[32] He believed, furthermore, that it would be possible to maintain areas suitable for interior pack trips and protection of wild life along with "the normal use of the timber and other resources of the region." Jones saw no objection to classifying a much smaller region as a wilderness area, one "involving not over 8 townships," or 288 square miles (184,320 acres), instead of the one originally proposed by Leopold embracing some 1,376 square miles or 880,640 acres. He viewed the future recreational development of the District on the basis of the smaller region, and added this final and interesting remark:

> Naturally, such a classification should not be given wide out of State publicity, otherwise the curiosity created might induce a large number of parties to visit the area and thus defeat the real purpose for those who desire wilderness conditions.[33]

A whole year passed before the next written action was taken. Then on March 28, 1924, the *first* "Recreational Working Plan, Gila National Forest," was prepared for approval of the District Forester.[34] The plan had been "apparently written in final form, at least, by J. D. Jones, or his staff and was largely influenced by Leopold's recommendations."[35]

On June 3, 1924, the District Forester, Frank C. W. Pooler, gave it his approval.[36] The salient points of the plan, or policy statement, should be noted here, especially as they seem to reflect inconsistencies. Under the heading "Recreational Objectives and Factors," reference was made to the fact that there had been "for a number of years a strong sentiment for the retention in this region of a wilderness hunting area." The next statement was later shown by the Forester's office in Washington to be partially untrue.

> This is the last big chance to retain a region of this kind in approximately primitive conditions since all of the other National Forests have been invaded by settlement and automobile roads to such an extent that only comparatively small areas remain off the beaten path.[37]

Accordingly, a "Wilderness Area" was designated within the Gila National Forest where a recreational policy was to be followed "for a period of ten years unless earlier modified." The construction of forest roads was to be limited, and there would be an effort to "eliminate as many of the interior alienations as can be justified under the land exchange legislation."[38]

The next item reflected the early problem of defining a wilderness area not yet wholly resolved:

> Restrict within the *Wilderness Area* the construction of recreational buildings and improvements to simple log cabins or shelters for the use of travelers or hunters, such improvements to be covered under free permits providing for general public use. (Exception to the above policy may be made to take care of state fish hatcheries or other buildings for similar purposes for game and fish propagation.)

There followed two final declarations of interest:

> It is not believed that the Wilderness policy will affect grazing administration.

> This statement of policy is not intended to bar possible water power development within the *Wilderness Area* or the construction of roads in connection therewith.[39]

At a later date, someone added to the document an entry which advised that:

> Since the above was approved, the area has been modified to eliminate small portions included in working circle management plans, and this involved the roads specifically mentioned. It was the intention, also, to provide for construction of all roads actually necessary for protection.[40]

The notation referred to a revision of the 1924 plan, dated February 1, 1928, signed by Frank C. W. Pooler, District Forester.[41] The revised version noted that the designated wilderness area was "largely closed naturally to timber operations by reason of inaccessibility," but that it was "planned to secure data as to the location and amount of economically accessible timber within the wilderness area." An additional notation in the revision illustrated the limitations of the District 3 policy, or the lack of same:

> For the period ending Dec. 31, 1937, the area is closed to commercial timber cutting except for local needs as distinguished from general market. Prior to the specified date, field examinations will be undertaken and the closure against commercial cutting as above defined will be reconsidered in the light of existing public sentiment and the economic and wilderness conditions specifically involved.[42]

Whatever the apparent ambiguities in the Gila National Forest wilderness area policy by 1928, in 1929 the Washington Office of the Forest Service adopted an over-all policy for what it termed primitive areas. The policy was stated in "Regulation L-20: Primitive Areas," which became effective July 12, 1929.[43] The ORRRC investigators reported that although several "wilderness areas" had been identified before 1929, that classification had been at the option of the District Foresters. The change in designation of "wilderness areas" to the new term under Regulation L-20 of "primitive areas, could be accomplished only by the Chief of the Forest Service, an official formality which had its own built-in complications. No longer was the District Forester, at his own discretion, able to classify or modify those tracts of land which were subject to administration and management under the terms of Regulation L-20.[44]

There were some additional developments between 1924 and 1929 which need to be noticed for they also helped usher in the official recognition and national regulation of "primitive areas" in National Forests. They occurred as a result of a continuation of the controversy in the Superior National Forest. So it is necessary to consider that Forest again in a brief review of the second half of the "critical decade" 1919-1929.

CHAPTER IX

LET'S GET ORGANIZED!

Earlier chapters have shown that much had been accomplished between 1919 and 1924 to promote at least partial acceptance of the wilderness concept. This chapter will show that the recreation plan for the Superior National Forest, written by A. H. Carhart in 1921, which had operated to deter early destruction of wilderness values in that Forest, later acted as a yardstick for that purpose, and in the preparation of subsequent plans. This chapter will also review those major events between 1924 and 1929 which not only molded Forest Service policy for a portion of the Superior National Forest, but influenced subsequent development of recreational plans and Service Regulations for the protection of wilderness values in all National Forests as well.

Meetings at Eveleth and Duluth, Minnesota (February, 1924)

The Superior National Forest Boundary Extension Bill,[1] introduced in the United States Congress during late 1923, had been referred to the Committee on Public Lands early in 1924. That Committee called for a report on it from the Secretary of the Interior and the Secretary of Agriculture, both of whom had approved of that measure.[2] At that point persistent rumors in northern Minnesota of opposition to the bill had crystallized into a meeting of the representatives of the Commercial Clubs of the Range cities and other interests, at Eveleth, Minnesota, on February 14, 1924. The Club representatives approved a resolution at that meeting which expressed unalterable opposition to the Fuller Bill in any form as "unjust, unfair, confiscatory and detrimental to the best interests of northern Minnesota."[3]

The following day, another meeting was held at Duluth. At the meeting the Range cities were well represented. There they conferred with Colonel A. S. Peck, District Forster, District 2, to discuss the proposed boundary changes. The Commercial Club representatives displayed a map with "much reduced boundary lines" and with "little additions" beyond the exterior boundaries of the Forest at that time. Backers of the Bill were disillusioned at the opposition to the proposed extensions, previously supported by the Commercial Clubs. Arguments by the Proponents of the Superior National Forest Boundary Extension Bill failed to change the complexion of the resolution adopted by the commercial clubs.[4] The following year, an article in *Parks & Recreation* reported that the Extension Bill had been "definitely dropped."[5]

Despite the disappointment felt by the failure of that measure, the Superior National Forest Recreation Association continued to function, however feebly, during 1925. The next year saw increased activity and some positive action taken by the Secretary of Agriculture. But that action was not calculated to please Riis. In a letter from Riis to A. H. Carhart in March, 1926, he expressed fear that the Forest Service "will continue to build roads and won't be satisfied until they have all been built," and that the "fire hazards increase in proportion to every road built."[6] He wrote further that:

> All our efforts are simply lost if we are not able to make recommendations and is out of the question with the little time on hand. So please shoot . . . this along and look over my recommendation in connection with map mailed you. . . . Send this along within twenty-four hours.[7]

To that request Carhart replied:

> Hasten to send back map. My feeling is that the FS [Forest Service] is going ahead . . . in spite of anyone, and that is not to be wondered at. . . . FS has shown trend of their future action in the Ely-Buyck [road building project]. They promised me several times this would not go through. But now that the "storm" has passed they bring it up in their program again. . . . Have always contended that funds to build roads if put in launches and other water equipment would beat every kind of road for protection.[8]

That letter was preparatory to another meeting of the SNFRA and the Forest Service officials in which much of what was feared became policy. The letter continued:

> Way I feel about whole business is that FS is going to get roads it wants in spite of hellenhighwater. They're bureaucratic, and the Bureau outlasts individuals and "fanatic" organizations such as the SNFRA. They can wait for ten years and they bring forth their program again if we block them this time.[9]

But the Superior National Forest Recreation Association was not alone in opposing the further road building plans of the Forest Service. The Izaak Walton League had entered the fight at an early date and by 1926 it was conducting its own campaign to save the Superior National Forest. The ORRRC investigators found that the League had played a key role in that episode, for it later reported that in response to considerable pressure from public opinion, led by the League, the Forest Service developed a recreation management plan for a portion of the area in 1926.[10] That plan will be discussed presently.

Hearing at St. Paul, Minnesota (September 3, 1926)

The hearing held at St. Paul on September 3, 1926, was to a large extent a repeat performance of the prior meeting at Duluth, April 3, 1923; the participants at that conference had been representatives of the wild life organizations who advocated wilderness protection, local commercial interests and officers of the Forest Service. The details of the St. Paul hearing need not be rehearsed here, but the resultant nine-page policy statment by the Secretary of Agriculture at that time, W. M. Jardine, should be briefly summarized.[11] The final decision concerning the management plan for the Superior National Forest was deferred to Secretary Jardine, who on September 17, issued the "first policy statement for the so-called primitive area."[12] Jardine stated in that significant document, in part:

> The Department of Agriculture recognizes the exceptional value of large portions of the Superior National Forest, containing its principal lakes and waterways, for the propagation of fish and game, for canoe travel, and for affording recreational opportunities to those who seek and enjoy wilderness conditions. It will be the policy of the Department to retain as much as possible of the land which has recreational opportunities of this nature as a wilderness. In these areas no roads will be built as far as the Forest Service can control the situation, and no recreational developments will be permitted on public lands except waterway and portage improvements

> and such simple camp ground facilities as may be needed to prevent the escape of fire or protect sanitary conditions. The purpose of this program is to conserve the value of the Superior National Forest as a game and fish country and as a national playground . . . off the beaten paths, just as far as essential facilities for the prevention and control of forest fires and as existing settlement and private land ownership will permit. Not less than one thousand square miles [or 640,000 acres] containing the best of the lakes and waterways will be kept as wilderness recreation areas.[13]

The statement also provided for the harvesting of timber under "scientific methods of cutting and a continuous yield of forest products" in accordance with the "fundamental purpose of the National Forests prescribed by law." Such harvesting would be carried out "with the preservation of natural screens along lake shores, camp grounds and similar areas," and was declared "not inconsistent with preserving opportunities for wilderness recreation."[14] Those were the main provisions of the policy.

But there were some other facets of the Secretary's policy statement which wilderness preservationists viewed as an open invitation to further road building in areas they believed should ultimately be absorbed into the consolidated and extended Forest of the lake country. For example, the statement declared that the following two items were essential to carrying out of the "whole program for the Superior National Forest,"

> (1) effective protection from fire, and (2) the consolidation of land ownership in the Government. The fire hazard to which the National Forest is subject has in some seasons been severe. . . . Therefore the administration of the Forest Service must be so organized and equipped as to hold the fire loss to a minimum. . . . [Fire control] is just as essential to wilderness recreation and

> wild life as to any other purposes of the National Forest.[15]

The need for lookout stations was recognized as well as the means of reaching fires once discovered, including transportation routes by water and land. Then the matters particularly considered at the hearing held on September 3rd were briefly reviewed. Jardine wrote that they

> dealt with the public highways within or adjacent to the National Forest on whose construction aid has been requested from the Department under the provisions of the Federal Highway Act of 1921. . . . The Department . . . must recognize its obligation as defined by [that Act] in so far as public highways are proposed which are of service to the Forest.[16]

With those prefatory comments, Jardine proceeded to enunciate another phase of highway policy, one to which the SNFRA and the Izaak Walton League took strong exception:

> The public highway which has been proposed from time to time, extending from Ely to Gunflint Lake, is outside of the boundaries of the Superior and traverses private lands which, on account primarily of mineral resources, will not bc added to the National Forest. The major portion of this road, extending from the Fernberg Lookout to Gunflint Lake, has not been placed on the Forest Highway system and no project for its construction is now under consideration.
>
> The 7-mile section connecting the present road eastward from Ely with the Fernberg Lookout, approximately one mile from the National Forest boundary, was previously placed upon the Forest Highway system because of the service which it was believed this road would render to the administration and protection of the Forest.[17]

The Secretary then explained that a fresh study of the situation disclosed that about 150,000 acres of Government land had to be protected from the Fernberg Lookout station. Under those conditions, he approved the extension of the existing road seven miles to the station as a Forest highway project in accordance with the plan originally determined upon. He believed the extension would not impair the wilderness area program for that Forest.[18]

Jardine declared in his final sentence:

> The general plan for protection roads on the Superior will be carried out by the Forest Service as herein defined, with the dominating purpose of retaining as much as possible of the Forest area in a wilderness condition and constructing only such roads as mature judgment and study show to be essential to redeem the responsibility of the Department for protecting this valuable region from forest fires.[19]

Secretary Jardine's policy statement was apparently a confirmation of the Plan of Management for the area, approved June 30, 1926, by Acting Forester E. A. Sherman.[20] The new policy, while specifically applicable to the Superior National Forest, was to help shape the attitude of the Forest Service officials toward wilderness preservation throughout the nation. Nevertheless, it had been preceded by certain significant comments on wilderness and its place in the over-all management plans for National Forests in the Annual Report of the Forester, Greeley, for 1926. He wrote:

> One consequence of the increasingly intensive use of the national forests for recreation is a growing sentiment in favor of the preservation of wilderness areas; that is, areas maintained as nearly in a state of nature and as free from highways, summer-home communities, resorts, and forms of industrial occupancy and use as the minimum requirements of national forest protection and management will permit. The Forest Service is sympa-

> thetic with the general conception of preserving . . . a number of areas especially adapted to the wilderness form of recreational use and wildlife propagation. The idea has merit and deserves careful study, but its correlation with the other obligations and requirements of national forest administration must be carefully worked out before definite steps are taken to give any areas a wilderness status.[21] It is inapplicable where the limitation of road construction and other forms of development or utilization of forest resources would be unjust to dependent local communities or to the States. No general policy can be applied, specific situations must be weighed individually . . . The "wilderness idea," as applied to national forests, will be greatly promoted if in its application to individual areas reasonable flexibility is allowed in providing for really urgent needs of the State or local communities.[22]

The above was the first instance of a Chief Forester issuing such a statement relative to the wilderness concept and its application.

Paving the Way to Nationwide Regulation and Protection of Wilderness Values in the National Forests

Between 1926 and the summer of 1929 when Forest Service Regulation L-20 was promulgated, many significant developments connected with the wilderness movement occurred, but only a few highlights of the period can be included here.

There was for instance, a letter written by Riis to Jardine, just prior to the policy statement of 1926, in which he made a last attempt to influence the Secretary to modify the proposed road building plans for the Superior National Forest.[23] Following the Jardine statement, Riis wrote a letter to George H. Selover of the Minneapolis Chapter of the Izaak

Walton League, dated October 13, 1926, which gave Riis's version of the outcome of the St. Paul Conference. The letter is intriguing for what it does not say as well as for what it does. He wrote:

> Frankly, I did not state the case plain and strong enough, as you know I spent the afternoon of the day following the Conference [September 4, 1926], with Col. Greeley, . . . and Col. Peck. From all that was transpired, taking it by and large, I am thoroughly convinced that the Forest Service simply gave us audience as a matter of courtesy, with no idea of modifying their program in the least. No doubt you have read Secretary Jardine's decision, which is so much in keeping with all that Col. Greeley said that one wonders how much Jardine had to do with it.[24]

Reaction to the Jardine policy for the Superior National Forest set in, and the participants in the movement to save the Superior National Forest wrote to each other and to members of the Forest Service in an effort to curtail the approved road construction, and water power development plans which had come to light in July, 1925.[25] On November 15, 1926, A. H. Carhart wrote to his friend A. G. Hamel, then Forest Supervisor of the Superior National Forest, "regarding the battle that has been waged to hold the wilderness values in the Superior Region."[26] Carhart reminded Hamel that the "first move of the scrap against making the Superior Forest a cut and dried type of National Forest," had been taken by the SNFRA "modeled on the San Isabel Association," of which Hamel had been a part. He then pleaded with Hamel to give the approved road program for the Superior National Forest "time to soak in before you form any judgment."[27]

But it would require more than persuasion to alter Forest Service policy. Frederick Law Olmsted, President, American Society of Landscape Architects, and the Society's Chapter in Minneapolis was "pegging" at the problem as were members of the Izaak Walton League.[28]

The June, 1927, issue of *Field and Stream* carried a plea written by Carhart which again brought many of the facts about the Superior National Forest situation to the public eye.[29] Not so obvious to the American public were the subtle, but definite, changes taking place in the Forest Service attitudes towards wilderness values. The *Report of the Forester* for the year 1927 reflected that the efforts of the various organizations and persons mentioned throughout this study had borne fruit, for it declared:

> As our population grows and land use becomes more intensive, there will be an increasingly felt need for wilderness areas where refreshment of body and spirit may be obtained in the surroundings of unspoiled nature. . . . It is not too soon to give thought to future social requirements along these lines and to make definite provisions for them. . . . It will, therefore, be the aim to keep substantial portions and some of the outstanding scenic features of the national forests available for forms of recreation impossible where automobile roads, commercial enterprises, and other popularizing facilities for use are encouraged. . . . The Forest Service plans to withhold these areas against unnecessary road building and forms of special use of a commercial character which would impair their wilderness character.[30]

The issue over the development and commercialization of the Superior National Forest was kept alive in the closing years of the 1920's in various ways. For example, James F. Gould, Commissioner of Game and Fish for the State of Minnesota, had become involved in the investigation of the dynamiting incident at Brule Lake, and had learned of the existence of Carhart's report on the Superior National Forest.[31] He wrote to Forester Greeley for a copy of the report which he had been informed contained "some very interesting and illuminating information and some recommendations relative to the handling of timber and other things in this area."[32] The reply from the Washington office of the Forest Service stated that the report could not be found, but referred Gould to Carhart in Denver.[33] There followed an exchange of letters between Gould, Carhart, and several mutual acquaintances in the Izaak Walton League and the American Society of Landscape Architects, all who had received copies of Carhart's 1919 and 1921 reports on the Superior National Forest.[34]

Carhart's 1919 and 1921 reports regarding the Superior, after some seven to nine years of seeming to "gather dust," had in reality remained quite alive. They had stood the test of time. A letter to Carhart from the Assistant District Forester, District 2, in Denver, dated February 23, 1928, brought out this point:

> Contrary to your impression, the recreation plan you conceived for the Superior has not been allowed to accumulate dust but rather has been a very live document and as time has gone by has formed the basis for the preparation of the controlling plan governing recreation and other activities within that Forest. While the wording in that plan may not be identical with that used by you, yet the fundamental policies are the same, which I presume will be the source of some satisfaction to you. . . . I believe our present plan provides for the utmost in coordinated use and for the ultimate development for the most attractive recreation ground that will meet with your ideas, to a large extent, of the capitalization of the social value of a Forest of this character.[35]

The Assistant District Forester's account of the use to which Carhart's reports had been put within the Forest Service demonstrated their key role in wilderness preservation policy formation. Another, and possibly more important, role for those reports, was the part they played in the ultimate passage in 1930 of the Shipstead-Newton, Nolan Act.[36] That Act withdrew from entry for commercial purposes the lands in the area which became known as the Boundary Waters Canoe Area in northern Minnesota, and provided for protection of recreation values.[37] Carhart's contributions in the early stages of the formation of the Quetico-Superior Council of Minneapolis, associated with the Izaak Walton League of America, need not be detailed here, but the pressure which that organization brought to bear on the Forest Service and the United States Congress cannot be exaggerated. The successful passage of the Shipstead-Newton-Nolan Act in 1930, and the policy changes towards wilderness areas in the closing years of the 1920's reflected the influence of the Izaak Walton League and its various associated organizations.[38]

In the *Report of the Forester* for the year 1928, the newly-appointed Chief Forester, R. Y. Stuart, remarked that

> the study of the so-called "wilderness areas" or areas believed to be most useful if retained in a condition of relative undevelopment, continued throughout the year, and in one district was completed. It is not proposed unduly to curtail timber cutting, grazing, water development, mining, or other forms of use incompatible with the public enjoyment of their major values.[39]

The foregoing reference to the study of the so-called "wilderness areas" that had continued throughout the year, and that "in one district was completed," failed to state that an area or areas had been established or designated. To that year, 1928, the *only* area which had come to the attention of the Washington office of the Forest Service and to the Secretary of Agriculture had been the border lake country in the Superior National Forest. Acting Forester Sherman had approved the Recreation Plan for the Superior National Forest, June 30, 1926, and that plan was given final approval by Secretary of Agriculture Jardine, September 17, 1926.[40] The files of the Gila National Forest, District 3, Albuquerque, New Mexico, reflected *no coordination with the Washington office of the Secretary of Agriculture between 1924 and 1928 concerning the "wilderness area" in that Forest.*[41] More will be reported on this topic in the succeeding chapter of this study.

By the year 1929 the Forest Service had taken some positive steps to regulate and protect "wilderness areas" on a nationwide basis. As a result of the first nationwide inventory to locate and delineate such areas, certain minimum standards of size and quality had to be set. The task of arriving at the formula for the Forest Service was delegated to L. F. Kneipp, Chief of the Branch of Lands, Washington office of the Service.[42] Kneipp wrote an article, which described the process and of finding that formula. Some pertinent excerpts from the article, which apparently was written during February, 1929, some five months before Regulation L-20 appeared, follow:

> The "wilderness" discussion was at its height. The Forester became curious. Just how far have the National Forests been invaded with joy-riding highways, polluted with the malodorous fumes of burned gasoline, . . . degraded with the modern types of resorts catering to a depraved taste for jazz, bathtubs, bridge and dinner clothes? . . . The Chief of Lands . . . passed the buck to Engineering, whose capable guide decided that Miss Mary M. Murphy possessed the requisite qualities of accuracy, capability, patience, and good nature and sentenced her to the job of digging up the facts.[43]

The article explained that one of the treasures of the Engineering Branch was its set of "quarter inch maps," upon which was recorded each Forest Supervisor's "wildest flights of fancy as to the ultimate road and trail system for his Forest," including construction progress. Those maps were adopted as the basis for the study, with any and every road, "existing or ever having existed," as the guiding principle. The latter was adopted so as to minimize the possibility that "some hardy soul might some day lay an accusing finger upon . . . the map and assert that he had driven his car to that point."[44]

Then it was decided that 10 townships (360 square miles, or 230,400 acres), was the smallest area deserving of consideration. Kneipp then explained:

> So Miss Murphy set to work. The road map of each Forest was subjected to almost microscopic examination. The merest suspicion of the existence of a road disqualified an area. . . . Single areas sometimes extended into 4 Forests, or two States or two districts, and careful coordination was essential. . . . The results were surprising. At present there are 74 areas, ranging from 360 to 10,859 square miles in extent, which so far as can be determined are without roads. The grand total area is 85,750 square miles, or an average of 1,159 square miles per area. If the proposed Forest Road System, as at present conceived, were 100 per cent completed, there would still be 61 areas ranging in extent from 360 square miles to 5,000 square miles, with a total area of 52,920 square miles and an average of 868 sections per area. These figures are exclusive of Alaska.[45]

Kneipp summed up the situation in the National Forests as "not so bad as some had feared." He noted that

> at present one-third of the gross acreage of the National Forests, exclusive of Alaska, is in roadless areas of more than 230,000 acres in extent. . . . Nobody who owns a good pair of shoes, pack or a riding saddle need throw them away because of a fear there will be no place to use them; nor is there any danger that Forest officers will wholly lose the use of their pedal extremities.[46]

On July 12, 1929, Forest Service Regulation L-20 became effective, affording for the first time in history of the United States nationwide regulation and protection for wilderness values in the National Forests, subject to approval of the Chief of the Forest Service. When fiscal year 1929 ended on June 30, 1929, it marked the end of an era. The Forester's report put it this way:

> The year marked the initiation of steps to preserve permanently within the national forests specimen areas of virgin timber representing the major forest types of each region, so that there may be preserved for scientific reference and study a well-chosen series of examples of the biological balances or complexes which originally obtained. Promiscuous recreational use of such areas would alter their character, and so defeat their purpose. But to provide for the forms of recreation for which wilderness surroundings are essential a second series of much larger areas is now being selected and established, within which primitive conditions of subsistence, habitation, transportation, and environment will permanently be maintained to the fullest practicable degree.[47]

With the promulgation of Regulation L-20, wilderness preservation in the National Forests was on a much surer footing than ever. Implementation of that measure was to prove difficult, subject to the vicissitudes of the times. The next chapter of this study will explain the steps taken by the Forest Service to establish formally the "Primitive Areas" authorized by that Regulation, and will be limited to the three *de facto* applications already discussed.

CHAPTER X

HERE COMES THE JUDGE!

The year 1929 brought the "Critical Period"[1] in the wilderness preservation movement to an end. For the first time in its history, the Forest Service issued a regulation which permitted the establishment of "Primitive Areas" within National Forests, subject to the approval of the Chief of the Service. This chapter will be limited to a discussion of the three areas, previously discussed, where *de facto* applications of the wilderness concept had been completed with the approval of the District Foresters concerned. While Regulation L-20 remained in force until it was superseded in 1939, this chapter will detail only those events related to the formal establishment of such areas authorized by that Regulation between 1929 and 1933.

Formal Establishment of "Primitive Areas" under Forest Service Regulation L-20 (July 12, 1929)

When the Forest Service promulgated its Regulation L-20, which became effective July 12, 1929, the nation was enjoying the overweening prosperity of the decade. The first inkling that the boom might be over came in early September of that year, and by mid-October the great bull market was at an end. The worst period of panic on the stock market was from October 24 through 29, and by then the "Great Depression" had been ushered in to remain until about 1940.[2]

It may be relevant, therefore, to emphasize that while the Eighteenth Amendment had been described as "the child of the First World War" and its repeal as "the child of the Great Depression," the same should not be said of the wilderness preservation movement which paralleled the years 1919-1933.[3] Though the end of World War I is perhaps a convenient starting point for the wilderness preservation movement and recreational development in the National Forests, action to establish and regulate "Primitive Areas" was initiated prior to the onset of the Great Depression by about three months, as evidenced by the issuance of Regulation L-20. That conservation measure was carried out by President Herbert Hoover's administration through Chief Forester R. Y. Stuart, and was by no means an invention of the New Deal.[4] The Hoover-Stuart team during the years 1929-1933 was somehow reminiscent of the Roosevelt-Pinchot combination in the early conservation movement of the Progressive Era.

When Regulation L-20 was initially distributed to the Forest Service Districts, it was accompanied by a set of mimeographed supplementary instructions outlining more specific guidelines in the administration of the primitive areas.[5] The latter instructions were "more revealing of wilderness concepts of the Service at that time than the regulation to which they applied." For example, under the heading "Utilization Policy," appeared the following:

> The establishment of a primitive area ordinarily will not operate to withdraw timber, forage or water resources from industrial use, since the utilization of such resources, if properly regulated, will not be incompatible with the purposes for which the area is designated. Where

> special circumstances warrant a partial or complete restriction of the use of timber, forage or water, that fact will be set forth in the plan of management for the area.[6]

The basic Regulation was amended on August 7, 1930, but those minor changes need not be described. Of interest and pertinence, however, were the provisions of the Regulation as to its implementation. It stated in part:

> The Chief of the Forest Service shall determine, define and permanently record . . . a series of areas to be known as primitive areas, and within which . . . will be maintained primitive conditions of environment, transportation, habitation, and subsistence, with a view to conserving the value of such areas for purposes of public education . . . and recreation.[7]

According to "A National Plan for American Forestry," called the "Copeland Report" and dated March 13, 1933, there were at that time thirty-eight "established, partly established and potential wilderness areas."[8] Eleven of those thirty-eight areas were reported to be "Established" in the National Forests. Two minor discrepancies were noted in that report, namely, the *omission* of the *Flat Tops Primitive Area* in the White River National Forest, Colorado, and the *erroneous inclusion* of the *Gila Primitive Area* as "Established" rather than "Partly Established."[9] Further, the ORRRC investigators found that "sixty-three primitive areas were identified by 1933 on national forests, ranging in size from 5,000 acres to a little over a million acres."[10] Incidentally, the available *evidence* demonstrates that even from a strictly technical standpoint, *the Gila Primitive Area was far from being the first such area to be formally established in the National Forests; it was rather among the last.* As the Nation was closing its banking institutions, so the National Forests were being closed to further commercialization and industrial development which would threaten wilderness values.[11]

The problems of management subsequent to establishment of primitive areas are illuminated by the circumstances attendant to the final approval of the formal classification of the three *de facto* areas as "Primitive Areas" and by key developments in their history during the following generation.

Boundary Waters Canoe Area. The area now known as the Boundary Waters Canoe Area (hereafter cited as BWCA) is located in the Superior National Forest, Minnesota. The BWCA was originally called a "Wilderness Area" in accordance with the Jardine formal policy statement of 1926. The BWCA has always been considered a "special case," and since 1926 has had its Plans of Management formally *determined, defined,* and *permanently recorded* by the Washington office of the Forest Service, and the Secretary of Agriculture,[12] As with all other plans for the National Forests, following the Crash in 1929, there was a delay in complying with Regulation L-20. The Recreation Plan and Report for the Superior National Forest was forwarded to Washington November 28, 1931, and was returned February 15, 1932, approved by the Chief Forester.[13] The latter action was a formality in compliance with Regulation L-20. However, it should be noted that the Shipstead-Newton-Nolan Act of 1930 had entered the picture at about the same time. That Congressional Act was passed to promote the better protection and highest public use of lands of the United States and adjacent lands and waters in northern Minnesota, and also had to be considered.[14]

Under L-20 the BWCA was changed from a "Wilderness Area" to a "Primitive Area," and in 1938 to a "Roadless Primitive Area,"[15] In 1958, the present name, BWCA, was selected as being more representative of the area. While the nomenclature has changed, fundamental policies of management have not changed. Succeeding plans of management to 1965 have been "largely a rededication of the policies as approved for the original Wilderness Area."[16] Probably, the BWCA remains the most complicated and varied of all regions in the National Forests, and from a management standpoint will likely remain a "special case."[17]

Flat Tops Primitive Area. The Flat Tops Primitive Area is located in the White River National Forest, Colorado, and is contiguous to but does *not* include Trappers Lake, on the shores of which the wilderness concept was born and first applied in the National Forests.[18] The story behind the region of Trappers Lake, familiarly called "White River County," is one of the most colorful in the history of Colorado. Before proceeding with an account of the formal establishment of the Flat Tops Primitive Area under Regulation L-20, the presentation of a necessarily abbreviated chronology of selected facts and highlights in the history of the development of that region may help clarify statements and data to follow.[19]

In the very same month and year of the signing of the Declaration of Independence, July, 1776, the Spanish friars, Silvestre Velez de Escalante and Francisco Atanasio Dominguez, trekked out of Santa Fe, New Mexico, with a small party in search of a northern route to Monterey, California. They crossed the Colorado River somewhere west of Grand Junction, and finally reached the White River near the present site of Rangely, the furthest north of Spanish penetration. Their route was south and west of the White River National Forest. At that time, all of what became Colorado west of the continental divide was largely an unknown wilderness occupied by the Utes, Cheyenne or Arapahoe. In the early and mid-nineteenth century, several other exploratory trips were made in the region, but none actually penetrated the Flat Tops area.[20]

Oliver Preble Wiggins, a one-time scout with Kit Carson claimed that he was the first white man to visit Trappers Lake, about thirty miles north of Glenwood Springs, and that he considered it almost "inaccessible, because of the density of fallen timber."[21] Wiggins was accompanied by one partner, Egbert Johnson. In the two seasons of 1856-1858 they caught 800 beavers near the Lake, and gave it the name which has ever since clung to it.[22]

The first authentic maps of the region were the work of the famous Dr. F. V. Hayden, U.S. Geologist, in the 1860's and 1870's.[23]

Following the Civil War, tens of thousands of white settlers pushed into Colorado Territory and by 1876, one hundred years after Escalante and Dominguez, Colorado was admitted as a State. The Utes resented the encroachment of the white man and finally met it with armed resistance. As a result, the government separated the Ute tribes into three groups, and placed them on different reservations. The Northern Utes remained wit hthe White River Agency, established at the site of present day Meeker. The newly-appointed agent, Nathan C. Meeker, helped create unrest among the Indians under his charge. His major fault was his missionary zeal and his lack of understanding of the Ute. However laudable his ideals, there followed the Meeker Massacre and Ute War of 1879, the last major Indian uprising in the West.[24] It was followed by the almost complete removal of the Utes from Colorado.

Settlement in the vicinity of Glenwood Springs and the country adjacent to the Flat Tops swiftly followed that removal, especially after the military post was abandoned in 1883. By 1885, the town of Meeker contained some three hundred people, and in that year, a local newspaper reported that:

> two years ago there were no cattle in this valley, and it is estimated that at least twenty-five to thirty thousand head are grazing upon its abundant and nutritious grasses. . . . Game is very abundant, especially the black-tail deer, and the crystal waters of White River furnish an unfailing supply of the most delicious trout, weighing often from two to three pounds.[25]

The people of Meeker joined other Colorado citizens in a move to halt the rapid depletion of local forest land. Formed in 1884, the Colorado State Forestry Association met in Denver on January 2, 1886, to discuss the "preservation and extension of forests, and maintenance of water supply, in this State."[26] The Association's united, state-wide effort produced results, for on March 3, 1891, Congress authorized the President to establish forest reserves from the public domain. On October 16 of that year, the White River Plateau Timberland Reserve was set aside by executive order of President Benjamin Harrison. The first such reservation in Colorado, and the second in the United States, it embraced an area of 1,198,080 acres. Congressional action taken June 4, 1897, placed it under the administration of the General Land Office of the Department of Interior. President Theodore Roosevelt changed its name to White River Forest Reserve, June 28, 1902, and on February 1, 1905, the administration of forest reserves was transferred to the Forest Service, U. S. Department of Agriculture. Two years later, the name of that reserve was change to "White River National Forest" by Act of Congress. The District Office in Denver was established January 1, 1909, and ten years later, the first Recreation Engineer was employed.[27]

Earlier discussion has documented sufficiently the events which occurred at Trappers Lake from 1919 through 1922. Subsequent developments there were affected by the fact that the previous policy approved by District Forester A. S. Peck for Trappers Lake was continued throughout the 1920's. Evidence to support that claim is found in the restricted development of that area, in actions taken to disapprove applications for homesites and in the cancellation of permits for sites already surveyed.[28] In addition, several permits for cabins, built in 1916, 1917, and 1920, were cancelled and the cabins destroyed. The following quotation is most explicit:

> From my field notes it is evident that we [Forest Supervisor Lewis R. Rist, Assistant Forest Supervisor Karl L. Janouch, and Forest Examiner Fred R. Johnson] conclu-

> ded that the area above Trappers Lake should be reserved for wilderness purposes. This was further corroborated by later findings in the Supervisor's Office at Glenwood Spings [in] a letter from Regional Forester Allen S. Peck to Supervisor James Blair, under date of Oct[ober] 12, 1923, stating that the Forest Service should not plan to continue the road beyond its terminus at Forest Inn (¼ mile below Trappers Lake).[29]

Forest Supervisor Lewis R. Rist, who replaced James A. Blair in 1928, approved the Recreation Management Plan for the White River National Forest on December 17, 1929. He then forwarded it to Washington, where on March 5, 1932, the Flat Tops Primitive Area was granted the final approval of the Chief of the Forest Service, R. Y. Stuart, under Regulation L-20.[30]

When Forester Stuart approved that plan, the Flat Tops tract contained about 117,800 acres, but curiously it did not contain Trappers Lake, the location where the precedent for preservation of all such areas had been set in 1919.

Jack J. McNutt, former Chief, Reclassification Section, Regional Office, USFS, explained the decision to exclude that lake from the Primitive Area in 1929.[31] McNutt stated substantially that Trappers Lake was only one of three areas which had been selected on April 4, 1927, by the Bureau of Reclamation as potential water power sites. Specifically, all lands within one-quarter mile of Trappers Lake and Big Fish Lake, Marvine Creek and Marvine Lake, and the North Fork of the White River, were assigned a "Power Site Classification" that has continued to the present.[32] In addition, there were "various proposals to raise the outlet of Trappers Lake to make it a much greater storage reservoir." Despite those classifications, McNutt commented, "Trappers Lake will be recommended for inclusion in the 'Flat Tops Wilderness' when it is reclassified from its present Primitive Area status."[38] The basis for such reclassification appears to arise from a Forest Service report of 1964 that the Bureau of Reclamation was no longer considering a dam site at Trappers Lake, because the lake "leaks like a sieve," and because of the potential adverse public reaction to a reservoir at that site.[34] The Bureau apparently indicated a willingness to recommend that part or all of the 1160-acre withdrawal be revoked.[35]

The section of the same report headed "Trappers Lake Addition (1389 acres)," included the following "justification statements" for the proposed addition of that unit:

> The principal attraction and wilderness value of this area is the 313-acre lake, the scenic escarpment surrounding the basin, and the cutthroat trout fishery the basin and lake supports.
>
> Trappers Lake is the second largest natural lake in Colorado and the largest that is still in a primitive environment. . . . In addition to its unique wilderness beauty, the lake and its inlets are the largest natural cutthroat trout fishery in Colorado. However, without regulation and protective management this last stronghold of Colorado's only native fish may not long exist.[36]

The report then referred to studies conducted over the previous five years by the Colorado State Department of Game, Fish, and Parks, which found that fishing pressure had increased so drastically, and that if the trend continued unchecked, it would soon become impossible for the cutthroat population to reproduce itself adequately.[37]

Seeming to echo the plea of an earlier day, the report stressed the fact that "new campground and sanitation facilities must be provided in the vicinity to adequately and safely handle not only the present use but the increased future use." The statement concluded with the following observations:

> Wilderness classification of the 1389 acres including the lake and its inlets would be the strongest and most permanent protection possible for the present scenic and fishery values that we offer. . . . With any other type

> of classification, no matter how good our intentions may be, the Forest Service cannot guarantee such complete protection forever. It is seldom we have the opportunity to protect so much by classifying so little acreage (1.4% of the total existing area).[38]

The White River Valley has long been known for its outstanding recreational features. An enthusiastic reporter for the *Meeker Herald* remarked that "probably no part of the United States is better known for its wonderful big game hunting than the White River Valley."[39] The region first received wide publicity in 1901 when Theodore Roosevelt, then Vice President of the United States, successfully hunted mountain lions in the valley. That publicity has continued throughout the years as there is no place in the State of Colorado where there is finer deer and elk hunting, and each season hunters also take home a number of bear.[40]

The Flat Tops Primitive Area was so named because of its high, comparatively flat topography. The name of Flat Tops originated among the early settlers of the surrounding Colorado, White, and Yampa River Valleys, and quite as naturally, it was applied to the tract when the Primitive Area was established. Nevertheless, the Area, which is located on a great plateau averaging in elevation from 8,000 to 12,250 feet, is by no means "flat," for among its many peaks, twelve of them range from 11,176 to 12,493 feet in height. The Area forms an important part of the Upper Colorado River watershed, and its watershed values are particularly high because of heavy snow pack and the related irrigation use downstream.[41]

The Flat Tops Primitive Area has been managed as a Primitive Area under Regulation L-20 since 1932. It has been studied and the completed proposal to reclassify the area to wilderness status as the Flat Tops Wilderness under the Wilderness Act of 1964 was forwarded to Congress for action. The report was signed and recommended for approval by Edward P. Cliff, Chief of the United States Forest Service on July 26, 1967, and was approved by the then Secretary of Agriculture Orville L. Freeman on August 11, 1967. The Wilderness Act of 1964 will be discussed briefly in the concluding chapter, the Epilogue. As of May 4th, 1972, Congress has not acted on the Flat Tops Wilderness Report.[42]

Gila Wilderness Area. The Gila Wilderness Area is located in the Gila National Forest, New Mexico, and has enjoyed much publicity under that title. A 1952 official report concerning that area explained that

> although its classification under Regulation L-20 made it technically a primitive area, the Gila has from the first been called a wilderness area, and for convenience we will continue to call it that.[43]

Following the promulgation of Regulation L-20, the revised Recreational Working Plan, Gila National Forest, was forwarded to the Washington office for approval. In a letter to Regional Forester Pooler from Forest Service headquarters, dated May 20, 1930, the reaction in Washington to the proposed Gila Primitive Area was given. It read in part:

> In considering this and other reports submitted by your District it may be well to review the basic purposes of this movement. In substance, there is widespread concern in the minds of many people and members of organizations with reference to the rapid modification of all parts of the United States leading to the elimination of the primitive conditions under which the pioneer growth of the Nation took form. . . . The special plans for the future administration of wilderness areas should be specific and, in large degree, prohibitive; that is, there preferably should be a series of unequivocal statements as to what will be done, so that there can be no innocent infiltration of new conditions through which primitive values of the area eventually will be destroyed.[44]

Later in that letter, the Washington office suggested that the "Gila and other classification reports be again scrutinized by your office," and "after you have considered the report which is being returned," the Washington office would be "glad to again give it consideration."[45]

The following year, after an exchange of several letters on the subject, Forester R. Y. Stuart wrote a memorandum to Assistant Forester L. F. Kneipp stating that "the Region will make some modifications to the report . . . and submit it to Washington for our further consideration." Stuart's main criticism of the report and recommendation was the "prohibition placed upon timber use by the report as being in conflict with the established primitive area policy." He stated that his interpretation of the policy was that while it was "well to gauge as closely as practicable when there may be economic need for any of the timber included in a primitive area," the determination of that time did not call for prohibition of cutting within that time. Stuart emphasized the point that "we should not select as primitive areas, areas that contain merchantable timber economically desirable in the near future."[46]

Another year passed and then Regional Forester Pooler wrote a terse note to Washington on March 22, 1932, which stated that while the areas proposed for consideration as primitive areas in Region 3 were being protected and handled with a view to ultimate approval, little progress had been made in getting such approval.[47] That letter brought results, for in a few days the Forester replied that after extended consideration of all the facts related to the establishment of the Gila Primitive Area within the Gila National Forest, he had given the proposal his approval. His approval was a qualified one, however.[48] He added that "in conformity with the prevailing practice you may now proceed to have the report written in final form on atlas folio sheets for permanent filing in this office." Further, he instructed that in preparing such reports "several Regions recently have adopted the practice of concluding the report with a rather formal statement of the action by the Forester." Consequently, when the final report was prepared it concluded with the following definite certification of action taken by the Forester as follows:

> By virtue of the authority vested in me by Regulation L-20 of the Secretary of Agriculture, relating to the use, occupancy, protection and administration of the National Forests, I hereby designate as the Gila Primitive Area the lands situated within the Gila National Forest which are described in the revised report submitted by L. R. Lessel Forest Supervisor under date of March 9, 1931, and shown on the map accompanying said report; and hereby direct that the future management and administration of said lands shall be in conformity with the purposes and principles of Regulation L-20 and the instructions thereunder, and with the plan of management prescribed in the report above referred to, or such subsequent amendment thereof as may be approved or authorized by the Forester.[49]

The March 9, 1931 Report was approved by the Forester on June 8, 1933.[50] That certification has been revised repeatedly since 1933 to conform to subsequent changes in the Gila area boundaries and Service Regulations, which need not be detailed here.

This chapter has shown that during the period 1929-1933, the first nationwide regulation of Primitive Areas was effected under Forest Service Regulation L-20. That measure has been the foundation of all subsequent management plans in the national Forests governing such areas. The stated mission of the Forest Service to produce timber and protect watershed was an obstacle which had to be overcome before the additional use of the Forests as recreation grounds could be realized. Regulation L-20 was inadequate particularly because it was not sufficiently restrictive in the developments permitted in the Primitive Areas. But a beginning had been made, and time would bring a maturation of the thinking necessary to the ultimate establishment in 1964 of a National Wilderness Preservation System worthy of the name.

EPILOGUE: NOW THAT WE'RE ORGANIZED, WHAT'LL WE DO?

The wilderness preservation movement which began in the United States in 1919 culminated in 1929 in the first nationwide program of regulated protection of wilderness values in National Forests. Centuries of changing philosophic attitudes toward wilderness areas finally resulted in emergence of a pragmatic plan which not only protected the Nation's remaining wilderness, but accommodated other demands in surrounding wildlands that would threaten the core wilderness area.

The movement may be said to have started when the Forest Service employed its first professionally trained landscape architect following World War I. Officially termed a Recreation Engineer and at heart an aesthetic conservationist, Arthur Hawthorne Carhart formulated the first *written plans* for human use and recreational development in National Forests in 1919. In the same year he prepared the first written blueprint which spelled out the wilderness concept as it is understood today.

While there had been recognition of the value of National Forests for recreation prior to, during and immediately after World War I, there existed no active program for their development for such a purpose, and no practical plan or policy regarding the preservation of wilderness values in the

National Forests had been formulated or even proposed. On the eve of World War I, Forest Service officials noted the increasing use of National Forests as playgrounds, and manifested a growing awareness of the recreational uses of the Forests. In 1916, National Forests scattered from Maine to California and from the Gulf of Mexico to the Canadian Line were visited by 2,000,000 people; the National Forests of Colorado alone had received more than 600,000 visitors during the previous summer.

The introduction into the Forest Service of a landscape architect in 1919 brought new concepts of forest management into our National Forests. For the first time, men professionally trained in landscape architecture and those trained in forestry began to communicate, and the Forest Service began to plan for the preservation of aesthetic values. Not only did the Forest Service launch an active program for the development of forest recreation in 1919, but as a by-product gave birth to the basic formula for wilderness preservation, the exclusion of man-made structures in designated areas protected by a surrounding regional plan.

The first regional plan undertaken anywhere in the National Forests was written by Arthur H. Carhart in 1919 and pertained to the recreational development of the San Isabel National Forest, Colorado. The second such plan was written by him in the same year for the Superior National Forest, Minnesota. Carhart was the first peripatetic planner of Forest recreation in the National Forests in District 2 of the United States Forest Service. His plans were far-reaching in scope and implication. The San Isabel National Forest of Colorado was the first Forest to receive the benefit of planned development of the unit Forest by a competent, professional landscape architect. Colorado can claim that distinction in Forest recreation with pride.

In the interest of historical accuracy, let the record be corrected to reflect that the wilderness concept was the brain child of Arthur Carhart *not* Aldo Leopold, and that the wilderness concept was born and the principle was *first applied in the summer of 1919 at Trappers Lake,* White River National Forest, Colorado. Assigned to make a survey of the Trappers Lake area to plot several hundred home sites on the lake shore and to plan a "through" road around the lake, Carhart completed the surveys pursuant to his instructions but made it known to his immediate supervisor that he opposed further "improvement where natural landscape would suffer." After some discussion, the Denver District Office of the Forest Service agreed that the Trappers Lake area should remain roadless, and that the many applications for homesite permits around the lake should not be honored. That was an unprecedented step in Forest Service history.

In 1920 the first extensive report on recreation was sent to Washington from the Denver office of the Service. It discussed the factors which were believed to have precipitated the unprecedented demand for National Forest recreation following World War I. Given among the factors were: the war factor which introduced men to outdoor life; the disappearing local camping areas; the increase of wealth among large bodies of citizens; the curtailment of travel to Europe during World War I; the increased production and ownership of automobiles; and the establishment of great trunk-line roads leading to National Forest territory. The year 1920 brought a somewhat ambivalent recognition of recreational development as a "major activity" of the Forest Service, and the publication of articles about recreation in nationally distributed magazines written by A. H. Carhart.

There were countervailing forces to National Forest recreation and wilderness preservation policy in 1921. That year, the National Park Service openly opposed the expenditure of federal funds for the development of recreational facilities in the National Forests. Concurrently, however, there existed a greater but less obvious deterrent to such development, known as the "good roads movement." The latter, by that year, had influenced legislation so that federal funds were not only available for the construction of roads and highways into and through the National Forests, but there was an unexpended accumulation of such funds running into millions of dollars. The existence of unexpended forest-road construction funds, primarily to promote fire suppression, may have militated against proposals for the exclusion of such roads in favor of wilderness preservation. The evidence helps explain why the Washington office of the Forest Service found its fire protection mission and its over-all public service considerations difficult to reconcile with the demands made by conservationists interested in wilderness protection.

At the turn of the century the Federal government entered the picture in Minnesota forestry in a substantial way. By 1909, President Theodore Roosevelt proclaimed the establishment of the Superior National Forest. The President's Proclamation did not include, however, the central strip of the choice lake country on the international border between Basswood Lake and Saganaga Lake, now known as the Boundary Waters Canoe Area, which was not added until 1936. The ownership status in the latter area produced controversy and management problems not yet solved.

The second *de facto* application of the wilderness concept in the United States took place in the Superior National Forest in Minnesota. Its origin could be traced to Recreation Engineer Arthur Carhart's "Preliminary Report" of 1919. It advanced a step further when in 1921 Carhart paid a second visit to that Forest, and drafted a second, or revised, report. Out of this plan came the first major dispute over road building in National Forests, and the dispute concerned the Boundary Waters Canoe Area. The Boundary Waters Canoe Area Review Committee reported to Secretary of Agriculture Orville L. Freeman in December, 1964, that the first attempt to indicate and to develop guiding principles for that area was made in 1919 when Arthur H. Carhart was employed as a landscape architect for the Forest Service. Carhart's plan for the Superior National Forest was formally approved in 1922, two years before the one proposed by Aldo Leopold for the Gila National Forest, New Mexico, which was not formally approved until June 3, 1924.

The first appropriation of Federal funds expressly for recreational development in National Forests was made in 1922 when Congress authorized the expenditure of $10,000 for recreation purposes. The amount was considered incidental by at least one Forest Service official, but it was the beginning of formal recognition by Congress of Forest recreation.

At the end of 1922, A. H. Carhart resigned from the Forest Service because he felt that there had not been adequate development of the plans he had prepared; in fact, he had been repeatedly told that the Service could supply neither funds nor organization to implement his plans. When he resigned, a certain cycle of accomplishment had been finished in recreation work in National Forests. Principles, methods and plans on which that work could progress for several decades had been demonstrated and have since stood the test of time. When he left the Service, Acting Forester E. A. Sherman wrote that Carhart had done "so much to establish the recreation use of the National Forests on a high plane of public service" that he wished Carhart would "stay to do a little more." Sherman remarked further that with each passing year the Forest Service would approach "more closely to the exacting standards which you set for yourself and which I am free to admit should govern the entire Service."

The foregoing chapters have demonstrated that in the 1920's the aims of the two professional disciplines, namely, forestry and landscape architecture, were difficult to achieve in the Forest Service. Carhart felt that by leaving the Service he would be free to help to overcome what seemed to be a losing battle for recreational development and wilderness preservation. Even before leaving the Forest Service, Carhart had carefully laid the ground work for the crusade he was to carry on following his resignation. Armed with information he had gained while in the Service and through his affiliation with the American Institute of Park Executives, Carhart wrote to P. B. Riis, the Institute's Chairman of the Department of Wild Life Preservation, about the proposed road construction in the Superior National Forest. Since Carhart could not openly precipitate the formation of a movement to protest those roads, and in order not to compromise or cut off his continuing source of information within the Forest Service, he secured the assistance of P. B. Riis while he remained in the background. It should be emphasized that Carhart's motives were unselfish, above reproach, and his actions reflected profound loyalty to his fellow man and to the Nation. He sought neither monetary reward nor personal aggrandizement.

The year 1929 brought the "Critical Period" in the wilderness preservation movement to an end. For the first time in its history, the Forest Service issued a regulation which required the final approval of the Chief of the Forest Service to formally establish "Primitive Areas" within National Forests. Until Regulation L-20 became effective on July 12, 1929, establishment of "wilderness" or "primitive" areas had been accomplished on the responsibility of the District Foresters concerned. Thus official action to establish and regulate "Primitive Areas" was a *fait accompli* at the highest administrative level prior to the onset of the Great Depression by about three months. Regulation L-20 was carried out by President Herbert Hoover's administration through Chief Forester R. Y. Stuart, and was not, therefore, an invention of the New Deal. The Hoover-Stuart team during the years 1929-1933 was somehow reminiscent of the Roosevelt-Pinchot combination in the early conservation movement of the Progressive Era. Under its leadership the three *de facto* areas were formally established as "Primitive Areas." The Boundary Waters Canoe Area, Superior National Forest, Minnesota, was established by Secretary of Agriculture W. M. Jardine, September 17, 1926, and a revised version of that plan was approved

February 15, 1932. The Flat Tops Primitive Area, adjacent to Trappers Lake, White River National Forest, Colorado, was formally established, March 5, 1932, by the Chief of the Forest Service, R. Y. Stuart. The Gila Primitive Area, Gila National Forest, New Mexico, was approved as such by Forester Stuart, June 8, 1933, during the first "Hundred Days" of the New Deal.

For an evaluation of the accomplishments and experience of the wilderness preservation movement in the period 1919-1933, a sketch of developments subsequent to that time will provide useful perspective.

Regulation L-20, dated July 12, 1929, was amended slightly on August 7, 1930, and served as the basis of forest management plans until it was superseded by regulations issued on September 19, 1939.[1] More concise than Regulation L-20, subsequent regulations indicated that the concepts of wilderness were crystallizing, for developments previously permissable in primitive areas were categorically excluded from wilderness and wild areas.[2] The essence of the three pertinent 1939 regulations follows:

> Regulation U-1: 'Upon recommendations of the Chief, Forest Service, national forest lands in single tracts of not less than 100,000 acres may be designated by the Secretary [of Agriculture] as "wilderness areas," within which there shall be no roads or other provision for motorized transportation, no commercial timber cutting, and no occupancy under special use permit for hotels, stores, resorts, summer homes, organization camps, hunting and fishing lodges, or similar uses . . . Wilderness areas will not be modified or eliminated except by order of the Secretary [of Agriculture].'
>
> Regulation U-2: 'Suitable areas of national forest land in single tracts of less than 100,000 acres but not less than 5,000 acres may be designated by the Chief, Forest Service, as "Wild areas," which shall be administered in the same manner as wilderness areas. . . . The procedure for establishment, modification or elimination of

> wild areas shall be as for wilderness areas, except that final action in each case will be by the Chief [Forester].' Regulation U-3: 'Suitable areas of national forest land, other than wilderness or wild areas, which should be managed principally for recreation use.'[3]

The process of reclassifying primitive areas to place them under the newer regulations was interrupted by the outbreak of World War II, but between 1939 and 1941, of the seventy-six primitive areas established under L-20, three were reclassified as wilderness areas, and six were reclassified as wild areas.[4]

The U-regulations imposed a type of formal zoning procedure on the Forest Service and gave lands classified under them "greater security than would be enjoyed were zoning to proceed informally." However, between 1939 and 1962, because of continuing exploitation, the ORRRC investigators concluded in the latter year that

> It is difficult to avoid the conclusion that new legislation specifically directed at and with clear mandates toward preserving wilderness units. . . will be necessary if wilderness areas are to be maintained.[5]

The ORRRC investigators attributed the problems in maintaining wilderness commitments to the lack of uniform control and the lack of full jurisdiction over lands supervised by the Forest Service and the National Park Service. They cited the example of the South Yellowstone-Teton-South Absaroka Wilderness Tract located in four separate administrative jurisdictions; one in a part of Yellowstone National Park, another in a primitive area and two others in wilderness areas within National Forests. The fragmentation of control was compounded by the fact that the Teton Wilderness Area was under the regional authority for the Teton National Forest, Ogden, Utah, while the adjacent South Absaroka Wilderness Area and Stratified Primitive Area were under the Regional Forester in Denver, Colorado, and Yellowstone National Park was under regional authority at Omaha, Nebraska. That tract, therefore, was administered by agencies under the Secretary of Agriculture and the Secretary of Interior, and by three different regional authorities in the National Parks and Forest Services. Similar conditions reportedly existed "for almost every tract" and for other areas as well. Owing to the lack of uniform control and imperfect coordination of management activities, entry by recreationists could occur in a tract through either a Park or a National Forest.[6] But lack of full jurisdiction was seen as a more serious problem in retaining wilderness conditions, especially in the National Forests, because unlike areas in the National Park System, where resource developments must be authorized by Congress, reserved wilderness in the Forests was subject to water and power development without specific Congressional approval. Not the least of the problems in maintaining wilderness conditions in the National Forests are those incidental to mining.[7]

The introductory chapter of this study pointed out that under Act of Congress, Public Law 85-470, President Dwight D. Eisenhower appointed the Outdoor Recreation Resources Review Commission in 1958 to survey the nation's outdoor recreation resources, and that the findings of the Commission were reported to President John F. Kennedy in January, 1962. In an article published in January, 1965, Senator Clinton P. Anderson explained in part how that Commission came into being, and furnished some of the background concerning the introduction and ultimate passage of the Wilderness Bill.[8] He credited a speech made by the late Howard Clinton Zahnizer, Executive Director, The Wilderness Society, as the opening statement in the drive for a "program to serve not only our own human needs but also those of the generations to follow." According to Senator Anderson, Zahnizer's address on "The Need for Wilderness Areas" before the American Planning and Civic Association in Washington, D. C. on May 24, 1955, "touched off a train of circumstances which led finally to introduction of the Wilderness Bill."[9] There is no need to rehearse the complicated legal procedure involved in the passage of the Wilderness Act of September 3, 1964, but some of its implications for the future of the nation's wilderness areas should be noted here.

Having secured the necessary legislation to convert *de facto* wilderness areas into *de jure* ones, has the fight been won? The late Howard Zahnizer wrote as follows when passage of the Wilderness Act seemed assured:

> We are establishing for the first time in the history of the earth a program, a national policy, whereby areas of wilderness can be preserved. That will not be the end of our efforts. That is just the beginning.[10]

The passage of the law establishing the new National Wilderness Preservation System in 1964 marked a significant stride toward the desired goal of preserving the remaining wilderness, but that passage is to be regarded as merely a stride and not the achievement of the goal. Laurance S. Rockefeller, Chairman, ORRRC Commission, has indicated that cooperative, scientific planning by conservation-minded Foresters and citizens must be continuous to insure wilderness preservation.[11]

In January, 1965, Stewart M. Brandborg, Executive Director, The Wilderness Society, wrote that when President Lyndon B. Johnson approved the Wilderness Bill on September 3, 1964, he "brought to a successful culmination one of the Nation's longest and most hard-fought conservation battles."[12] Brandborg declared that the Act gave clear direction and

> a firm legal foundation for those in the Federal agencies who manage areas of wilderness for the "preservation of their wilderness character" so that they are "affected primarily by the forces of nature." The administrators of these agencies are now in a much stronger position to protect wilderness than they were before passage of the

> Act. As they proceed to implement its policies, they now have—for the first time—a full opportunity to develop long-range programs which will assure adequate protection of the wilderness resource.[13]

The same author also emphasized that an important part of the programs under the Act would be "development of plans" which would provide for "various uses of wilderness areas without impairing the natural environment or wild character of the lands involved," *features provided for in Arthur H. Carhart's recreational plans written half a century before.*[14]

President Johnson, in a message transmitting the Wilderness Act embodying the National Wilderness Preservation System, dated February 8, 1965, remarked in part:

> The wonder of nature is the treasure of America. What we have in woods and forest, valley and stream, in the gorges and the mountains and the hills, we must not destroy. The precious legacy of preservation of beauty will be our gift to posterity. . . . Only in our country have such positive measures been taken to preserve the wilderness adequately for its scenic and spiritual beauty. In the new conservation of this century, our concern is with the total relation between man and the world around him. Its object is not only man's material welfare but the dignity of man himself. . . . Generations of Americans to come will enjoy a finer and more meaningful life because of these actions taken in these times.[15]

This view, embodied in an Act of Congress in 1964 and in a Presidential declaration in 1965, has now become widely accepted. But in the decade of the 1920's it was a distinctly minority position. With the vision of a statesman, Arthur Hawthorne Carhart had written in 1919:

> There is no question in my mind but that there is a definite point in different types of country where man-

> made sructures should be stopped . . . the question of how best to do this is perhaps the real question, rather than shall it be done.[16]

Likewise, it may not be so important to know *who* first conceived the wilderness idea, as to recognize that it was conceived at all. Victor Hugo wrote that there is no army so powerful as an idea whose time has come. Yet evolution is a slow process, for as Einstein has noted, though in a somewhat different context, everything has changed in recent times except our ways of thinking about them.

It would appear that among the men who were ahead of their time in planning for recreational development and the preservation of wilderness areas in our National Forests, Arthur H. Carhart was in the front rank. Surely it would seem seasonable to conclude from the evidence presented in this study that if Gifford Pinchot was the "Father of the Forest Service," then Arthur Carhart might be considered among the most eligible candidates for the title, "Father of the Wilderness Concept."

But Carhart's collaborators should not go unnoticed, for without their support the wilderness idea itself may well have remained only an obscure idea. The contributions of men like Carl J. Stahl, Paul B. Riis, Will O. Doolittle, to name a few outstanding pioneers, and such organizations as The Izaak Walton League of America, The Quetico-Superior Council, the American Society of Landscape Architects, and countless other outdoor organizations, likewise cannot be exaggerated. Their unselfish efforts, particularly during the "Critical Period" in the wilderness preservation movement, 1919-1929, should be recognized. Despite the inertia in favor of other uses of the National Forests, the bureaucracy responsible for their care was to respond constructively to a new idea.

But how constructively did the U. S. Forest Service respond to the innovation? It will be recalled that in the opening chapter, *supra,* it was emphasized that establishing a federal agency does *not* bring a full solution to the problem which the agency is to handle. Interpreting and applying the law under which it operates, the agency may find that it lacks sufficient power or encounters such conditions that it may be unable to carry out the basic assignment for which it was created.

The above generalization was made in 1965 when the author's basic research was completed. It was based on the author's personal experience and on the hard facts taught by history. If past is prologue, as we have heard all our lives, then it was merely a reasonable assumption—*not* a profound prognostication. This may be seen readily by utilizing the Flat Tops Primitive Area as an example of the lack of sufficient power—or prerogative—possessed by the U. S. Forest Service in carrying out its assigned mission in regard to the Wilderness Act. Perhaps this is good; perhaps not. It is the long-range effect that matters.

When the Forest Service initially proposed the reclassification of the Flat Tops Primitive Area to Wilderness, a hearing was held in Glenwood Springs, Colorado, on October 10, 1966, with the hearing record held open to receive late written reports until November 14, 1966. In all, eighty-nine oral presentations were made and over 350 letters were received from interested parties. Sentiment ran overwhelmingly for the addition of the area to the new Wilderness Preservation System, with a majority favoring an even larger Wilderness than the present Flat Tops Primitive Area. The list of participants was impressive and too extensive for the purpose here intended. Suffice it to say that the hearing record overlapped and duplicated considerably. Many of the individuals who gave statements were members of groups, organizations, or associations. It became difficult to assess whether the testimonials were made by individuals or groups who really knew the area or made by those who testified on the basis of principle alone. As of May, 1972, the hearings of the Flat Tops Primitive Area continued.

At a conference of the Rocky Mountain Social Science Association at the University of Utah in Salt Lake City on

April 29, 1972, the author attended a Workshop on The Environmental Crisis: Modern Romanticism or Realistic Confrontation. The paper presented by Professor Fred Erisman of Texas Christian University, Fort Worth, Texas, was entitled, "The Environmental Crisis and Present-Day Romanticism." In his summary statement, Erisman opined that the rhetoric of the environmental crisis focuses on at least three fundamental principles:

> the effects of a technological society; the need for some modification of human life in such a society; and the recognition that, because the terrestrial ecosphere is a closed system, the fortunes of all things are related.

Erisman noted some curious side effects to those principles—some potentially detrimental side effects. A sizable following of the "new/now" movement has attracted intensely romantic Americans, young and old, who would remake society into a new world in the manner of Emerson and Thoreau. He did not doubt the group's allegiance to environmental reform but he questioned their rejection of much that is necessary to science. Accordingly, Erisman felt that there must be a truce between scientists and romantics because they need each other. Romantics, in sum, must accept some scientific discipline or there seems little hope, or as he stated: "What remains is the poignant sight of a well-meaning people, weighted down, like Henry Adams, by the rubbish of 140 years of seductively persistent tradition, saying the right things, trying to do the right things, for the most woefully wrong reasons." It is devoutly hoped that the well-meaning people at the ongoing Wilderness Act reclassification hearings are doing more than following tradition or slavishly following principle alone. Even a cursory review of the reports prepared by the Department of Agriculture to determine the suitability of the 34 Primitive Areas and other National Forest areas for reclassification manifestly demonstrated the opportunities for all to be heard. Those words in turn must be acted upon in good faith. Meanwhile, however, timbering, mining, and other types of developments are taking place—and not all of them merit a good report card.

Nothing happens in a vacuum. The seamless cloth of history is composed of many threads each contributing to the ultimate pattern and quality of the fabric. If the quality of our life is to be improved or, indeed, even maintained at its present level, our available resources must not be misused, for when we misuse or misplace a resource—any resource—we are polluting our environment. To the extent that we have ignored the "handwriting on the wall," as it were, and to the extent that we continue to delay our response to the current "Distant Early Warnings" of concerned citizens, then to that extent is our total pursuit of happiness threatened.

In every walk of life there are pivotal points: we can either stagnate at dead center, or strike out with vigor and make a bold new departure. Pragmatic plans for the management of our natural heritage *have been proposed* over the decades by men (and women) of vision. We must choose either to wither or to thrive in this the only finite environment we possess.

President Thomas Jefferson in his First Inaugural Address given on March 4th, 1801, made an appeal designed to "Bring us together":

> . . . Let us, then, with courage and confidence pursue our own . . . principles, . . . possessing a chosen country, with room enough for our descendants to the hundredth and thousandth generation; entertaining a due sense of our *equal right* to the use of our own faculties, . . . to honor and confidence from our fellow citizens, resulting not from birth but from our *actions* . . . with all these blessings what more is necessary to make us a happy and prosperous people? Still one thing more, fellow citizens—a wise and frugal government, which shall *restrain men from injuring one another,* which shall leave them otherwise free to regulate their own pursuits of industry and improvement . . . This is the sum of good govern-

> ment, and this is necessary to *close the circle* of our felicities. [emphases added]

The contemporary political issue over "Law and Order" is an outgrowth of the need to "restrain men from injuring one another." Injury comes in various forms; it is not just the all-too-common assault and battery variety inflicted in one way or another by a known assailant. Knowingly or unknowingly *all* citizens are injured every time an individual or group of individual citizens acquire their "unequal share" to land, *i.e.,* federally-owned land of which by birth we own "co-equal shares." Knowingly or unknowingly *all* citizens are injured when any plan is carried out which diminishes the public land intended for their benefit as shareholders in the Corporation Doing Business As: The United States of America. For this reason alone every citizen should show concern for the plans being considered by the federal government to establish policy and administer his or her land. One way to kill unwanted plans is to study them to death. Proposals to manage the remaining wilderness are not lacking. Action is.

The quiet revolution that began with Arthur Carhart is now not so quiet—nor is it a one-man show. The modern Wilderness Preservation Movement has blossomed into a not-too-sonorous chorus; there is a confusion of voices so great that the Forest Service is not procrastinating so much as it is experiencing delay in carrying out a vital program. That delay could have unfortunate repercussions in the form of loss of precious wilderness pockets. The pressure of events may eventually dictate the course of "emergency action" the government will be obliged to take to attempt to recover the *un*recoverable. Procrastination can lead to paralysis, and paralysis to extinction.

NOTES

PROLOGUE

1. Address by James Anderson, Bureau of Land Management representative, delivered at the Conference on Natural Areas of the Southwest, held November 7, 1964, at Santa Fe, New Mexico. A similar feeling was expressed by J. Michael McCloskey, Northwest Conservation Representative, Federation of Western Outdoor Clubs, Eugene, Oregon, at the Conference on Open Space, held September 26-27, 1964, at Breckenridge, Colorado. The present author attended both conferences.

2. Although the increase in population played a part in this development, it will not be discussed extensively as a separate force because it is beyond the scope of the present study. The population factor, however, is implicit in the presentation of the other interacting forces mentioned, and will be commented on when appropriate.

3. The System resulted from the passage of an Act "to establish a National Wilderness Preservation System for the permanent good of the whole people, and for other purposes," and "in order to assure that an increasing population, accompanied by expanding settlement and growing mechanization, does not occupy and modify all areas within the United States . . . leaving no lands designated for preservation and protection in their natural condition . . . for the American people of present and future generations the benefit of an enduring resource . . . of federally owned areas designated by Congress as 'wilderness areas.' " Public Law 88-577, 88th Congress, Session 4, September 3, 1964.

4. For a discussion of that rivalry see Donald C. Swain, *Federal Conservation Policy, 1921-1933* (Berkeley, 1963), 134-38.

5. Wesley M. Gewehr, *American Civilization* (New York, 1957), 381. This is one of many standard textbook accounts reflecting this erroneous belief.

6. The Wildlands Research Center, University of California, "Wilderness and Recreation—A Report on Resources, Values, and Problems," *Study Report 3 of the Outdoor Recreation Resources Review Commission* (hereafter cited as ORRRC, *Study Report 3*) (Washington, D.C., 1962), 3-39. Under Act of Congress, Public Law 85-470, President Dwight D. Eisenhower appointed the Commission in 1958 to survey the nation's outdoor recreation resources; the findings were reported to President John F. Kennedy in January, 1962, and have since been the bases of new legislation.

7. *Ibid.*, 3.

8. Frederick Jackson Turner, *Frontier and Section* (Englewood Cliffs, N.J., 1961), 37-62.

9. Frederick L. Paxson, *Postwar Years, Normalcy, 1918-1923* (Berkeley, 1948), 161-63, 381-82.

10. Richard Hofstadter, *The Age of Reform—From Bryan to F.D.R.* (New York, 1955), 302. Though Donald C. Swain did point out that the period 1921-1933 was a "time of preparation for greater forestry accomplishment in the future," his book did not point to the positive gains in the wilderness preservation in the National Forests but in the National Parks. Donald C. Swain, *Federal Conservation Policy, 1921-1933* (Berkeley, 1963), 29, 123-43.

11. Memorandum from A. H. Carhart, Recreation Engineer, District 2, United States Forest Service (hereafter cited as USFS), Denver, Colorado, to Aldo Leopold, Assistant District Forester, District 3, USFS, Albuquerque, New Mexico, December 10, 1919. Carhart Papers, Conservation Library Center, Denver Public Library, Colorado (hereafter cited as Carhart Papers).

12. Roderick W. Nash, "Man and Nature in America," *Forest History*, VII (Winter, 1964), 21-22. Nash's review concerned the book by Arthur A. Ekirch, Jr., *Man and Nature in America* (New York, 1963), which he stated was a "rehash" of "widely documented portions of American history such as the campaigns for forest conservation and the national parks."

13. See, for example, Hans Huth, *Nature and the American—Three Centuries of Changing Attitudes* (Berkeley, 1957). Huth's book contains a useful bibliography. See also, Stewart L. Udall's *The Quiet Crisis* (New York, 1963), for another meritorious monograph containing even more up-to-date developments.

14. The Librarian of Congress, "Outdoor Recreation Literature: A Survey," *Study Report 27 of the Outdoor Recreation Resources Review Commission* (hereafter cited as ORRRC Study Report 27) (Washington, D,C., 1962), 1-3.

15. John Muir, "A Plan to Save the Forests," *Our National Parks* (Boston, 1901), 337. Muir wanted to "preserve" the forests, whereas Pinchot subscribed fully to the nineteenth-century school of applied science which espoused the "gospel of efficiency" in the utilization of forest lands.

16. Samuel P. Hays, *Conservation and the Gospel of Efficiency: The Progressive Conservation Movement, 1890-1920* (Cambridge, 1959), 67-68, 189-98, *et passim.*

17. United States Department of Agriculture, Forest Service, *Wilderness.* Pamphlet 459 (Washington, 1963), 3. It also identified Henry David Thoreau as one of the first Americans who spoke out for the preservation of wildlands "just over 100 years ago."

18. *Ibid.*

19. Robert Sterling Yard, "Saving the Wilderness," *The Living Wilderness,* V (July, 1940), 3.

20. Harvey Broome, "Origins of the Wilderness Society," *The Living Wilderness,* V (July, 1940), 13.

21. *Ibid.*, citing Aldo Leopold, "The Last Stand of American Wilderness," *American Forests and Forest Life,* XXXI (October, 1925), 599-604.

22. *Ibid.*, citing Robert Marshall, "The Problem of Wilderness," *The Scientific Monthly, XXX* (February, 1930), 141-48.

23. Broome, *The Living Wilderness,* V (1940), 13.

24. Aldo Leopold, "Origin and Ideals of Wilderness Areas," *The Living Wilderness,* V (July, 1940), 7.

25. *Ibid.*, citing Aldo Leopold, "The Wilderness and Its Place in Forest Recreational Policy," *Journal of Forestry,* XIX (November, 1921), 718-21. For a summary of this article, see below, pp. 229 ff.

26. Aldo Leopold, "Origin and Ideals of Wilderness Areas," *The Living Wilderness,* V (July, 1940), 7.

27. ORRRC, *Study Report* 3, 20.

28. *Ibid.*, 21. These regulations were listed as U-1, U-2, and U-3, and remained in effect until 1964 when they were superseded by the Wilderness Act (PL 88-577).

29. See, for example, the unpublished Master's Thesis of Alice W. Scheffey, "The Origin of Recreation Policy in the National Forests—A Case Study of the Superior National Forest," The University of Michigan, 1958; and Burton H. Atwood, "Controversy in the Boundary

Waters Canoe Area," (Illinois: The Izaak Walton League of America Endowment, August 10, 1964). (Mimeographed.)

30. ORRRC *Study Report 27*, 99-125.

31. *Ibid., Study Report* 3, 279-87.

CHAPTER I

HEAD FOR THE WOODS

1. The conference was held in District 2, at the Denver office of the United States Forest Service (hereafter cited as USFS), Colorado.

2. *District 2 Minutes of Supervisors' Meeting, January 29-February 3, 1917*, USFS, Denver, 118-19. Conservation Library Center, Denver Public Library, Colorado (hereafter cited as CLC, DPL).

3. *Ibid.*, 121-28.

4. *Ibid.*, 121.

5. *Ibid.* According to A. H. Carhart, it was W. I. Hutchinson who designed the first poster for the Forest Service, carrying the slogan, "The National Forests—The People's Playground." This slogan has since been changed to read, "The National Forests . . . AMERICA'S PLAYGROUNDS." Author's interview with A. H. Carhart, October 30, 1964.

6. *Ibid.*, 122.

7. *Ibid.*

8. *Ibid.*, 123-28.

9. *Ibid.*, 128. William E. Leuchtenburg has observed that the "enormous increase in efficiency of production" was "in part the result of the application of Frederick W. Taylor's theory of scientific management," that "in 1914 . . . Henry Ford had revolutionized industrial production by installing the first moving assembly line with an endless-chain conveyor; three months later his men assembled an automobile, down to its smallest parts, in 93 minutes. A year before it had taken 14 hours. . . . The summit of technological achievement was reached on October 31, 1925, when Ford rolled a completed automobile off his assembly line every ten seconds." W. E. Leuchtenburg, *The Perils of Prosperity, 1914-1932* (Chicago, 1958), 179-80.

10. *District 2 Minutes, 1917*, 129.

11. Frank A. Waugh, *Recreation Uses on the National Forests* (Washington, 1918), 1-37. Waugh was head of the School of Landscape Engineering at Dartmouth College, N.H., and a personal friend of Edward A. Sherman, Assistant Forester, USFS, Washington, D.C.

12. *Ibid.*, 4, citing Houghton Townley, *English Woodlands* (London, 1910), 1.

13. Waugh, *Recreation Uses on National Forests*, 4-5,

14. *Ibid.*, 5.

15. *Ibid.*, 6.

16. *Ibid.*, 10-11.

17. *Ibid.*, 13. This practice began when National Monuments were created under the Antiquities Act of June 8, 1906. The Act authorized the President to declare by proclamation "historic landmarks, historic and prehistoric structures, and other objects of historic or scientific interest that are situated upon the lands owned by or controlled by the Government of the United States." *United States Code,* Title 16, IV (Washington, 1958), 431-433.

18. *Ibid.*, 35-36.

19. *Ibid.*, 37.

20. Letter from A. H. Carhart to E. A. Sherman, Assistant Forester, USFS, Washington, D.C., February 12, 1919. Carhart Papers.

21. Author's interview with A. H. Carhart, October 9, 1964.

22. Letter from District 5, USFS, San Francisco, December 30, 1918. Carhart Papers.

23. Letter from District 2, USFS, Denver, to A. H. Carhart, December 30, 1918. Carhart Papers.

24. Letter from E. A. Sherman, Assistant Forester, USFS, Washington, D.C., to A. H. Carhart, February 8, 1919. Carhart Papers.

25. Letter from District 2, USFS, Denver, to A. H. Carhart, February 11, 1919. Carhart Papers.

26. It is noteworthy that District 2 at that time enclosed the National Forests located in Colorado, Wyoming, Nebraska, South Dakota, Northern Michigan and Minnesota. On May 1, 1929, the Secretary of Agriculture approved a change in the official designation of the nine Forest Service Districts, the District Foresters, and other District Officers, so that Region and Regional superseded the term "district."

United States Department of Agriculture, Forest Service, *Report of the Forester to the Secretary of Agriculture for the Fiscal Year Ended June 30, 1930*, September 25, 1930 (Washington, 1930), 14.

27. A. H. Carhart, "Your Scenic Attractions," *The Bulletin, District 2*, USFS, Denver, III (May, 1919), 12, CLC, DPL.

28. The Wheeler National Monument, located in the Rio Grande National Forest, near Creede, Colorado, was established by proclamation, December 7, 1908 (35 Stat. 2214). The 300 acre Monument was abolished by Public Law 81-652, approved August 3, 1950. *U.S. Statutes at Large,* 81 c. 2 S, 1950-51, LXI (Washington, 1952), 405.

29. Carhart, *The Bulletin, District 2*, III (1919), 12.

30. *Ibid.*

31. *Ibid.*

32. Author's interview with A. H. Carhart, October 9, 1964.

33. Letter from E. A. Sherman, Assistant Forester, USFS, Washington, D.C., to A. H. Carhart, July 10, 1919. Carhart Papers. The citizens of Pueblo used private funds to build the camps referred to by Sherman.

34. *Ibid.*

35. A. H. Carhart, *General Working Plan, Recreational Development of the San Isabel National Forest, Colorado*, December, 1919. Carhart Papers. See also, A. H. Carhart, "Municipal Playgrounds in the Forests," *Municipal Facts Monthly*, II, July, 1919), 9, 14, which heralded the fact that the Denver office of the Forest Service was the first to receive a recreation engineer, and that "Colorado towns thus receive mountain parks."

36. *Ibid.*, 1.

37. *Ibid.*, 2.

38. Grace L. Nute's *Caesars of the Wilderness* (New York, 1943), describes early voyages by canoe and portage in this area.

39. A. H. Carhart, *Preliminary Report, Recreation Reconnaissance, Superior National Forest, Minnesota, 1919*. Carhart Papers.

40. *Ibid.*, Card placed inside the front cover.

41. *Ibid.*, 76.

42. *Ibid.*, 77.

43. *Ibid.*, 78.

44. *Ibid.*, 79.

45. Author's interview wtih A. H. Carhart, October 9, 1964.

46. A. H. Carhart, "Landscape Appreciation," *The Bulletin, District 2*, III (November, 1919), 11-13. CLC, DPL.

47. *Ibid.*, 12.

48. *Ibid.*, 13.

49. The short-title for Public Law 88-577 is "The Wilderness Act," and the terms may be used interchangeably.

CHAPTER II

TAKE ONE GIANT STEP FOR MANKIND

1. Author's interview with A. H. Carhart, September 23, 1963. Figure 7 shows the location of the proposed road. Paul J. Rainey brought to the United States the first motion pictures of African wildlife, and William McFadden loaned money to Ernest W. Marland for the first Marland oil well at Ponca City, Oklahoma.

2. Congress authorized the Secretary of Agriculture to grant permits to "responsible persons or associations to use and occupy suitable spaces or portions of ground in the national forests for the construction of summer homes, hotels, stores, or other structures, needed for recreation or public convenience," by Public Law 63-293, approved March 4, 1915. *Index to Federal Statues*, 63 c. 3 S, 1915-16 (Washington, 1916), 1101.

3. Memorandum from A. H. Carhart, "Memorandum for Mr. Leopold, District 3," District 2, USFS, Denver, Colorado, to Aldo Leopold, Assistant Forester, District 3, USFS, Albuquerque, New Mexico, December 10, 1919. Carhart Papers.

4. From the preamble to The Constitution of the United States of America.

5. Memorandum from A. H. Carhart to Aldo Leopold, December 10, 1919, 1. Carhart Papers.

6. *Ibid.*

7. Acting in response to an inquiry by the President of the United States, J. Wesley White of the Forest Service office in Duluth, Minnesota, was conducting research at the CLC, DPL, October 13-16, 1964,

when the author interviewed him. White has "worked for ten years in the acquisition of property in the B.W.C.A. [Boundary Waters Canoe Area]," and much remains to be done, according to him and Burton H. Atwood, Secretary-Treasurer, The Izaak Walton League of America Endowment. See footnote 16, Prologue, *supra.*

8. Memorandum from A. H. Carhart to Aldo Leopold, December 10, 1919, 1. Carhart Papers.

9. Adrienne Koch and William Peden, *The Life and Selected Writings of Thomas Jefferson* (New York, 1944), 323.

10. Memorandum from A. H. Carhart to Aldo Leopold, December 10, 1919, 1-2. Carhart Papers.

11. *Ibid.*, 2.

12. This phrase caught the attention of Samuel T. Dana, Dean Emeritus, School of Natural Resources, the University of Michigan, Ann Arbor, Michigan, and a Presidential Commissioner for the ORRRC Report, while he visited CLC, DPL, on September 29, 1964. The author interviewed Dana who stated he was intrigued by the use of the words *medium scenic.* Dana also stated he had had no prior knowledge of the existence of this memorandum.

13. Memorandum from A. H. Carhart to Aldo Leopold, December 10, 1919, 3. Carhart Papers.

14. *Ibid.* The difficulties of defining "stopping points" has remained a central problem.

15. *Ibid.*, 3-4.

16. A. H. Carhart, *Planning for America's Wildlands* (Harrisburg, 1961). It was published under the sponsorship of the National Audubon Society, the National Parks Association, the Wildlife Management Institute, and the Wilderness Society.

17. *Ibid.*, Foreword.

18. Memorandum (L Uses), White River [National Forest], District 2, USFS, Denver, Colorado, February 1, 1920, Carhart Papers. Throughout this book will appear parenthetic designations and symbols, such as "L Uses," utilized in the USFS filing system.

19. *Ibid.*, 1.

20. *Ibid.*, 2.

21. *Ibid.*, 2-3.

22. *Ibid.*, 3.

23. *Ibid.*, 5.

24. *Ibid.*, 6.

25. *Ibid.*

26. Memorandum (L Recreation), White River, District 2, USFS, April 7, 1920. Carhart Papers.

27. *Ibid.*, 1.

38. *Ibid.*, 2.

29. *Ibid.*, 8-9.

30. *Ibid.*, 9.

31. *Ibid.*, 10-11.

32. Note to A. S. Peck from A. H. Carhart, undated. Carhart Papers.

33. Note to A. S. Peck from F. Morrell, undated. Carhart Papers.

34. Note to A. H. Carhart from A. S. Peck, undated. Carhart Papers.

35. United States Forest Service, *A Vacation Land of Lakes and Woods—The Superior National Forest* (Washington, 1919), 8-10.

36. *Ibid.*

CHAPTER III

JUST FOR THE FUN OF IT

1. Letter from E. A. Sherman to A. H. Carhart, March 12, 1920. Carhart Papers.

2. Letter from E. A. Sherman to A. H. Carhart, October 9, 1920. Carhart Papers.

3. Author's interview with A. H. Carhart, August 27, 1964.

4. Report, *Digest of L*, Recreation, District 2, USFS, December 3, 1920, 1. Carhart Papers.

5. *Ibid.*, 3; also see ORRRC *Study Report 3*, pages 126-38, where this factor is considered.

6. *Digest of L, Recreation*, December 3, 1920, 4. Carhart Papers.

7. *Ibid.*

8. *Ibid.*

9. *Ibid.*, 5.

10. *Ibid.*

11. William E. Leuchtenburg, *The Perils of Prosperity, 1914-32* (Chicago, 1958), 178-203.

12. *Ibid.*, 2.

13. *Ibid.*, 6.

14. "1st-Class Machine—Car Came of Age Half Century Ago," *The Denver* [Colorado] *Post*, November 15, 1964.

15. *Ibid.*

16. Leuchtenburg, *Perils of Prosperity*, 185-86.

17. *Ibid.*, 178-79.

18. *Ibid.*, 184-85. A measure to provide aid to the states in "the construction of rural post roads and for other purposes," was approved July 11, 1916; Public Law 64-156. *U.S. Statutes at Large*, 1915-1917, 64 c. 1 s., XXXIX (Washington, 1917), 355-59.

19. *Ibid.*, 194.

20. *Digest of L, Recreation,* December 3, 1920, 16. Carhart Papers.

21. *Ibid.*, 17.

22. *Ibid.*, 38-39. Fiscal year 1922 began July 1, 1921.

23. *Ibid.*, 39-40.

24. *Ibid.*, 47.

25. *Ibid.*, 48.

26. Some two thousand photographs taken by Carhart are filed in the Washington headquarters of the United States Forest Service. Author's interview with A. H. Carhart, October 16, 1964, and inventory lists of Forest Service photographs, CLC, DPL.

27. A. H. Carhart, "Recreation in the Forests," *American Forestry,* XXVI (May, 1920), 268-72.

28. *Ibid.*, 268.

29. *Ibid.*

30. *Ibid.*, 270.

31. In 1960, Congress enacted the Multiple Use Act which enlarged the purposes for which National Forests were established by including "outdoor recreation." The act also directed that "due consideration shall be given to the relative values of the various resources in particular areas." *United States Code*, Title 16, Supplement II (Washington, 1958), 528-531.

32. *Ibid.*, 271.

33. *Ibid.*, 271-72.

34. Arthur H. Carhart, "The Department of Forest Recreation," *American Forestry*, XXVI (September, 1920), 549.

35. In a chapter headed "The Big Red Scare," Frederick Lewis Allen described the many "radical" movements or fears of the period following World War I. He recorded that there were "ugly rumors of a huge conspiracy against the government and institutions of the United States. . . . They seriously thought . . . that a Red revolution might begin in the United States the next month or next week." F. L. Allen, *Only Yesterday* (New York, 1931), 32.

36. Arthur H. Carhart, "Vacation Opportunities in Your National Forests," *American Forestry*, XXVI (September, 1920), 549-53.

37. *Ibid.*, 552-53. Today "Smokey," the bear, urges the same precautions to be taken: "Remember—Only you can PREVENT FOREST FIRES! AND LEAVE YOUR CAMP CLEAN." Quoted from USFS poster.

38. Arthur H. Carhart, "Auto Camp Conveniences," *American Forestry*, XXVI (September, 1920), 553-57.

39. *Ibid.*, 553.

40. *Ibid.*, 557.

41. A. H. Carhart, "What is Recreation's Next Step?," *American Forestry*, XXXVI (October, 1920), 593.

42. *Ibid.*, 593-94. The National Park Service was founded in 1916 in the Department of the Interior. Note the favorable comment about the National Parks.

43. *Ibid.*, 595.

44. *Ibid.*, 595-96.

45. *Ibid.*, 597.

46. *Ibid.*, 598.

47. The proposals made in this article should be compared with those in "Outdoor Recreation for America," ORRRC Summary Report of Recommendations, 121-26.

48. Letter from A. S. Peck, District Forester, District 2, USFS, Denver, to The Forester, USFS, Washington, D.C., December 6, 1920, Carhart Papers.

49. A. H. Carhart, "Live Game and Forest Recreation," American Forestry, XXVI (December, 1920), 723.

50. *Ibid.*, 723-25.

51. *Ibid.*, 726.

52. *Ibid.*, 727.

53. A. H. Carhart, *Recreational Plan, San Isabel National Forest, Colorado*, District 2, USFS, Denver, 1920, Carhart Papers.

54. *Ibid.*, 50.

55. *Ibid.*, 51-52.

56. *Ibid.*, 53.

57. John C. Miller, *Origins of the American Revolution* (Stanford, 1959), 484.

58. Memorandum (L Supervision—Service Standard), USFS, Washington, D.C., December 2, 1920. This memorandum was signed by L. F. Kneipp. Kneipp replaced E. A. Sherman as head of the Branch of Lands and Recreation.

59. *Ibid.*, 6.

60. *Ibid.*, 7.

61. *Ibid.*

62. *Ibid.*

CHAPTER IV

NOT SO FAST!

1. Memorandum for the Forester (L Supervision), District 2, USFS, Denver, January 17, 1921. Carhart Papers.

2. *Ibid.*

3. *Ibid.*, 1-2.

4. The total number of National Forests and the acreage they contained differ slightly in the various sources quoted, but these minor variances have no direct bearing on the purposes of this study.

5. Memorandum for the Forester, January 17, 1921, 2. Carhart Papers.

6. *Ibid.*, 2-3.

7. *Ibid.*, 3. Under the heading: "OUR NATIONAL PARKS ARE NOT LUXURIES," Stephen T. Mather commented further on this impression later that year, when he reported, "And yet only this summer the question 'Are not our national parks luxuries?' was asked in all seriousness by a Federal official during a conference that touched upon the expenditures of Government funds for the upkeep and maintenance and further development of the parks." Department of Interior, National Park Service, *Report of the National Park Service to the Secretary of the Interior for the Fiscal Year Ended June 30, 1921, and the Travel Season 1921* (Washington, 1921), 13.

8. See footnote 5, Chapter I, *supra.*

9. Memorandum for the Forester, January 17, 1921, 4. Carhart Papers. James William Good was the Republican Representative from Iowa. Elected to the Sixty-first and six succeeding Congresses, he served from March 4, 1909, until his resignation on June 15, 1921. Appointed Secretary of War in Hoover's cabinet, he served from March 5, 1929, until his death in Washington, D.C., November 18, 1929. *The Biographical Diretory of the American Congress, 1774-1949* (Washington, D.C., 1950), 1219.

10. *Ibid.*

11. "Visitors to Colorado Spent $500 Million Last 12 Month," *The Sunday Denver* [Colorado] *Post,* October 25, 1964, 79.

12. A brochure entitled, *Ski Colorado*, prepared by the Colorado Winter Sports Committee, Capitol Building, Denver, Colorado, undated. By actual count, twenty-two of the thirty-three developed ski areas were located in the National Forests of Colorado.

13. United States Department of Agriculture, Forest Service, *Skiing.* Pamphlet 525 (Washington, 1964), 3.

14. Memorandum for the Forester, January 17, 1921, 5. Carhart Papers.

15. *Des Moines* [Iowa] *Register*, January 11, 1921.

16. *Rocky Mountain News*, Denver, Colorado, January 11, 1921. For a discussion of rivalry between the Forest Service and the National Park Service, see also, Donald C. Swain, *Federal Conservation Policy, 1921-1933* (Berkeley, 1963), 134-38.

17. Memorandum for the Forester, January 17, 1921, 6. Carhart Papers.

18. *Ibid.*, 7.

19. *Ibid.*

20. Horace M. Albright was Mather's assistant and in 1929 became Director of the National Park Service following Mather's illness. Stephen T. Mather died January 22, 1930. *National Cyclopedia of American Biography*, XXVI (New York, 1937), 210.

21. Memorandum for the Forester, January 17, 1921, 8. Carhart Papers. See also, Resolution 4, "First National Conference on State Parks," *Report of the National Park Service*, June 30, 1921, 32-33.

22. Memorandum (L Recreation, District 2, USFS, Denver, January 20, 1921, 1. Carhart Papers.

23. *Ibid.*

24. *Ibid.*, 2-3.

25. *Ibid.*, 4.

26. *Ibid.*, 5.

27. Letter from Wallace I. Hutchinson to A. H. Carhart, February 10, 1921. Carhart Papers.

28. *Ibid.* Smith Riley was formerly the District Forester in Denver.

29. *Ibid.* See also "Needs of the Park System," *Report of the National Park Service*, June 30, 1921, 120, in which S. T. Mather stated that he had made a "personal investigation of the conditions in many of the national parks . . . reflecting on what problems should be met first."

30. Letter from James Sturgis Pray to A. H. Carhart, April 23, 1921, 1. Carhart Papers. Additional information about the suggested $50,000 appropriation for recreational facilities will be presented later in this study.

31. *Ibid.*

32. *Ibid.*, 2. Frederick Law Olmsted was President of the Board of Trustees of the American Society of Landscape Architects and Chair-

man of the Committee on National Parks and National Forests. See Chapter III, page 56, *supra.*

33. *Ibid.*

34. *Ibid.*, 3.

35. *Ibid.*

36. *Ibid.*, 4.

37. Letter from A. H. Carhart to J. S. Pray, May 2, 1921. Carhart Papers.

38. Letter from J. S. Pray to A. H. Carhart, June 10, 1921, 1-2. Carhart Papers.

39. *Ibid.*, 1.

40. *Ibid.*, 2.

41. *Ibid.*

42. Orlando B. Douglass, M.D., "The Relation of Public Parks to Public Health," *Second Report of the American Park and Outdoor Art Association,* Minneapolis, Minnesota, June 22, 23, 24, 1898. Attachment to letter from J. S. Pray to A. H. Carhart, June 10, 1921. Carhart Papers.

43. Allen T. Burns, "Relation of Playgrounds to Juvenile Delinquency," *Playgrounds and Juvenile Delinquency*, Bulletin 385, Community Service, Inc., 1 Madison Avenue, New York City. Burns, Dean of the Chicago School of Civics and Philanthropy, presented a digest of this study to the Second Playground Congress, 1908. Attachment to letter from J. S. Pray to A. H. Carhart, June 10, 1921. Carhart Papers.

44. J. Horace McFarland, "The Reason for Parks," from the Proceedings of the Twelfth Annual Convention of the American Association of Park Superintendents held at Harrisburg, Pa., August 9-10, and at Gettysburg, Pa., August 11, 1910. Attachment to letter from J. S. Pray to A. H. Carhart, June 10, 1921. Carhart Papers.

45. Letter from Phelps Wyman to A. H. Carhart, July 21, 1921. Carhart Papers, and interview with A. H. Carhart, October 9, 1964. Wyman was a member of the Board of Trustees of the ASLA.

46. A. H. Carhart, "Denver's Greatest Manufacturing Plant," *Municipal Facts Monthly*, IV (September-October, 1921), 3-7. This organ was published by the City and County of Denver for the information of its residents.

47. *Ibid.*, 4.

48. *Ibid.*

49. *Ibid.*, 5. For a follow up article, see also, A. H. Carhart, "Going to the Glaciers," *Municipal Facts Monthly*, V (March-April, 1922), 7-9. The latter article told how the "people of Boulder have taken the lead in the development of the Glacier region" through their "Recreation Association." Such associations played a vital role in the establishment of recreation in the National Forests.

50. Letter from Frank A. Waugh to A. H. Carhart, November 12, 1921. Carhart Papers. Waugh, in 1921, was Head of the Division of Horticulture, Massachusetts Agricultural College, Amherst, Massachusetts.

51. Letter from A. H. Carhart to F. A. Waugh, December 12, 1921. Carhart Papers.

52. *Ibid.*

53. Robert C. Lucas, "The Quetico-Superior Area: Recreational Use in Relation to Capacity" (unpublished Ph.D. Thesis, The University of Minnesota, 1962), 64, citing James P. Gilligan, "The Development of Policy and Administration of Forest Service Primitive and Wilderness Areas in the Western United States" (unpublished Ph.D. Thesis, The University of Michigan, 1954), 75.

54. United States Department of Agriculture, Forest Service, *Report of the Forester to the Secretary of Agriculture for the Fiscal Year Ended June 30, 1916* [hereafter cited as *Report of the Forester*], October 2, 1916 (Washington, 1916), 1.

55. *Ibid.*, 23. The amounts of these two appropriations were combined in subsequent *Reports of the Forester*, and referred to as the "Ten Per Cent Fund." The ten per cent fund was derived from the receipts in the National Forests for the previous year, and began with the Department of Agriculture appropriations acts of August 10, 1912, and March 4, 1913.

56. *Report of the Forester*, October 1, 1917, 23. For the purpose of this study, Section 8 of the Federal-Aid Road Act of 1916 will be designated as category two.

57. *Ibid.*, 24.

58. *Report of the Forester*, October 1, 1918, 1.

59. *Ibid.*, 10-11.

60. *Ibid.*, 11.

61. *Ibid.*, 28.

62. *Report of the Forester*, October 8, 1919, 18. It should be emphasized here that the first Recreation Engineer, A. H. Carhart, reported for duty on March 1, 1919, and that he regularly apprised Assistant Forester E. A. Sherman in Washington, through personal correspondence and official reports, of plans he had prepared to develop and protect recreational resources in the National Forests. *The Forester's Report* helps fix the period when recreation began to receive significant notice in the Forests, and should be compared with Carhart's writings in mid-1919.

63. *Ibid.*

64. *Ibid.*, 19.

65. *Ibid.*, 21.

66. *Ibid.*, 23.

67. *Ibid.*, 25.

68. *Report of the Forester*, October 4, 1920, 1.

69. *Ibid.*, 19-20.

70. *Ibid.*, 21.

71. *Ibid.*, 22-23.

72. *Ibid.*, 24.

73. *Report of the Forester*, October 6, 1921, 33.

74. *Ibid.*, 34.

75. *Report of the Forester*, September 30, 1922, 40.

76. *Ibid.*

77. *Ibid.*

78. *Ibid.*, 41.

79. *Report of the Forester,* 1922-1930, inclusive.

80. *Report of the Forester*, October 4, 1923, 41.

81. Letter from the Good Roads Association, Inc., Birmingham, Alabama, to Governor Merritt C. Mechem, Santa Fe, New Mexico, February 25, 1921. State of New Mexico, Records Center and Archives, Santa Fe, N.M.

82. *Ibid.*

83. *Ibid.*

84. Letter from Henry C. Wallace, Secretary of Agriculture, to Governor Merritt C. Mechem of New Mexico, April 18, 1921. State of New Mexico, Records Center and Archives, Santa Fe, N.M.

85. *Ibid.*

86. Letter from the Good Roads Association, Inc., Birmingham, Alabama, to Governor M. C. Mechem, Santa Fe, New Mexico, February 23, 1922. N.M. Records Center, Santa Fe, N.M.

87. *The United States Good Roads Bulletin*, II, (December, 1923), 12, *et passim.* N.M. Records Center, Santa Fe, N.M.

88. *Ibid.*

89. *Ibid.*, 2, *et passim.*

90. *Report of the Forester*, October 4, 1923, 38.

91. *Ibid.*, 39-40.

CHAPTER V

TAKE ANOTHER STEP

1. A. H. Carhart, *Preliminary Report, Recreation Reconnaissance, Superior National Forest, Minnesota,* 1919. Carhart Papers.

2. Under the caption "Service Notes" appeared a notice that "Arthur H. Carhart left May 2 for St. Paul and Ely, Minn., to outline a comprehensive recreational plan for the Superior Forest." *The Review, District 2*, USFS, Denver, II (May, 1921), 19, CLC, DPL.

3. A. H. Carhart, *Recreation Plan, Superior National Forest, Minnesota*, 1921. Carhart Papers.

4. For additional data concerning the Superior National Forest and the Boundary Waters Canoe Area see: *The Report of the Boundary Waters Canoe Area Review Committee*, Duluth, Minnesota, submitted to the Secretary of Agriculture, December 15, 1964; The unpublished Ph.D. Thesis of Robert C. Lucas, "The Quetico-Superior Area: Recreational Use in Relation to Capacity," The University of Minnesota, 1962; The unpublished Master's Thesis of Alice W. Scheffey, "The Origin of Recreation Policy in the National Forests—A Case Study of the Superior National Forest," The University of Michigan, 1958; and a study by Burton H. Atwood, Secretary-Treasurer, The Izaak Walton League of America Endowment, "Controversy in the Boundary Waters Canoe Area," August 10, 1964.

5. Theodore Christian Blegen, *The Land Lies Open* (Minneapolis, 1949), 14-15.

6. William Watts Folwell, *A History of Minnesota,* I (St. Paul, 1956), 6.

7. *Ibid.*, I, 7-10.

8. Ray Allen Billington, *Westward Expansion—A History of the American Frontier* (New York, 1960), 131.

9. Samuel E. Morison, *Sources and Documents Illustrating the American Revolution, 1764-1788* (London, 1961), 3, xvii-xx.

10. Folwell, *A History of Minnesota,* I, 65.

11. Thomas P. Abernethy, *Western Lands and the American Revolution* (New York, 1959), 3, 362, *et passim.*

12. Folwell, *A History of Minnesota,* I, 69-70.

13. R. A. Billington, B. J. Loewenberg, and S. H. Brockunier, *The Making of American Democracy—Readings and Documents,* I, (New York, 1950), 94-95.

14. *Ibid.*, 96-97. Similar provisions were carried forward in the Act authorizing the inhabitants of the Territory of Minnesota to form a State government, and in the Constitution of that State. Atwood, "Controversy in the Boundary Waters Canoe Area," August 10, 1964, 4.

15. Henry B. Parkes, *The United States of America—A History* (New York, 1955), 156.

16. Thomas A. Bailey observed that unknown to the negotiators, the area contained a large part of the magnificent iron-ore deposits of Minnesota, which became one of the foundation stones of America's industrial might. "In losing 5000 square miles of pine forest in Maine, while gaining 6500 square miles of priceless ore-bearing land, Webster drove an infinitely better bargain than he or anyone else then realized." T. A. Bailey, *A Diplomatic History of the American People* (New York, 1958), 214.

17. Billington, *Westward Expansion,* 479.

18. Blegen, *The Land Lies Open,* 230.

19. Folwell, *A History of Minnesota,* I, 213.

20. *Ibid.*

21. *Ibid.*, 236; Blegen, *The Land Lies Open,* 97.

22. Billington, *Westward Expansion,* 480.

23. *United States Statutes at Large*, 32nd and 33rd Congress, December 1851-March 1855, I (Boston, 1855), 1109. See also, Folwell, *A History of Minnesota*, I, 306.

24. *United States Statutes at Large*, X (1855, 1165); Folwell, *A History of Minnesota*, I, 307.

25. Folwell, *A History of Minnesota*, I, 307-08.

26. Blegen, *The Land Lies Open*, 98.

27. Folwell, *A History of Minnesota*, II, 109.

28. *Ibid.*, II, 391-93.

29. *Ibid.*, II, 190.

30. Glanville Smith, "Minnesota, Mother of Lakes and Rivers, *National Geographic Magazine*, LXVII (March, 1935), 263-318.

31. Theodore C. Blegen, *Minnesota, A History of the State* (Minneapolis, 1963), 253.

32. *Ibid.*, 322-25.

33. Folwell, *A History of Minnesota*, I, 128. Hans Huth noted that "the idea of creating state parks was not a new one, for as far back as 1891 Minnesota had set aside Itasca Park, where the headwaters of the Mississippi originate. In the same year the park idea had been taken up by some public-minded men in Massachusetts, among whom were Charles W. Eliot, Oliver Wendell Holmes, Thomas Wentworth Higginson, Frederick Law Olmsted, and Francis Parkman. They established 'The Trustees of Public Reservations' with the idea of providing by private endowment for the 'preservation and dedication to public enjoyment of such scenes and sites in Massachusetts as possess either uncommon beauty or historical interest.' " Hans Huth, *Nature and the American* (Berkeley, 1957), 199.

34. Folwell, *A History of Minnesota,* I, 128-29.

35. *Ibid.*, I, 112-15.

36. Blegen, *The Land Lies Open*, 13.

37. Frederick Jackson Turner, *Frontier and Section* (Englewood Cliffs, N.J., 1961), 37.

38. Blegen, *The Land Lies Open*, 234.

39. Blegen, *Minnesota, A History of the State*, 315-16, 405.

40. Blegen, *The Land Lies Open*, 221-23.

41. *Ibid.*, 224.

42. Blegen, *Minnesota, A History of the State*, 405.

43. *Ibid.*, 404-405.

44. Blegen, *The Land Lies Open*, 217-19.

45. The state was shocked to learn that in the summer of 1894 a total of 413 persons had burned to death. Blegen, *Minnesota, A History of the State*, 405.

46. *Ibid.*, 328-29.

47. That acreage formed the nucleus for the Chippewa National Forest, established in 1908. "History," *Report of the Boundary Waters Canoe Area Review Committee* [hereafter cited as BWCARC Report], Duluth, Minnesota, December 15, 1964, 3. Secretary of Agriculture Orville L. Freeman appointed the BWCA Review Committee on May 21, 1964, to review the prescribed management plan for the BWCA in the Superior National Forest.

48. The approximate acreages and dates of those withdrawals were: 500,000 acres on June 30, 1902; 141,000 acres on August 18, 1905; and 518,700 acres on April 22, 1908. *Ibid.*

49. *Ibid.*

50. The lands outside the proclaimed boundaries of the Superior National Forest, about 137,000 acres, were formally released from withdrawal on September 22, 1909. *Ibid.*

51. *Ibid.*

52. The Weeks Act provided for protection of watersheds by authorizing the purchase of lands at headwaters of navigable streams. *United States Statutes at Large*, 61st Congress, XXXVI (Washington, 1911), 961-963. The first expansion of the Superior National Forest under that act occurred in 1912 when, by Presidential Proclamation No. 1215, about 380,000 acres were added. *BWCARC Report,* December 15, 1964, 4.

53. *Ibid.*

54. *Ibid.*

55. *Ibid.*, 5. This view is at variance with previous statements. See Prologue, pages 6-8, *supra.* It should also be noted that Carhart's *Recreational Plan for the San Isabel National Forest,* Colorado, was the first such studied plan of management, and antedated the Superior National Forest Plan for 1919 by several months. Wilderness protection was included in the 1919 San Isabel plan as well. See Chapter I, pages 22-23, *supra.*

56. *Ibid.* The rationale, here expressed, should be compared with the Multiple Use Principle under which the Forest Service has recently been operating. The Multiple Use Act of 1960 "was a belated endorsement of an expansion that had occurred long before. The growth of this idea of Forest Wilderness directly concerns the Boundary Waters Canoe Area, which was one of the first and most important areas of established wilderness." Lucas, "The Quetico-Superior Area," Ph.D. Thesis, 1962, 62-63.

57. *Ibid.*

58. *Ibid.*

59. A. H. Carhart, *Recreation Plan, Superior National Forest, Minnesota*, 1921. Carhart Papers.

60. *Ibid.*, 3.

61. *Ibid.*, 5.

62. *Ibid.*, 5-6.

63. *Ibid.*, 6.

64. *Ibid.*, 14.

65. *Ibid.*, 15.

66. *Ibid.*, 29.

67. *Ibid.*, 57.

68. Letter (U-Recreation), from USFS, Washington, D.C., to Region 9, USFS, Milwaukee, Wisconsin, November 18, 1955. H. A. Svensen, Assistant Forester, Region 9, stated that the issue of whether or not Carhart's report had ever received formal approval arose in 1955 when that Regional Office attempted to write a history of its development. Author's interview with H. A. Svensen, February 3, 1965.

69. *The Recreational Working Plan, Gila National Forest*, was submitted March 28, 1924, and approved by District Forester F. C. W. Pooler on June 3, 1924. Region 3, USFS, Albuquerque, New Mexico.

70. A. H. Carhart, *Timber in Your Life* (Philadelphia, 1955), 145.

71. *Ibid.*

72. *Ibid.*, 146. The "upheaval" referred to will be discussed at length presently. But now it should be pointed out that the $53,000 was for the construction of a road from Ely to the Fernberg Fire Lookout Tower paralleling the Kawishiwi River. ORRRC, *Study Report 27*, 114.

73. A. H. Carhart, *Timber in Your Life*, 147. The Small group referred to was the Superior National Forest Recreation Association, which will be discussed in a later chapter.

CHAPTER VI

WHAT'S IT ALL ABOUT?

1. See Chapter III, page 56, *supra.*

2. See Chapter IV, pages 68-69, *supra.*

3. Letter from Everett L. Millard, 69 W. Washington Street, Chicago, Illinois, to A. H. Carhart, February 15, 1922. Carhart Papers.

4. The letter mentioned activities during 1922 in which Carhart had participated, and referred to other persons engaged in promoting recreational developments in the nation. Frank Culley had been Frank A. Waugh's star pupil in landscape design, Carhart's former instructor at Iowa State College, and later, for almost a decade, Carhart's partner in professional landscape design and city planning in Denver. Author's interview with A. H. Carhart, October 9, 1964.

5. Letter from A. H. Carhart to J. S. Pray, March 11, 1922. Carhart Papers.

6. ORRRC, *Study Report 27*, 116. The First National Conference on Outdoor Recreation met in Washington, D.C., May 22-24, 1924. The "permanent" organization lasted for about four years. It was officially terminated July 1, 1929. *Ibid.*, 116-117. See also, Donald C. Swain, *Federal Conservation Policy, 1921-1933* (Berkeley, 1963), 135-56.

7. Frank A. Waugh, "What is a Forest," *Journal of Forestry*, XX (March, 1922), 209-14.

8. *Ibid.*, 209. It would appear that the definition must have had *some* foundation or it would not have been so widespread.

9. *Ibid.*

10. *Ibid.*, 210, citing Houghton Townley, *English Woodlands and Their Story* (London, 1910); and John Manwood, *Treatise and Discourse of the Laws of the Forest* (London, 1598).

11. *Ibid.*, citing William Gilpin, *Remarks in Forest Scenery and Other Woodland Views*, II (London, 1834), 94.

12. *Ibid.*, citing John Charles Cox, *The Royal Forests of England* (London, 1905), 5.

13. *Ibid.*, 211.

14. *Ibid.*, 213-14. Waugh's conclusion was not completely valid; primitive people did, after all, make their *homes* in the forest. His definition of a forest is defensible, however.

15. Letter from J. S. Pray to A. H. Carhart, May 27, 1922, 1-2. Carhart Papers. Carhart's letter of April 29, 1922, was not among the documents examined.

16. *Ibid.* See Chapter V, pages 106-106, *supra.*

17. *Ibid.*, 2-3. The statement was quoted from a letter apparently sent to Pray by Sherman.

18. *Ibid.*, 3.

19. Letter from A. H. Carhart to J. S. Pray, June 12, 1922, 1. Carhart Papers.

20. *Ibid.*, 2.

21. *Ibid.*, 5-6.

22. *Ibid.*, 6. The Bureau of Outdoor Recreation was authorized by the Land and Water Conservation Act, PL 88-578, signed into law by President Lyndon Baines Johnson, September 3, 1964.

23. *Ibid.*, 6.

24. *Ibid.*, 7.

25. Letter from A. H. Carhart to E. A. Sherman, June 29, 1922, 1. Carhart Papers.

26. Carhart apparently wanted the Chief Forester to wage a "bare knuckles" battle with Congress.

27. *Ibid.*, 2-3.

28. *Ibid.*, 4.

29. Author's interview with A. H. Carhart, November 18, 1964.

30. Letter from E. A. Sherman to A. H. Carhart, July 5, 1922, 1. Carhart Papers.

31. *Ibid.*, 2.

32. *Ibid.* It is interesting to note that Carhart planned to quit at the end of the year in which the first forest recreation funds were authorized, 1922.

33. *Ibid.*

34. *Ibid.* The following year, another $15,000 was authorized for the installation of "sources of pure-water supply, fireplaces, toilets, garbage pits, and other simple facilities required for public health and comfort and reasonable security against fire"; "To date the total sum appropriated to meet these requirements has been only $25,000." *Report of the Forester*, October 4, 1923, 37.

35. *Ibid.*, 3.

36. Letter from A. H. Carhart to A. E. Sherman, July 19, 1922. Carhart Papers.

37. *Ibid.*, 2.

38. *Ibid.*, 3-6.

39. Letter from A. H. Carhart to A. S. Peck, July 3, 1922, 1. Carhart Papers. This letter was written while Carhart was on a field trip at Lander, Wyoming.

40. *Ibid.*, 2.

41. *Ibid.* For a lucid account of the needs in recreation which had been proposed by Carhart earlier in 1922, see his illustrated article, "Minimum Requirements in Recreation," *American Forestry*, XX (January, 1922), 31-36.

42. Letter from A. S. Peck to A. H. Carhart, August 2, 1922, 1-2. Carhart Papers.

43. *Ibid.*

44. Memorandum (L Recreation), District 2, USFS, Denver, November 27, 1922. Carhart Papers.

45. *Ibid.*

46. Memorandum (L Recreation), District 2, USFS, Denver, November 28, 1922, 1-5. Carhart Papers.

47. Memorandum (L Recreation), District 2, USFS, Denver, November 29, 1922, 1-3. Carhart Papers.

48. *Ibid.*, 1-2.

49. *Ibid.*, 3.

50. Letter from Frank A. Waugh to A. H. Carhart, December 19, 1922. Carhart Papers.

51. *Ibid.*

52. Arthur H. Carhart, "Recreation in Forestry," *Journal of Forestry*, XXI (January, 1923), 10-14.

53. *Ibid.*

54. *The Review (USFS, Rocky Mountain Region), District 2*, IV (January, 1923), 15. CLC, DPL.

CHAPTER VII

O.K., ALL YOU CATS, KEEP OUT!

1. Letter (DA Appointments), from A. H. Carhart, Recreation Engineer, District 2, USFS, Denver, to The Forester, Washington, D.C., December 2, 1922. Carhart Papers.

2. *Ibid.*, 1.

3. *Ibid.*, 1-2.

4. *Ibid.*, 2.

5. Letter (O Personnel, Carhart, Arthur H.), from E. A. Sherman, Acting Forester, USFS, Washington, D.C., to A. H. Carhart, December 20, 1922, 1-2. Carhart Papers.

6. *Ibid.* Recreation had been put upon a "well organized basis from a District standpoint, but from a Forest [Service] standpoint, the activity is not as well defined as it might be." Minutes (O Special), Supervisor's Meeting, Rocky Mountain District, USFS, Denver, March 1, 1923. National Archives, Federal Records Center, Denver, Colorado, Container No. 37702.

7. Letter, Sherman to Carhart, December 20, 1922, 1-2.

8. Letter from A. H. Carhart to E. A. Sherman, February 13, 1923, 1-3. Carhart Papers. See Appendix A for the complete text of this letter.

9. Letter from E. A. Sherman to A. H. Carhart, February 21, 1923. Carhart Papers.

10. Letter from A. H. Carhart to E. A. Sherman, February 27, 1923. Carhart Papers. See Appendix B for the complete text of this letter.

11. *Ibid.*

12. Letter from E. A. Sherman to A. H. Carhart, March 6, 1923. Carhart Papers. See Appendix C for the complete text of this letter.

13. Letter from A. H. Carhart to J. S. Pray, June 17, 1922, 1-3. Carhart Papers.

14. *Ibid.*, 1.

15. *Ibid.*, 2.

16. *Ibid.*

17. *Ibid.*

18. *Ibid.* Since this letter was captioned "CONFIDENTIAL," it would perhaps be more accurate to note that Carhart really meant "I don't *dare* to be associated" with such a movement. See Chapter VI, page 112, *supra.*

19. Author's interview with A. H. Carhart, March 22, 1965.

20. Letter from A. H. Carhart to P. B. Riis, Chairman of the Department of Wild Life Preservation, American Institute of Park Executives, Rockford, Illinois, December 6, 1922, 1-7. Carhart Papers. Riis became President of the Superior National Forest Recreation Association, an organization patterned after the San Isabel National Forest Recreation Association. See Chapter III, page 44, *supra.*

21. *Ibid.*, 1.

22. *Ibid.*, 2.

23. *Ibid.* Donald Hough was a former Ranger in the Superior National Forest, an outdoor writer, and later Director of Publicity for the Izaak Walton League of America. Hough, incidentally, became Secretary of the Superior National Forest Recreation Association.

24. At that time, Will H. Dilg was employed in the Commercial Department of the magazine, *Outer's Recreation.* It was later sold because of financial difficulties, and merged into the magazine, *Outdoor Life.* According to A. H. Carhart, Dilg then wanted to start a "sportsman's organization," and through Dilg's urgings, The Izaak Walton League of America was formed. Author's interview with A. H. Carhart, March 19, 1965. See also, *Union List of Serials* (New York, 1943), 2115, for data concerning the periodicals mentioned.

25. Letter from A. H. Carhart to P. B. Riis, December 6, 1922, 2. Carhart Papers.

26. *Ibid.*, 3.

27. *Ibid.*

28. *Ibid.*

29. Will O. Doolittle was Secretary of the American Institute of Park Executives and Editor of the Institute's publication, *Parks and Recreation.* Dootlittle, as Editor, gave the movement the first speaker's platform to shout from, and thus rendered an invaluable service. Author's interview with A. H. Carhart, March 22, 1965.

30. Letter from A. H. Carhart to P. B. Riis, December 6, 1922, 4. Carhart Papers.

31. *Ibid.*, 4-5.

32. *Ibid.*, 5.

33. *Ibid.*, 6.

34. *Ibid.*

35. *Ibid.*, 7.

36. *Ibid.*

37. A partial list of those persons and organizations would include: The Izaak Walton League of America, Friends of Our Native Landscape, American Historic and Scenic Preservation Society, the Prairie Club, the Ecological Society of America, the Associated Mountaineering Club of North America, State of Iowa Board of Conservation, James Oliver Curwood, the Honorable Gifford Pinchot, the Mississippi Valley Chapter of American Society of Landscape Architects, Minnesota Forestry Association, Municipal Art League of Chicago, Game Conservation Society, Roosevelt Wild Life Experiment Station, American School of Wild Life Protection, Iowa Conservation Association, Harvard Graduate School of Landscape Architecture, Duluth Chamber of Commerce, Rotary Club and Taxpayers League of Duluth, Commercial Clubs of Tower and Ely and a number of game protective associations and other individuals noted in conservation work nationally. "National Needs Recognized at Superior National Forest Conference," *Parks & Recreation* (May-June, 1923), 438.

38. Letter from E. A. Sherman, Acting Forester, Washington, D.C., to P. B. Riis, Department of Wild Life Preservation, American Institute of Park Executives, Rockford, Illinois, February 13, 1923, 1. Carhart Papers. See Appendix D for the complete text of this letter.

39. *Ibid.*, 1-3.

40. William T. Hornaday was at that time Director of the Zoological Park, Bronx, New York.

41. Theodore Wirth was at that time President of the American Institute of Park Executives, Rockford, Illinois.

42. Letter from L. H. Pammel, Iowa State College, to P. B. Riis, Rockford, Illinois, February 7, 1923. Carhart Papers.

43. *Ibid.*

44. Letter from J. A. O. Preus, Governor of Minnesota, to Le Roy Jeffers, Associated Mountaineering Clubs of North America, New York City, New York, February 13, 1923. Carhart Papers.

45. Letter from P. B. Riis to J. A. O. Preus, February 19, 1923. Carhart Papers.

46. Letter from Henry C. Wallace, Secretary of Agriculture, Washington, D.C., to P. B. Riis, February 23, 1923. Carhart Papers.

47. Letter from A. H. Carhart ot P. B. Riis, February 28, 1923. Carhart Papers.

48. *Ibid.*, 2.

49. Letter from E. A. Sherman to P. B. Riis, February 20, 1923, 1. Carhart Papers. See Appendix E for the complete text of this letter.

50. *Ibid.*

51. *Ibid.*, 2.

52. Letter from P. B. Riis to E. A. Sherman, February 24, 1923. Carhart Papers.

53. Letter from A. H. Carhart to P. B. Riis, February 26, 1923. Carhart Papers.

54. *Ibid.*, 2. The idea of extending and consolidating the northern Minnesota region was eventually embodied in the Shipstead-Newton-Nolan Act of 1930. This letter, perhaps, represents its proximate origin.

55. *Ibid.*

56. *Ibid.*

57. George E. Mowry noted that the October, 1902, issue of McClure's Magazine carried Lincoln Steffens' article "Tweed Days in St. Louis," which is usually cited as the start of muckraking, and often given credit for initiating a great wave of civic reform. George E. Mowry, *The Era of Theodore Roosevelt: 1900-1912* (New York, 1958), 64.

58. No author shown, "A Lakeland Wilderness Refuge," *Parks & Recreation* (November-December, 1922), 176. Because of Carhart's plan

to remain "undercover" during the protest, this article was sent by P. B. Riis in Rockford, Illinois, to W. O. Doolittle in Minot, North Dakota, for publication. In Riis's handwriting appeared a note to Carhart as follows: "Mailed Lakeland Wilderness, [and] Birth of a Wilderness [and] Maps of Superior with Roads: from Committee—no names—*of course you will be there.*" Carhart Papers, and Author's interview with A. H. Carhart, March 19, 1965.

59. Emerson Hough, "Wild Life in Danger," *Parks & Recreation* (November-December, 1922), 175-176. Hough's article had originally appeared in the *Philadelphia Public Ledger*, and was reproduced by permission.

60. No author shown, "A Lakeland Wilderness Refuge," *Parks & Recrecreation* (November-December, 1922), 176. See also footnote 58, immediately *supra.*

61. *Ibid.*

62. *Ibid.*

63. It may be informative to mention that in August, 1963, the articles which had appeared from 1922 through 1927 in *Parks & Recreation*, published by the American Institute of Park Executives, were photostated and bound for the Conservation Library Center, Denver Public Library, under the title, *The Superior National Forest: A Supreme "Wilderness" Area.* A statement on the front cover stated that those articles had been published "in advocacy and support of the efforts to conserve for all time this splendid international area—to keep it free from undesirable and commercial encroachments, to retain it as a permanent undefiled place for canoeing, fishing, Nature study and limited camping,—a place where one may strengthen and invigorate himself in surroundings and under conditions afforded by an unspoiled America." The numerous photographic illustrations in the collection of articles have since been annotated by Arthur H. Carhart. He initialed and dated explanatory notes about the photographs in late August, 1963, identifying many of them as ones he had personally taken during his trips to the Superior National Forest in 1919 and 1921. CLC, DPL.

64. "Conference at Duluth," *Parks & Recreation* (March-April, 1923), 322.

65. Paul B. Riis, "Birth of a Wilderness," *Parks & Recreation* (March-April, 1923), 311-15. This article was actually written by A. H. Carhart. See footnote 58, Chapter VII, immediately *supra.* See also E. N. Munns, U.S. Department of Agriculture Miscellaneous Publication No. 364, *A Selective Bibliography of North American Forestry* I (Washington, 1940), 1003, which understandably credited P. B. Riis

with authorship of this article. Munn's directory recorded "forest influences" and was useful as a tool in this study.

66. Riis, "Birth of a Wilderness," *Parks & Recreation* (March-April, 1923), 315. See also footnotes 58 and 65, immediately *supra.*

67. *Ibid.*, plus the following articles by the Committe on Preservation of Wild Life: "The Lure of the Superior"; "America's Paramount Water-Travel Playground"; "Facts about the Superior National Forest"; "The Part of Good Citizens"; and "Conference at Duluth," 316-22.

68. Committee on Preservation of Wild Life, "National Needs Recognized at Superior National Forest Conference," *Parks & Recreation* (May-June, 1923), 437. That article also mentioned that "detail plans of the proposed road project came to hand in early winter," a statement which corroborated evidence presented earlier in this study.

69. *Ibid.*, 438.

70. *Ibid.*

71. P. B. Riis, "Recreational Development of National Forest," *Parks & Recreation* (July-August, 1923), 500-01.

72. *Ibid.* See also Chapter IV, page 80, *supra,* and ORRRC *Study Re port 27,* 114.

73. *Ibid.*, 501.

74. Committee Preservation Wild, "National Needs Recognized," *Park & Recreation* (May-June, 1923), 438.

75. *Ibid.*

76. *Ibid.*, 438-39.

77. Author's interview with A. H. Carhart, March 22, 1965.

78. Charles Guyton, "Waltonism, 1928: Our Hats Off to the Old—Our Coats Off to the New," *Outdoor America*, VI (February, 1928), 34-35. Izaak Walton was born at Stafford, England, on August 9, 1593, and died in 1683. He wrote "*The Compleat Angler*, or the Contemplative Man's Recreation, being a discourse of Fish and Fishing, not unworthy the perusal of most Anglers, of 18 pence price." First printed in London, 1653. The earliest American publisher still in business was probably Lippincott with their reprint of 1844. Paul Faulkner, "Three Hundred Years of the Compleat Angler," *Outdoor America* (September-October, 1953), 4-14.

79. The *Izaak Walton League Monthly* was published from August, 1922 through August, 1923, when it was superseded by *Outdoor America. Union List of Serials* (New York, 1943), 2115.

80. Emerson Hough, "Time to Call a Halt," *Izaak Walton League Monthly* (August, 1922), 1.

81. Zane Grey, "Vanishing America," *Izaak Walton League Monthly* (September, 1922), 1.

82. Letter from A. H. Carhart to J. S. Pray, May 12, 1923. Carhart Papers. At the time, Charles H. Ramsdell, Minneapolis Chapter, ASLA, had wanted his organization to be selected by Riis to publish the official news for the SNFRA. Author's interview with A. H. Carhart, March 19, 1965.

83. Donald Hough, "The Superior National Forest to be Saved Forever," *Izaak Walton League Monthly* (April, 1923), 379-81; 430-31; P. B. Riis, "Paradise Regained," *IWL Monthly* (June, 1923), 527. See also, "Superior National Forest Data," *IWL Monthly* (June, 1923), 559.

84. "History," *Report of the Boundary Waters Canoe Area Review Committee*, Duluth, Minnesota, December 15, 1964, 6.

85. A. H. Carhart, "The Superior Forest: Why It is Important in National Recreation System," *Parks & Recreation* (July-August, 1923), 502-504. See also, A. H. Carhart, "156,000,000 Acres—Count 'em," *Outdoor America* (October, 1923), 80-81, 122-23.

86. No author shown, "Superior National Forest Boundary Extensions," *Parks & Recreation* (November-December, 1923), 168-70. See also, Donald C. Swain, *Federal Conservation Policy, 1921-1933* (Berkeley, 1963), 14-15. The fate of the Superior National Forest Boundary Extension Bill (or the Fuller Bill as it came to be known), will be discussed in a later chapter.

87. See Chapter V, pages 104-106, *supra.*

CHAPTER VIII

TAKE A THIRD STEP

1. Aldo Leopold was born January 11, 1886, at Burlington, Iowa. He was trained in forestry at Yale receiving his Master of Forestry in 1909. He served as Assistant District Forester in southwestern United States from 1909 until 1924 when he transferred to the U.S. Forest

Products Laboratory, Madison, Wisconsin, to become Associate Director during the period 1924-1928. From 1928 to 1933 he conducted various game surveys, and in the latter year was appointed Chairman of the Department of Wildlife Management, University of Wisconsin. He died of a heart attack near his summer home at Baraboo, Wisconsin, April 21, 1948, after two hours of fighting a bad grass fire on a neighbor's land. Paul L. Errington, "In Appreciation of Aldo Leopold," *Journal of Wildlife Management*, XII (October, 1948), 341-50.

2. Aldo Leopold's "The Wilderness and its Place in Forest Recreational Policy," *Journal of Forestry*, XIX (November, 1921), 718-21, was the first expression of his views on wilderness protection. His publications from 1920 through 1925 were predominantly short articles on ornithology, hunting and game management, forestry in relation to game management, erosion control, ecological consequences of forest fires, and the one on wilderness values cited. His next published articles on the subject of the wilderness appeared in 1925. *Ibid.*, 342. See also, Prologue pages 7-8, *supra.*

3. Leopold, *Journal of Forestry*, XIX (1921, 718).

4. *Ibid.*

5. When Leopold wrote this article there were no "Recreation Plans," as such, in District 3, and in all probability he was alluding to those plans prepared by A. H. Carhart of which he had knowledge. Writing in 1955, Carhart stated: "While I was still writing my report on the Superior [National Forest in the late summer of 1921], Aldo Leopold, then Regional Forester at Albuquerque, visited the Denver headquarters. As we talked for several hours we discovered both had arrived at conclusions that were almost identical. Leopold was particularly interested in saving the best of the remaining wilderness areas. I talked of the dominant use principle, and wilderness set aside to preserve its values was an application of that principle. Soon Leopold began to preach the need for retaining primitive lands we still had in the nation for the type of recreational use they supplied. He did great service in developing this idea into positive action." A. H. Carhart, *Timber in Your Life* (Philadelphia, 1955), 147.

6. Leopold, *Journal of Forestry*, XIX (1921, 718-19).

7. *Ibid.*, 719.

8. *Ibid.*

9. *Ibid.*

10., *Ibid.*, 719-20.

11. *Ibid.*, 720.

12. *Ibid.*, 720-21.

13. *Ibid.*, 721.

14. It should be noted that in both instances, that is, in his article of November, 1921, and in the one he wrote in July, 1940, Aldo Leopold, candidly and quite factually, stipulated the "Southwest," by which he meant New Mexico and Arizona, as the area in which the former article was proposing and the latter proposed the establishment of wilderness areas. Leopold never claimed to have originated the idea for the National Forests. Others seem to have attributed that origin to him posthumously. See Prologue, pages 7-8, and Chapter VIII, page 157, *supra.*

15. Letter (D Supervision-Datil, Inspection), Datil National Forest, Magdalena, New Mexico, to the District Forester, District 3, USFS, Albuquerque, New Mexico, September 1, 1922. This document antedates the one referred to by Aldo Leopold in his July, 1940 article in the *Living Wilderness*, by twenty days. National Archives, Federal Records Center, Denver, Colorado [hereafter cited as Denver FRC], FRC Container 37098. No other documents dated earlier than September 1, 1922, are known to be in existence for the Gila Wilderness Area. Author's interview with Fred H. Kennedy, Regional Forester, Region 3, and Norman P. Weeden, Chief, Recreation Branch, Division of Recreation and Lands, Region 3, USFS, Albuquerque, New Mexico, November 4, 1964.

16. To reduce cost of administration, the Datil National Forest, New Mexico, was divided between the Gila and the Cibola National Forests. *Report of the Forester*, September 1, 1932, 10.

17. Letter, Datil National Forest, New Mexico, September 1, 1922, Denver FRC.

18. *Ibid.*

19. Aldo Leopold, Report on Proposed Wilderness Area (L Recreation-Gila, Wilderness Area), District 3, USFS, Albuquerque, N.M., October 2, 1922. Denver, FRC. It is noteworthy that Aldo Leopold's initials or signature element appear on no other documents related to the Gila Wilderness Area after October 2, 1922, though he is referred to in the third person after that time. He left District 3 on June 15, 1924, for Madison, Wisconsin.

20. *Ibid.*, 1-3.

21. *Ibid.*, 1. Here again, Leopold stessed "in the Southwest," presumably with a purpose.

22. *Ibid.*,

23. *Ibid.*, 1-2.

24. *Ibid.*, 2.

25. See Chapter II, page 31, *supra.*

26. Memorandum (S Management Plans, Gila, Policy Statement), (L Recreation, Gila, Wilderness Area), District 3, USFS, Albuquerque, N.M., November 28, 1922. Denver FRC.

27. *Ibid.*, 1.

28. *Ibid.*, 1-2.

29. *Ibid.*, 2.

30. *Ibid.* Census figures for the State of New Mexico in 1920 reflected a population of 360,350 persons, compared with 423,317 in 1930. *The World Almanac and Book of Facts* (New York, 1964), 253.

31. M. M. Cheney was Assistant to the Solicitor, Law Branch, District 3; John D. Jones was another Assistant District Forester, District 3. Memorandum (L Recreation, Gila, Wilderness Area), Memorandum for Mr. Pooler, District 3, USFS, Albuquerque, N.M., March 1, 1923. Denver FRC.

32. *Ibid.*, 1-2.

33. *Ibid.*

34. No author shown, Recreational Working Plan, Gila National Forest, District 3, USFS, Albuquerque, N.M., submitted for approval, March 28, 1924. Denver FRC.

35. Copy of handwritten note from Zane G. Smith, staff member, District 3, to Rex King, Assistant District Forester, District 3, USFS, Albuquerque, N.M., undated. This was, however, in response to an inquiry initiated by the Washington office, USFS, by Memorandum (U-Recreation, R-3, Gila, Gila Wilderness Area) (I-Cooperation, Wilderness Society), October 13, 1948.

36. Recreational Working Plan, Gila National Forest, District 3, USFS, Albuquerque, New Mexico, June 3, 1924, 2. Denver FRC.

37. *Ibid.*, 1.

38. *Ibid.*, 1-2. While forest roads were to be limited, provision was made for "consideration of all meritorious projects." Also, the "Forest Service with such cooperation as it can secure from County and other sources," would construct a "recreational loop road for the towns of Silver City, Fort Bayard, Central, Burley, Santa Rita and the other

small community towns and open up this area for general camping and summer home use."

39. *Ibid.*, 2.

40. *Ibid.*

41. Recreational Working Plan, Gila National Forest, District 3, revised, February 1, 1928.

42. *Ibid.*, 2.

43. Regulation L-20 was slightly amended on August 7, 1930, and remained in effect until September 19, 1939, when it was superseded by Regulations U-1, U-2, and U-3 (a). ORRRC *Study Report 3,* 20.

44. *Ibid.*, 20-21.

CHAPTER IX

LET'S GET ORGANIZED!

1. That Bill was referred to as the Fuller Bill in the literature of the time. See Chapter VII, page 150, *supra.*

2. P. B. Riis, "Superior National Forest Recreation Association," *Parks & Recreation* (March-April, 1924), 409-10.

3. *Ibid.*, 410.

4. *Ibid.*

5. P. B. Riis, "Superior National Forest News," *Parks & Recreation* (March-April), 380-81.

6. Letter from P. B. Riis to A. H. Carhart, March 30, 1926. Carhart Papers.

7. *Ibid.*

8. Letter from A. H. Carhart to P. B. Riis, April 2, 1926. Carhart Papers.

9. *Ibid.*

10. ORRRC *Study Report 3*, 313-14.

11. W. M. Jardine, Secretary of Agriculture, USDA, Washington, D.C., "The Policy of the Department of Agriculture in Relation to

Road Building and Recreational Use of the Superior National Forest, Minnesota," September 17, 1926, 1-9.

12. "History," *BWCA Review Committee Report*, December 15, 1964, 5-6. It should be noted that to that time, management plans for National Forests were concluded at the option and decision of the District Forester concerned; the issue over road building in the Superior National Forest involved the Secretary of Agriculture directly for the first time in 1923 and again in 1926.

13. Jardine, "The Policy in Relation to Road Building and Recreational Use of the Superior National Forest," September 17, 1926, 1-2.

14. *Ibid.*, 2.

15. *Ibid.*, 2-3.

16. *Ibid.*, 3-6.

17. *Ibid.*, 6.

18. *Ibid.*, 6-8.

19. *Ibid.*, 8-9.

20. The Superior Roadless Area Report, approved June 27, 1938 by Acting Chief Forester Earle H. Clapp, contained the following statement: "The Superior Wilderness Area approved by Acting Forester E. A. Sherman, June 30, 1926, was given final approval by Secretary of Agriculture September 17, 1926." Author's interview with H. A. Svensen, Assistant Forester, Region 9, USFS, Milwaukee, Wisconsin, April 12, 1965; and Letter from H. A. Svensen to author, April 14, 1965.

21. This statement was made before the Jardine policy statement of September 17, 1926.

22. *Report of the Forester for the Year Ended June 30, 1926*, October 11, 1926, 34.

23. Letter from P. B. Riis to W. M. Jardine, September 10, 1926. Carhart Papers.

24. Letter from P. B. Riis to George H. Selover, October 13, 1926. Carhart Papers.

25. On July 25, 1925, there was a dynamiting incident at Brule Lake. A company interested in water power development had blasted an opening at the outlet of that lake to increase the water supply in South Brule River at the expense of lowering the level of the Temperance River and surounding lakes. This was known as the "E. W. Backus Scheme" in conservation circles, but cannot be detailed here. For a

brief account see A. H. Carhart, "Our Superior Forest," *Field and Stream* (June, 1927), 42-44, 75, 98.

26. Letter from A. H. Carhart to A. G. Hamel, November 15, 1926. Carhart Papers.

27. *Ibid.* A. G. Hamel had been the Forest Supervisor of the San Isabel National Forest, Colorado, in 1919.

28. Letter from A. H. Carhart to Frederick Law Olmsted, February 14, 1927. Carhart Papers.

29. Carhart, "Our Superior Forest," *Field and Stream* (June, 1927), 42-44, 75, 98.

30. *Report of the Forester*, September 1, 1927, 32.

31. Letter from J. F. Gould, Commissioner of Game and Fish, State of Minnesota Department of Conservation, St. Paul, Minnesota, to Forester W. B. Greeley, USFS, Washington, D.C., January 16, 1928. Carhart Papers.

32. *Ibid.*

33. Letter from E. Burkholder, Publication Distribution, USDA, Forest Service, Washington, D.C., to James F. Gould, Commissioner of Game and Fish, St. Paul, Minnesota, January 23, 1928. Carhart Papers.

34. Letter from A. H. Carhart to Charles H. Ramsdell, Febuary 4, 1928; and Letters from C. H. Ramsdell to A. H. Carhart, January 31 and February 7, 1928, are examples. Carhart Papers.

35. Letter from E. W. Tinker, Assistant District Forester, District 2, USFS, Denver, Colorado, to A. H. Carhart, February 23, 1928. Carhart Papers.

36. "History," *BWCARC Report*, December 15, 1964, 6.

37. *ORRRC Study Report 27*, 114-15.

38. The Quetico-Superior Council of Minneapolis, associated with the Izaak Walton League of America, was replaced in 1934 when President Franklin D. Roosevelt created the Quetico-Superior Committee. The Committee has been extended by succeeding Presidents to advise on matters concerning the roadless areas in the Superior National Forest. *Ibid.*, 115, 128; and "History," *BWCARC Report*, December 15, 1964, 6-7.

39. *Report of the Forester*, September 1, 1928, 38-39.

40. See Chapter IX, page 173, *supra.*

41. Author's perusal of the active files of the Gila National Forest, Albuquerque, New Mexico, and author's interview with Regional Forester Fred H. Kennedy, Region 3, and Norman P. Weeden, Chief, Recreation Branch, Division of Recreation and Lands, Region 3, USFS, Albuquerque, N.M., November 4, 1964; plus author's examination of the dead files pertaining to the Gila National Forest, November 12, 1964. National Archives, Federal Records Center, Denver, Colorado, FRC Containers 8264 and 37098.

42. Letter from A. S. Peck, District Forester, District 2, USFS, Denver, Colorado, to A. H. Carhart, February 13, 1929, with undated draft of article written by L. F. Kneipp, "These Tame National Forests." Carhart Papers.

43. L. F. Kneipp, "These Tame National Forests," undated.

44. *Ibid.*, 1.

45. *Ibid.*

46. *Ibid.*, 2.

47. *Report of the Forester*, Sepetmber 3, 1929, 40.

CHAPTER X

HERE COMES THE JUDGE!

1. The historian John Fiske applied the term "Critical Period" to the years 1783-1788, a period pre-eminently the turning point in the development of political society in the western hemisphere. John Fiske, *The Critical Period of American History*, 1783-1789 (Boston, 1888), 55.

2. John D. Hicks, *Republican Ascendancy, 1921-1933* (New York, 1960), 223-24.

3. *Ibid.,* 262. The Eighteenth Amendment which prohibited the manufacture, sale, or transportation of intoxicating liquors was ratified January 29, 1919, and the Twenty-First Amendment which repealed it was ratified December 5, 1933.

4. Donald C. Swain has pointed out that American historians have written a number of books and articles on the subject of conservation, concentrating on the years up to 1921. Swain noted that "perhaps because the first year of the Harding administration produced a climax for the Pinchot group, 1921 has become a convenient terminal point for studies of conservation. Historians and conservation writers alike

expatiate on the Roosevelt-Pinchot era and then skip gracefully to the New Deal resource program, assuming that the intervening years, 1921-1933, were an unimportant interlude." Donald C. Swain, *Federal Conservation Policy, 1921-1933* (Berkeley, 1963), 5-6.

5. *ORRRC Study Report 3*, 20-21.

6. *Ibid.*, citing Mimeographed supplement to Forest Service Administrative Manual sent to Forest Service Districts, June 29, 1929, and kept in use during 1930.

7. *Ibid.*, 20.

8. The "Copeland Report" was published under the title *A National Plan for American Forestry* (Washington, 1933), 474-76. A recent study found that "under authorization of an administrative regulation, L-20, set up in 1929, three primitive areas were established in 1930, with an aggregate of 360,444 acres. By 1939 there were 73 such areas, totaling 13,643,599 acres." Michael Nadel, "The Pace of Wilderness Classification," *The Living Wilderness* (Winter-Spring, 1964), 16.

9. *Ibid.*, 476.

10. ORRRC *Study Report 3*, 19.

11. James MacGregor Burns, *Roosevelt: the Lion and the Fox* (New York, 1956), 166-67.

12. ORRRC *Study Report 3*, 313-16. Author's interview with H. A. Svensen, Assistant Forester, Region 9, USFS, Milwaukee, Wisconsin, April 12, 1965; and Letter from H. A. Svensen to the author, April 14, 1965.

13. Author's interview with H. A. Svensen, Assistant Regional Forester, Region 9, USFS, Milwaukee, Wisconsin, April 12, 1965.

14. "History," *BWCARC Report*, December 15, 1964, 7-9.

15. *Ibid.* Letter from H. A. Svensen to the author, April 14, 1965.

16. The Superior National Forest Plan of Management has been revised repeatedly to include a series of extensions and modifications to the Forest in 1930, 1933, 1935, 1936 and again in 1965, but those changes need not be detailed here. "History," *BWCARC Report*, December 15, 1964, 6-7. See also Chapter IX, pages 170-73, *supra.*

17. For a current map of the BWCA, see Figure 14.
In a news release dated January 12, 1965, Secretary of Agriculture Orville L. Freeman stated that he had taken action "to nearly double the land area where timber cutting is prohibited in the Boundary Waters Canoe Area in the Superior National Forest in Minnesota,

thereby placing within the zone about 90% of the water surface of the entire area." The Secretary's action was an adoption of one of the major recommendations made by the *BWCARC Report*, December 15, 1964.

18. For a current map of the Flat Tops Primitive Area, White River National Forest, see Figure 8.

19. Though numerous histories of Colorado have been written, none pertains specifically to the White River National Forest, Trappers Lake, or the Flat Tops Primitive Area, under one cover. The author would like, at some future date, to write a monograph based on data collected during the conduct of the research for this study. In the meantime, the brief exposition here presented will be a series of not clearly connected facts, a condition which calls for the indulgence of the reader.

20. "Meeker Massacre—Last Major Indian Uprising in the West," *Meeker* (Colorado) *Herald*, August 18, 1960, 3; and various documents regarding the Flat Tops Primitive Area, White River National Forest, in the files of the Meeker Ranger Station, Colorado.

21. F. C. Grable, *Colorado—The Bright Romance of American History* (Denver, 1911), 123.

22. "Trapping Beavers—When the Fur-Bearing Animals were Plentiful in Colorado," *The Denver* (Colorado) *Times*, February 9, 1902, 19; and Eugene Parsons, "Old Scout Wiggins," *The Trail* (December, 1910), 11, and Parsons, *A Guidebook to Colorado* (Boston, 1911), 126. See also, the unpublished Master's Thesis of Ruth Estelle Matthews, "A Study of Colorado Place Names," Stanford University, 1940, which reported that "what is now known as Trappers Lake also once bore the name Sweetwater Lake." The Indian legend related to "Sweetwater Lake" may be found in Kenneth Hotchkiss' "Mount Dam and the Legend of Toponas Rock." *The Trail,* XVI, (April, 1924), 18-19.

23. For maps of the region, see F. V. Hayden, *Geological and Geographical Atlas of Colorado* (Washington, 1881).

24. Frank Hall, *History of the State of Colorado* (Chicago, 1895), 284-87.

25. *The Meeker* [Colorado] *Herald* (August 15, 1885), 1. That was the first issue published by the *Herald.*

26. *The Meeker* [Colorado] *Herald* (January 9, 1886), 1.

27. United States Forest Service, *White River National Forest* (Oakland, 1941), October 11, 1941, 2-5.

28. Handwritten note by Fred R. Johnson, Forest Examiner, District 2, USFS, Denver, July 29, 1958, citing his Diary and Field Notes for the period June 17, 1929 through June 27, 1929. CLC, DPL.

29. *Ibid.*

30. Recreation Management Plan, White River National Forest, Regional Office, Region 2, USFS, Denver, December 17, 1929, formally approved by Chief Forester R. Y. Stuart, March 5, 1932.

31. Author's interview with Jack J. McNutt, Chief, Reclassification Section, Regional Office, Region 2, USFS, Denver, Colorado, April 23, 1965.

32. Power Site Classification (PSC #176), based on a survey conducted by the Bureau of Reclamation on April 4, 1927, pre-empted a total of approximately 1,160 acres of lake and river areas for the purpose stated. *Ibid.*

33. *Ibid.*

34. Preliminary Reclassification Report, Flat Tops Primitive Area, White River National Forest, February, 1964, 1.

35. *Ibid.*, 5.

36. *Ibid.*, 5-6.

37. *Ibid.*, 6. In the past five years 12,000 to 25,000 fish have been harvested annually (average of 18,000).

38. *Ibid.*

39. "White River Valley Noted for Hunting Throughout U.S.," *The Meeker* [Colorado] *Herald*, August 18, 1960, 3. In 1964, there were 1.3 million recreation visits made to the White River National Forest. *The Denver* [Colorado] *Post*, February 20, 1965, 4.

40. *The Meeker* [Colorado] *Herald*, August 18, 1960, 3.

41. Various reports and charts in the Meeker Ranger Station, White River National Forest, Region 2, USFS, Meeker, Colorado, September 15, 1964.

42. Author's interview with G. E. Weidenhaft, Branch Chief, Wilderness and Special Areas, Reclassification Section, Regional Office, Rocky Mountain Region, Denver, Colorado, May 4, 1972.

43. Statement Relating to the Gila Primitive Area and Proposing of the establishing of the Gila Wilderness Area under Regulation U-1, submitted at the Gila Wilderness Area Hearing, Silver City, New Mexico, August 7, 1952, 3.

44. Letter (L Classification, Gila (Datil)), from L. F. Kneipp, Assistant Forester, USFS, Washington, D.C., to Frank C. W. Pooler, Regional Forester, Region 3, USFS, Albuquerque, New Mexico, May 20, 1930, 1.

45. *Ibid.*, 2-4.

46. Memorandum (S Supervision, L Classification, Gila-Datil), from R. Y. Stuart, Forester, USFS, Washington, D.C., to L. F. Kneipp, Assistant Forester, USFS, Washington, D.C., June 30, 1931, 1-2.

47. Letter (L Classification, Primitive Areas) from F. C. W. Pooler, Regional Forester, Region 3, USFS, Albuquerque, N.M., to the Forester, USFS, Washington, D.C., March 22, 1932.

48. Letter (L Classification, Gila) from R. Y. Stuart, Forester, USFS, Washington, D.C., to F. C. W. Pooler, Regional Forester, Region 3, USFS, Albuquerque, N.M., March 28, 1932, 1.

49. *Ibid.*, 1-2.

50. Memorandum (L Classification-Gila Primitive Area), from Assistant Forester M. M. Cheney, Region 3, USFS, Albuquerque, N.M., to Forest Supervisor, Gila National Forester, Silver City, N.M., August 25, 1933.

EPILOGUE

1. ORRRC *Study Report 3*, 21. These regulations were listed as U-1, U-2, and U-3.

2. *Ibid.*

3. *Ibid.*

4. *Ibid.*

5. *Ibid.*, 316.

6. *Ibid.*, 307.

7. *Ibid.*, 310.

8. Clinton P. Anderson, Senator of New Mexico, "The Wilderness Act, A Constructive Measure," *The Living Wilderness* (January, 1965), 3-4. The Wilderness Act is Public Law 88-577, 88th Congress, Session 4, September 3, 1964. The details concerning the problems of maintaining wilderness commitments by the Forest Service are explained in ORRRC *Study Report 3*, 203-316, *et passim.*

9. *Ibid.*, 3. For a full record of the Wilderness Bill as introduced in the 88th Congress on April 3, 1963, based on the final report in the Legislative Calendar of the House Committee on Interior and Insular Affairs, see *Ibid.*, 35.

10. Howard Clinton Zahnizer, "The People and Wilderness," *The Living Wilderness* (January, 1965), 41.

11. Laurance S. Rockefeller, "What Kind of America?" *Audubon*, LXVI (November-December, 1964), 376-81.

12. Stewart M. Brandborg, "The Job Ahead Under the Wilderness Act," *The Living Wilderness* (January, 1965), 13.

13. *Ibid.*

14. *Ibid.*

15. Lyndon Baines Johnson, President of the United States, "Message from The President of the United States transmitting National Wilderness Preservation System," The White House, February 8, 1965, reproduced in *The Living Wilderness* (Winter, 1964-65), 2.

16. Memorandum from A. H. Carhart to Aldo Leopold, December 10, 1919, 3-4.

SELECTED BIBLIOGRAPHY

A. PRIMARY SOURCES

1. Letters and Other Personal Material

Carhart, Arthur Hawthorne, Papers, 1918-1930. MSS in the Conservation Library Center, Denver Public Library, Denver, Colorado.

Johnson, Fred R. Papers, 1919-1929. MSS in the Conservation Library Center, Denver Public Library, Denver, Colorado.

Mechem, Merritt C. Letters received 1921-1922. MSS in the State of New Mexico, Records Center and Archives, Santa Fe, New Mexico.

2. Government and Other Organizational Documents

A National Plan for American Forestry. Washington: Government Printing Office, 1933.

Boundary Waters Canoe Area Review Committee Report, Duluth, Minnesota, submitted to the Secretary of Agriculture, December 15, 1964. MSS in the files of the Regional Office, Region 9, United States Forest Service, Milwaukee, Wisconsin.

Biographical Directory of the American Congress, 1774-1949. Washington: Government Printing Office, 1950.

Index to Federal Statutes, 63rd Congress, 3rd Session, 1915-1916. Washington: Government Printing Office, 1916.

Index to Federal Statutes, 64th Congress, 1st Session, 1915-1917. Washington: Government Printing Office, 1917.

"Outdoor Recreation Literature: A Survey," *Study Report 27 of the Outdoor Recreation Resources Review Commission* by The Librarian of Congress. Washington: Government Printing Office, 1962.

"Outdoor Recreation for America," *Summary Report of Recommendations,* Outdoor Recreation Resources Review Commission. Washington: Government Printing Office, 1962.

United States Code, Title 16. Vol. IV. Washington: Government Printing Office, 1958.

———. Supplement II. Washington: Government Printing Office, 1958.

United States Department of Agriculture, Forest Service:

Carhart, Arthur H. "Your Scenic Attractions," *The Bulletin, District 2,* U.S. Forest Service, Denver, III (May, 1919), 12. MS in the Conservation Library Center, Denver Public Library.

———. "Landscape Appreciation," *The Bulletin, District 2,* U. S. Forest Service, Denver, III (November, 1919), 11-13. MS in the Conservation Library Center, Denver Public Library.

———. *General Working Plan, Recreational Development of the San Isabel National Forest, Colorado, December, 1919.* MS in the Carhart Papers, Conservation Library Center, Denver Public Library.

———. *Preliminary Report, Recreation Reconnaissance Superior National Forest, Minnesota, 1919.* MS in the Carhart Papers, Conservation Library Center, Denver Public Library.

———. *Recreation Plan San Isabel National Forest, Colorado, 1920.* MS in the Carhart Papers, Conservation Library Center, Denver Public Library.

———. *Recreation Plan, Superior National Forest, Minnesota, 1921.* MS in the Carhart Papers, Conservation Library Center, Denver Public Library.

Gila Wilderness Area (U-Classification)—General Files, Bound Reports and Newspaper Clippings, MSS in the National Archives, General Services Administration, Federal Records Center, Denver, Colorado, Container No. 8264.

Gila Wilderness Area (U-Classification)—Correspondence Files, 1922-1950. MSS in the National Archives, General Services Administration, Federal Records Center, Denver, Colorado, Container No. 37098.

Jardine, W. M. "The Policy of the Department of Agriculture in Relation to Road Building and Recreational Use of the Superior National Forest, Minnesota." Washington: (Processed), September 17, 1926.

Memorandum from Arthur H. Carhart, "Memorandum for Mr. Leopold, District 3," District 2, United States Forest Service, Denver, Colorado, to Aldo Leopold, Assistant Forester, District 3, United States Forest Service, Albuquerque, New Mexico, December 10, 1919. MS in the Carhart Papers, Conservation Library Center, Denver Public Library.

Memorandum (L Supervision-Service Standard), United States Department of Agriculture, Forest Service, Washington, D.C., December 2, 1920. MS in the National Archives, General Services Administration, Federal Records Center, Denver, Colorado, Container No. 81950.

Minutes, Supervisors' Meeting, January 29-February 3, 1917, District 2, United States Forest Service, Denver, Colorado, February 3, 1917. MS in the Conservation Library Center, Denver Public Library.

Minutes (O Special), Supervisors' Meeting, Rocky Mountain District (2) United States Forest Service, Denver, Colorado, March 1, 1923. MS in the National Archives, General Services Administration, Federal Records Center, Denver, Colorado, Container No. 37702.

Munns, E. N. Miscellaneous Publication No. 364, *A Selective Bibliography of North American Forestry*. Volume I. Washington: Government Printing Office, 1940.

National Parks and National Forests. Brochure. Washington: Government Printing Office, 1962.

"Preliminary Reclassification Report, Flat Tops Primitive Area, White River National Forest," Region 2, United States Forest Service, Denver, Colorado, February, 1964. MS in the Regional Office, Region 2, U.S. Forest Service, Denver.

Report of the Forester to the Secretary of Agriculture for the Fiscal Year Ended June 30, 1916, October 16, 1916. Washington: Government Printing Office, 1916.

Report of the Forester to the Secretary of Agriculture for the Fiscal Year Ended June 30, 1917, October 1, 1917. Washington: Government Printing Office, 1917.

Report of the Forester to the Secretary of Agriculture for the Fiscal Year Ended June 30, 1918, October 1, 1918. Washington: Government Printing Office, 1918.

Report of the Forester to the Secretary of Agriculture for the Fiscal Year Ended June 30, 1919, October 8, 1919. Washington: Government Printing Office, 1919.

Report of the Forester to the Secretary of Agriculture for the Fiscal Year Ended June 30, 1920, October 4, 1920. Washington: Government Printing Office, 1920.

Report of the Forester to the Secretary of Agriculture for the Fiscal Year Ended June 30, 1921, October 6, 1921. Washington: Government Printing Office, 1921.

Report of the Forester to the Secretary of Agriculture for the Fiscal Year Ended June 30, 1922, September 30, 1922. Washington: Government Printing Office, 1922.

Report of the Forester to the Secretary of Agriculture for the Fiscal Year Ended Junt 30, 1923, October 4, 1923. Washington: Government Printing Office, 1923.

Report of the Forester to the Secretary of Agriculture for the Fiscal Year Ended June 30, 1924, October 13, 1924. Washington: Government Printing Office, 1924.

Report of the Forester to the Secretary of Agriculture for the Fiscal Year Ended June 30, 1925, October 10, 1925. Washington: Government Printing Office, 1925.

Report of the Forester to the Secretary of Agriculture for the Fiscal Year Ended June 30, 1926, October 11, 1926. Washington: Government Printing Office, 1926.

Report of the Forester to the Secretary of Agriculture for the Fiscal Year Ended June 30, 1927, September 1, 1927. Washington: Government Printing Office, 1927.

Report of the Forester to the Secretary of Agriculture for the Fiscal Year Ended June 30, 1928, September 1, 1928. Washington: Government Printing Office, 1928.

Report of the Forester to the Secretary of Agriculture for the Fiscal Year Ended June 30, 1929, September 3, 1929. Washington: Government Printing Office, 1929.

Report of the Forester to the Secretary of Agriculture for the Fiscal Year Ended June 30, 1930, September 25, 1930. Washington: Government Printing Office, 1930.

Report of the Forester to the Secretary of Agriculture for the Fiscal Year Ended June 30, 1932, September 1, 1932. Washington: Government Printing Office, 1932.

Report of the Forester to the Secretary of Agriculture for the Fiscal Year Ended June 30, 1933, September 1, 1933. Washington: Government Printing Office, 1933.

Report of the Forester to the Secretary of Agriculture for the Fiscal Year Ended June 30, 1934, September 1, 1934. Washington: Government Printing Office, 1934.

Skiing. Pamphlet 525. Washington: Government Printing Office, 1964.

Waugh, Frank A. (Collab.) *Recreation Uses on the National Forests.* Washington: Government Printing Office, 1918.

————. *A Vacation Land of Lakes and Woods - The Superior National Forest.* Washington: Government Printing Office, 1919.

White River National Forest. Oakland: United States Forest Service, October 11, 1941. MS in the Meeker Ranger Station, White River National Forest, United States Forest Service, Meeker, Colorado.

Wilderness. Pamphlet 459. Washington: Government Printing Office, 1963.

United States Statutes at Large, 61st Congress, 3rd Session. Volume XXXVI. Washington: Government Printing Office, 1911.

United States Statutes at Large, 81st Congress, 2nd Session. Volume LXI. Washington: Government Printing Office, 1952.

United States Statutes at Large, 32nd & 33rd Congress, December 1851-March 1855. Volume X. Boston: Little, Brown & Company, 1855.

United States Department of Interior, National Park Service:

Report of the Director of the National Park Service to the Secretary of the Interior for the Fiscal Year Ended June 30, 1921. Washington: Government Printing Office, 1921.

"Wilderness and Recreation—A Report on Resources, Values, and Problems," *Study Report 3 of the Outdoor Recreation Resources Review Commission* by The Wildlands Research Center, University of California. Washington: Government Printing Office, 1962.

3. Periodicals

Anderson, Clinton P. "The Wilderness Act, A Constructive Measure," *The Living Wilderness* (January, 1965), 3-4.

Brandborg, Stewart M. "The Job Ahead Under the Wilderness Act," *The Living Wilderness* (January, 1965), 13-14.

Broome, Harvey, "Origins of the Wilderness Society," *The Living Wilderness,* V (July, 1940), 13-14.

Carhart, Arthur H. "Municipal Playgrounds in the Forests," [Denver] *Municipal Facts Monthly,* II (July, 1919), 7, 14.

————. "Recreation in the Forests," *American Forestry,* XXVI (May, 1920), 268-72.

————. "The Department of Forest Recreation," *American Forestry,* XXVI (September, 1920), 549.

————. "Vacation Opportunities in Your National Forests," *American Forestry,* XXVI (September, 1920), 549-53.

————. "Auto Camp Conveniences," *American Forestry,* XXVI (September, 1920), 553-57.

————. "What is Recreation's Next Step?," *American Forestry,* XXVI (October, 1920), 593.

————. "Live Game and Forest Recreation," *American Forestry,* XXVI (December, 1920), 723.

————. "Denver's Greatest Manufacturing Plant," [Denver] *Municipal Facts Monthly,* IV (September-October, 1921), 3-7.

————. "Minimum Requirements in Recreation," *American Forestry,* XX (January, 1922), 31-36.

————. "Going to the Glaciers," [Denver] *Municipal Facts Monthly,* V (March-April, 1922, 7-9.

————. "Recreation in Forestry," *Journal of Forestry,* XXI (January, 1923), 10-14.

————. "The Superior Forest: Why It is Important in National Recreation System," *Parks and Recreation,* VI (August, 1923), 502-04.

————. "156,000,000 Acres—Count 'em," *Outdoor America* (October, 1923), 80-81, 122-23.

————. "Our Superior National Forest," *Field & Stream* (June, 1927), 42-44, 75, 98.

Committee Preservation Wild, "A Lakeland Wilderness Refuge," *Parks & Recreation* (November-December, 1922), 176.

Committee Preservation Wild, "Conference at Duluth," *Parks & Recreation* (March-April, 1923), 322.

Committee Preservation Wild, "The Lure of the Superior"; "America's Paramount Water-Travel Playground"; "Facts about the Superior National Forest"; and "The Part of Good Citizens"; *Parks & Recreation* (March-April, 1923), 316-22.

Hough, Donald. "The Superior National Forest to be Saved Forever," *Izaak Walton League Monthly* (April, 1923), 379-81; 430-31.

Johnson, Lyndon Baines. "Message from the President of The United States Transmitting National Wilderness Preservation System," The White House, February 8, 1965, reproduced in *The Living Wilderness* (Winter, 1964-65), 2.

Leopold, Aldo, "Origin and Ideals of Wilderness Areas," *The Living Wilderness,* V (July, 1940), 7.

————. "The Wilderness and Its Place in Forest Recreational Policy," *Journal of Forestry,* XIX (November, 1921), 718-21.

Muir, John, "A Plan to Save the Forests," *Century,* XLIX (February, 1895), 631.

Nadel, Michael. "The Pace of Wilderness Classification," *The Living Wilderness* (Winter-Spring, 1964), 16-24.

Riis, Paul B. "Birth of a Wilderness," *Parks & Recreation* (March-April, 1923), 311-15.

————. "Paradise Regained," *Izaak Walton League Monthly* (June, 1923), 527.

————. "Recreational Development of National Forests," *Parks & Recreation* (July-August, 1923), 500-01.

————. "Superior National Forest Recreation Association," *Parks & Recreation* (March-April, 1924), 409-10.

————. "Superior National Forest News," *Parks & Recreation* (March-April, 1925), 380-81.

Rockefeller, Laurance S. "What Kind of America," *Audubon,* LXVI (November-December, 1964), 376-81.

Superior National Forest Recreation Association. "National Need Recognized at Superior National Forest Conference," *Parks & Recreation* (May-June, 1923), 438.

————. "Superior National Forest Boundary Extension," *Parks & Recreation* (November-December, 1923), 168-70.

Yard, Robert Sterling, "Saving the Wilderness," *The Living Wilderness,* V (July, 1940), 3-4.

Zahnizer, Howard Clinton. "The People and Wilderness," *The Living Wilderness* (January, 1965), 39-42.

4. *Newspapers*

Denver [Colorado] *Post,* February 20, 1965.

Denver [Colorado] *Times,* February 9, 1902.

Des Moines [Iowa] *Register,* January 11, 1921.

Meeker [Colorado] *Herald,* August 18, 1960.

————, August 15, 1885

————, January 9, 1886.

Rocky Mountain News Denver, Colorado, January 11, 1921.

Sunday Denver [Colorado] *Post,* October 25, 1964.

5. *Maps and Atlases*

Hayden, F. V. *Geological and Geographical Atlas of Colorado.* Washington: Government Printing Office, 1881.

United States Department of Agriculture, Forest Service:

Map of National Forests and National Parks.

Map of White River National Forest, Colorado.

Map of Superior National Forest, Minnesota.

Map of Gila National Forest, New Mexico.

6. *Miscellaneous*

Anderson, James. Address by the Bureau of Land Management representative at the Conference on Natural Areas of the Southwest, held at Santa Fe, New Mexico, November 7, 1964. The present author attended the conference.

Freeman, Orville L. News Release by the Secretary of Agriculture, Washington, D. C., regarding the Boundary Waters Canoe Area, Superior National Forest, Minnesota, January 12, 1965.

McCloskey, J. Michael. Address by the Northwest Conservation Representative, Federation of Western Outdoor Clubs, Eugene, Oregon, at the Conference on Open Space, held at Breckenridge, Colorado, September 26-27, 1964. The present author attended the conference.

Ski Colorado. Brochure prepared by the Colorado Sports Committee, Capitol Building, Denver, Colorado, undated.

Svenson, H. A. Letter from the Assistant Regional Forester, Region 9, U. S. Forest Service, Milwaukee, Wisconsin, to the author, April 14, 1965.

United States Good Roads Bulletin, II (December, 1923), 1-16. MSS in the State of New Mexico, Records Center and Archives, Santa Fe, New Mexico.

B. SECONDARY SOURCES

1. *Books*

Abernethy, Thomas Perkins. *Western Lands and the American Revolution*. New York: Russell & Russell, Inc., 1959.

Allen, Frederick Lewis. *Only Yesterday*. New York: Bantam Books, Inc., 1931.

Bailey, Thomas A. *A Diplomatic History of the American People.* New York: Appleton-Century-Crofts, Inc., 1958.

Billington, Ray Allen. *Westward Expansion—A History of the American Frontier.* New York: The MacMillan Company, 1960.

————, Loewenberg, Bert James, Brockunier, Samuel Hugh. *The Making of American Democracy—Readings and Documents.* Volume I (1492-1865). New York: Rinehart and Co., Inc., 1950.

Blegen, Theodore Christian. *The Land Lies Open.* Minneapolis: University of Minnesota Press, 1949.

————. *Minnesota, A History of the State.* Minneapolis: University of Minnesota Press, 1963.

Burns, James MacGregor. *Roosevelt: the Lion and the Fox.* New York: Harcourt, Brace & World, Inc., 1956.

Carhart, Arthur H. *Planning for America's Wildlands.* Harrisburg: The Telegraph Press, 1961.

————. *Timber in Your Life.* Philadelphia: J. B. Lippincott Company, 1955.

Cox, John Charles. *The Royal Forests of England.* London: Methuen & Co., 1905.

Ekirch, Arthur A., Jr. *Man and Nature in America.* New York: Columbia University Press, 1963.

Fiske, John. *The Critical Period of American History, 1783-1789.* Boston: Houghton, Mifflin and Company, 1888.

Folwell, William Watts. *A History of Minnesota,* Volume 1. St. Paul: Minnesota Historical Society, 1956.

Gilpin, William. *Remarks in Forest Scenery and Other Woodland Views.* 2 Vols. London: Originally printed for R. Blamire, 1791; reprinted 1834.

Gewehr, Wesley M. *American Civilization.* New York: McGraw-Hill Book Company, Inc., 1957.

Grable, F. C. *Colorado—The Bright Romance of American History.* Denver: The Kistler Press, 1911.

Hall, Frank. *History of the State of Colorado*. Chicago: The Blakeley Printing Co., 1895.

Hays, Samuel P. *Conservation and the Gospel of Efficiency: The Progressive Conservation Movement, 1890-1920*. Cambridge: Harvard University Press, 1959.

Hicks, John D. *Republican Ascendancy, 1921-1933*. New York: Harper & Brothers, 1960.

Hofstadter, Richard. *The Age of Reform—From Bryan to F.D.R.* New York: Alfred A. Knopf, Inc., 1955.

Huth, Hans. *Nature and the American—Three Centuries of Changing Attitudes*. Berkeley and Los Angeles: University of California Press, 1957.

Koch, Adrienne and Peden, William. *The Life and Selected Writings of Thomas Jefferson*. New York: Random House, 1944.

Leuchtenburg, William E. *The Perils of Prosperity, 1914-1932*. Chicago: University of Chicago Press, 1958.

Manwood, John. *Treatise and Discourse of the Laws of the Forest*. London: Thomas Wight and Bonham Norton, 1598.

Miller, John C. *Origins of the American Revolution*. Stanford: Stanford University Press, 1959.

Morison, Samuel E. *Sources and Documents Illustrating the American Revolution, 1764-1788*. London: Oxford University Press, 1961.

Muir, John. *Our National Parks*. Boston: Houghton, Mifflin and Company, 1901.

Mowry, George E. *The Era of Theodore Roosevelt: 1900-1912*. New York: Harper & Row, 1958.

Nute, Grace Lee. *Caesars of the Wilderness*. New York: D. Appleton-Century Co., Inc. 1943.

National Cyclopedia of American Biography. Volume XXVI. New York: James T. White and Company, 1937.

————. Volume XXXIV. New York: James T. White and Company, 1948.

Parkes, Henry Bamford. *The United States of Ameica—A History.* New York: Alfred A. Knopf, Inc., 1955.

Parsons, Eugene, *A Guidebook to Colorado.* Boston: Little, Brown, and Company, 1911.

Paxson, Frederick L. *Postwar Years, Normalcy. 1918-1923.* Berkeley: University of California Press, 1948.

Swain, Donald C. *Federal Conservation Policy, 1921-1933.* Volume LXXVI. Berkeley: University of California Press, 1963.

Townley, Houghton. *English Woodlands and Their Story.* London: Methuen & Company, 1910.

Turner, Frederick Jackson. *Frontier and Section.* Englewood Cliffs, N.J.: Prentice-Hall, Inc., 1961.

Udall, Stewart L. *The Quiet Crisis.* New York: Holt, Rinehart and Winston, 1963.

2. *Periodicals.*

Burns, Allen T. "Relation of Playgrounds to Juvenile Delinquency," *Playgrounds and Juvenile Delinquency.* Bulletin 385, Community Service Inc., 1 Madison Avenue, New York City, N.Y. Burns, Dean of the Chicago School of Civics and Philanthropy, presented a digest of this study to the Second Playground Congress, 1908.

Douglas, Orlando B. "The Relation of Public Parks to Public Health," *Second Report of the American Park and Outdoor Art Association,* Minneapolis, Minnesota, June 22, 23 and 24, 1898.

Errington, Paul L. "In Appreciation of Aldo Leopold," *Journal of Wildlife Management,* XXI (October, 1948), XII (October, 1948), 341-50.

Faulkner, Paul. "Three Hundred Years of The Compleat Angler," *Outdoor America* (September-October, 1953), 4-14.

Guyton, Charles. "Waltonism 1928: Our Hats Off to the Old—Our Coats Off to the New," *Outdoor America,* VI, (February, 1928), 34-35.

Hitchkiss, Kenneth. "Mount Dome and the Legend of the Toponas Rock," *The Trail, XVI* (April, 1924), 18-19.

McFarland, J. Horace. "The Reason for Parks," from the Proceedings of the Twelfth Annual Convention of the American Association of Park Superintendents, Harrisburg, Pa., August 9-10, and at Gettysburg, Pa., August 11, 1910.

Nash, Roderick W. "Man and Nature in America," *Forest History,* VII (Winter, 1964), 21-22.

Parsons, Eugene. "Old Scout Wiggins," *The Trail* (December, 1910), 5-13.

Smith, Glanville. "Minnesota, Mother of Lakes and Rivers," *National Geographic Magazine,* LXVII (March, 1935), 263-318.

Waugh, Frank A. "What is a Forest," Journal of Forestry, XX (March, 1922), 209-14.

3. *Unpublished Materials*

Atwood, Burton T. "Controversy in the Boundary Waters Canoe Area." Illinois: The Izaak Walton League of America Endowment, August 10, 1964. (Mimeographed.)

Gilligan, James P. "The Development of Policy and Administration of Forest Service Primitive and Wilderness Areas in the Western United States." Unpublished Ph.D. Thesis, The University of Michigan, 1954.

Lucas, Robert C. "The Quetico-Superior Area: Recreational Use in Relation to Capacity." Unpublished Ph.D. Thesis, The University of Minnesota, 1962.

Matthews, Ruth Estelle. "A Study of Colorado Place Names." Unpublished Master's Thesis, Stanford University, 1940.

Scheffey, Alice W. "The Origin of Recreation Policy in the National Forests—A Case Study of the Superior National Forest." Unpublished Master's Thesis, The University of Michigan, 1958.

4. Personal Interviews

Author's interview with Arthur H. Carhart during the period September, 1963-May, 1965.

Author's interview with Samuel T. Dana, Dean Emeritus, School of Natural Resources, The University of Michigan, Ann Arbor, Michigan, September 29, 1964.

Author's interview with Fred R. Kennedy, Regional Forester, Region 3, Albuquerque, New Mexico, November 4, 1964.

Author's interview with Richard E. McArdle, former Chief Forester, U. S. Forest Service, Washington, D.C., September 28, 1964.

Author's interview with Jack J. McNutt, Chief, Reclassification Section, Region 2, U.S. Forest Service, Denver, Colorado, October 5, 1964; April 23, 1965, and May 3, 1965.

Author's interview with H. A. Svensen, Assistant Regional Forester, Region 9, U.S. Forest Service, Milwaukee, Wisconsin, February 3, 1965, and April 12, 1965.

Author's interview with Norman P. Weeden, Chief, Recreation Branch, Division of Recreation and Lands, Regional Office, Region 3, Albuquerque, New Mexico, November 4, 1964.

Author's interview with G. E. Weidenhaft, Branch Chief, Wilderness and Special Areas, Reclassification Section, Regional Office, Rocky Mountain Region, Denver, Colorado, May 4, 1972.

Author's interview with J. Wesley White, Duluth Office, U.S. Forest Service, Duluth, Minnesota, October 13-16, 1965.

APPENDICES

APPENDIX A. Letter from A. H. Carhart to E. A. Sherman
February 13, 1923.

PERSONAL

February 13, 1923

Mr. E. A. Sherman,
Forest Service
Washington, D.C.

Dear Mr. Sherman:

Your good letter of December 20th last awaited my return to Denver the middle of last month. Since that time I have not had the opportunity to write saying how much I appreciated your kind words. I hope I have accomplished as much as you intimate and that I will be missed in Service Circles with genuine regret.

You need not regret the fact that I did not see the fire problems of 1, 4 and 6. I have been through those forests by rail and remember conditions to some extent. Furthermore I heard about a hundred times more about fire than the other men in the service ever heard about recreation so it was inevitable that I get a good understanding of the part fire protection plays in the work of the Forest Service.

One thing I think we all have genuine reason to regret is that the heads of the Service have not seen fit to put the time in conference and study on the growing recreation activity that it merits. In all of the four years I was in the Service there never was a time when Mr. Greeley, other leaders from Washington, a District Forester or other men who should be studying this move ever came to my office and sat down and dug into the problem of handling recreation on the National Forests.

The allotment of money at the present time is not so important. Constructive thought is. I could be thoroughly satisfied with not seeing any appropriations for forest recreation for another five years if in that time the members of the Service that must necessarily take the lead would put solid thought on this work to reach policies that are sound and which they know are sound. What we need for this work is an allotment of brains to its problems, not money to carry out amateur plans that are based on tree production, cow growing and other purely forestry problems rather than on service to humans.

The service is making a mistake in trying to approach everything from the board feet angle. This is the greatest weakness in their recreation policy—is in fact the basis for their lack of recreation policy. For there will never be sound recreation plans in the National Forests until they are approached strictly from the side of what service they may be to human service rather than how they are going to interfere with the cows and conifers. It is all very well to take timber and cattle into consideration when the other side of the question is worked out but the first approach to recreation designing must be from the human service side.

In all of the work that the Forest Service has tried to do in recreation the plan has been to make it conform with existing policies absolutely. There has been no attempt to find out if there should be some radically different method of handling the recreation than those applied to timber and cattle. The application of methods that are adapted to the cattle and timber business may be entirely alright but does the service KNOW this. I am positive it does not know nor has it occurred to the heads of the Service to study this phase of the problem.

Looking forward I see three probabilities in forest recreation. The heads of the service must so inform themselves that they can approach recreation planning with as much background for their decisions as they now have in the fields of forestry and grazing. Or there must be a body of men trained in landscape architecture built up in the Service so the weight of their thinking will bring the proper balance in the handling of National Forest lands. Or there will within a decade perhaps be formed a national recreation service to take over the planning and administration of all of the recreation resources of our national properties.

There is no question but that there are lines of work other than recreation which demand more money and man power. But in every case that I know of they at least are getting thought and study. All effort has been made to wring out the fundamentals in each, to sift the bared truth from the husks, but in recreation this has not been done. This is probably quite natural and proper. For every executive in the Service has the "forestry viewpoint." Having the background of training in wood production or cattle raising they are able to go into problems relating to them with sympathetic understanding. But with recreation the old basic training of the forester remains so that recreation is approached from the cattleman's or foresters' viewpoint. Of course with the more thorough understanding of the needs of the trees and cows they have received preference. What the Service should strive to do is to get a just balance of effort between the human use of the forests and other uses. This is impossible until the needs of the districts and some effective portion of the Washington office combine with their knowledge of grazing and forest growing a somewhat equally broad knowledge in the principles, values, problems, etc. of forest recreation or recreational landscape design.

This may sound rather odd to you but I am certain that you will give it the just thought it merits. Perhaps I am wrong on some points. But you must admit that I am in a position to speak with authority equal to any on this subject. I would gladly have thrashed these questions out in a conference but as you recall there has never been one at where this might have been done. The other questions which the forester understands so much better, which perhaps are not so baffling, have had the preference and recreation has been administered on principles based on steer and tree growing.

Do not get the idea that I am "soured" on the Service. I still think it one of the best of the governmental bureaus. The men in it are all splendid and I shall wish to count them my very best friends the rest of my days. I never expect to be associated with a like number of individuals in which each was so much of a member of God's nobility as I found in the Forest Service. But I do think that the Forest Service has a long way to go on the recreation development that is inevitable although recognizing recreation as a major use for seven years has not got far in the past. You may count on me to help in every possible manner to the greatest constructive effort in this field of forest use for the rest of my natural life. And if there comes a time when the Service may really need my help and is really ready for it I certainly would seriously consider any opportunity to aid.

With my very best wishes and regards, I am,

Very Sincerely,

(Signed) Arthur H. Carhart
900 Exchange Building
Denver, Colorado

APPENDIX B. Letter from A. H. Carhart to E. A. Sherman, February 27, 1923

February 27, 1923

Mr. E. A. Sherman
Forest Service
Washington, D.C.

Dear Mr. Sherman:

Your letter of the 21st came today.

I do not expect any Forest Service man to agree with my ideas and am not surprised that you do not. Still one cannot help but draw his own conclusions and he better be honest about it than evasive.

You know that I write you very freely. I want to always feel that I can do that. We may not agree but we can say plainly what we think and respect the other fellow's viewpoint. I wrote in that manner in my previous letter.

I am predisposed to grant any request you may make. But I hesitate to say "go ahead" on the sending of my letter to the various DFs. Would it do anything constructive? I feel that they would read it, rare back, squat on their haunches, show their teeth, expose the whites of their eyes, probably give voice to the classic that has been used on occasions vis. "To Hell with Carhart and his comical ideas", initial the letter and send it to files. Or would they really do a little probing into their approach to recreation problems to find if they consider human service or other work first and get some good out of it. I'll say honestly that I believe that such a letter to them would only thicken the passive resistance to constructive recreation planning rather than swing our men to a critical, self analysis viewpoint.

I am tempted to offer a suggestion. If there is any value to you in my letter cannot it be passed on in some manner through you without there being a copy of the letter sent to the DFs.

You may be assured I am ready to help in anything constructive for the Service in any manner. That is the reason I hesitate to approve sending my letter to you to the District Foresters. I'm afraid it would not cause constructive reaction.

Very Sincerely,

(Signed) Arthur H. Carhart
900 Exchange Building
Denver, Colorado

APPENDIX C. Letter from E. A. Sherman to A. H. Carhart, March 6, 1923.

UNITED STATES DEPARTMENT OF AGRICULTURE
FOREST SERVICE

Address Reply to
THE FORESTER
and refer to

Washington

O
Personnel,
Carhart, Arthur H.

March 6, 1923

Mr. Arthur H. Carhart,
900 Exchange Building,
Denver, Colorado.

Dear Mr. Carhart:

Your letter of February 27 is received.

Upon second thought I believe you are right in thinking that your letter of February 13, written wholly for my personal information, might not accomplish the purpose I had in mind when I suggested that copies of it be furnished the District Foresters. I, therefore, have dismissed the idea of such a distribution.

I still think the letter embodies much that our adminstrative officers should carefully ponder. However, your suggestion that anything of value to me in your letter be passed on in some manner through me without there being a copy of the letter sent to the District Foresters is rather difficult of adoption. The effect of the letter would lie in its complete presentation of your viewpoint. Since I am unable to entirely agree with you, either as to your facts or conclusions, I would have to qualify or modify the letter if presented in the way you suggest and thus would largely destroy its value for the purpose I had in mind.

Our continued correspondence on subjects in which we are mutually interested will be of value only in the event that both of us say plainly what we think even though we may not always agree. Unquestionably the conclusions which you draw should be stated honestly rather than evasively. Your assurance that you are ready to help in any manner in anything constructive for the

Forest Service is appreciated. I shall expect to hear from you from time to time.

Very sincerely yours,

(Signed) E. A. Sherman
Acting Forester.

APPENDIX D. Letter from E. A. Sherman to P. B. Riis, February 13, 1923.

UNITED STATES DEPARTMENT OF AGRICULTURE
FOREST SERVICE

Address Reply to
THE FORESTER
and refer to

Washington

L
Recreation, Superior

February 13, 1923

Mr. Paul B. Riis, Secretary
Department of Wild Life Preservation,
American Institute of Park Executives,
301 Shaw Street,
Rockford, Ill.

Dear Mr. Riis:

Mr. R. Y. Stuart, Commissioner of Forestry, Pennsylvania, has sent to this office a copy of your letter of January 24 to Governor Pinchot concerning proposed road construction in the Superior National Forest, Minnesota.

The question of the position which the Forest Service should take regarding road construction within the Superior National Forest first arose about two years ago when Mr. Carhart, then Recreation Engineer of the Forest Service, submitted his plan for the development of the recreational resources of that Forest. In this plan Mr. Carhart very strongly recommended that the Superior National Forest be regarded and developed exclusively as a canoe forest or, in other words, that transportation by canoe should be relied upon to the exclusion of all other methods. This idea made a strong appeal to many members of the Forest Service who had the pleasure of reviewing Mr. Carhart's report and there was a strong sentiment favorable to the adoption of his recommendations. Continued study made it evident, however, that the Forest Service would be unable to rigidly maintain this form of development and the principle underlying Mr. Carhart's entire report was with some reluctance abandoned.

In the first place, only a little over two-thirds of the land within the Superior National Forest is in Government ownership. The other third, amounting to 411,199 acres, is privately owned and widely distributed throughout the Government holdings. Furthermore, there are other very considerable areas of privately-owned land adjoining but outside of the National Forest boundaries, for which road transportation can be provided only by road construction over the National Forest Lands.

Congress, by the enactment of various statutes, has authorized States and Counties to build highways over publicly-owned lands and there is very grave doubt regarding the ability of the Forest Service to prevent States or Counties from exercising this long and well established legal right. Furthermore, the several good roads acts passed by Congress since 1916 make available for cooperation with the States in National Forest road construction, considerable sums of money which, in part, are apportioned to the various States on the basis of the acreage and value of the National Forest lands within their boundaries. One feature of this Federal aid in road construction is that it offsets, in large measure, the loss in taxes sustained by the States through the withdrawal of large areas for National Forest purposes. Under these acts each region which includes National Forests has a certain equitable interest in these road appropriations - an interest which could not be realized if the construction of roads within the National Forests were restricted or prohibited.

Another consideration is that upon the Government lands within the Superior Forest the mature timber has an approximate value of almost three million dollars.

The desirability of its utilization through lumbering may be open to question but the obligation of the Forest Service to protect it against destruction by fire or other agencies is clearly defined. While it is true the fire hazard within the Superior region is relatively low it nevertheless is real and continuing. Adequate protection and administration of this important timber resource cannot be accomplished on the basis of exclusive canoe transportation. Men and supplies cannot be moved by this means with sufficient rapidity and in sufficient numbers to meet the probable requirements of good protection.

Still another feature which must be considered is that parts of the Forest are so far removed from the general routes of canoe travel that their utilization would in no material way impair the attractiveness of the area. to the canoeist and nature lover. Even under the most intensive development that can be anticipated much of the forest area and many of the canoe routes will remain in a state of virgin wilderness. It must, I believe, be recognized that in a country such as the Superior Forest canoeing is a highly specialized and rather restricted form of outdoor amusement which can be indulged in only by those especially qualified to meet its hazards and its hardships. For the minority who demand this class of outdoor recreation the untouched portions of the Forest will continue to offer a wide and entirely unspoiled field of amusement and recreation. Upon this point, the District Forester at Denver, under date of February 5, makes this comment -

"No passable canoe routes of any kind along routes where our road plan contemplates roads, except Grand Marais-Gunflint which is already constructed about twenty-six miles north from Grand Marais, and section Ely-Gunflint under construction by counties."

These variously enumerated considerations finally led the Forest Service to the conclusion that the adoption of Mr. Carhart's plan of development would be impracticable and caused it to listen receptively and sympathetically to the requests of the State and County officials for cooperation in road development under the provision of the good roads acts. It is true that the local people are not unanimous in favoring or requesting cooperation in the construction of road projects but it does appear that the majority of the local people favor road construction and formal application for cooperation under the law has been received from the accredited representatives of these local people. As a result, the Secretary of Agriculture has approved the expenditure of certain amounts from Forest Road appropriations made available under the Federal Highway Act on three major road projects partly within the Superior Forest.

These road projects are the Ely-Buyck, the Ely-Fernberg section of the Ely-Gunflint road and the Grand Marais-Gunflint road. The approximate location of these projects is shown upon the attached forest map. All three projects are now on the County road system but it is entirely possible that after the completion of the low-type roads now contemplated, the State will designate one or more as State Highways and bring them up to the State standard. These are not new road projects. The Counties have been interested in them for many years and have already spent considerable sums in their construction and maintenance. The Counties are now prepared to provide approximately $174,000 for the betterment of these roads and are asking that there be alloted from the forest road funds a total amount for the three projects of $80,000. It is not clear that refusal by the Federal Government to cooperate to the extent indicated would prevent the eventual construction of the roads. Probably the most it would do would be to retard construction, while at the same time arousing bitter antagonism to a plan which failed to take into account the reasonable transportation needs of the local communities.

It may be of interest to note that the Ely-Gunflint road is almost entirely outside of the National Forest boundaries and that of the Grand Marais-Gunflint road approximately two-thirds of the entire length is outside of the Forest boundaries. Of the thirteen miles of road within the Forest boundaries eight and one-half is on patented privately-owned land. The correspondence which has developed on this subject seems to be generally based upon the thought that the Superior National Forest is exclusively a public property and that the question of road development lies wholly within the jurisdiction of the Federal and State authorities. This is not the case. Considering the Forest alone, the Government has a two-thirds interest only. If consideration is extended to embrace the surrounding adjacent land the Government holdings are in the minority. It would not be possible to rigidly suppress road construction and economic development upon the privately-owned lands and it therefore would be futile to attempt to carry through a program which would engender bitter opposition, destructive of the present spirit of cooperation, when every consideration indicates the eventual and inevitable failure of the program.

The members of the Forest Service are not as materialistic as they are sometimes represented to be and the conception of a great National Forest maintained as nearly as possible in a state of nature and traversible only by canoe made a strong appeal to our imaginations. We thoroughly appreciate and to a large extent share your viewpoint on this subject. We could not, however, in the face of all the considerations I have mentioned adopt or maintain an attitude of opposition to reasonable road development of a character authorized by law and generally encouraged by all of the Federal agencies. We, therefore, have given our approval to the very moderate road development plans presented by the State and County officials. In doing this, however, we have not in any way lost our appreciation of the other values present within the area and every effort will be made to prevent the unnecessary impairment of such value through unwise or unnecessary road construction.

Very sincerely yours,

(Signed) E. A. Sherman
Acting Forester.

APPENDIX E. Letter from E. A. Sherman to P. B. Riis, February 13, 1923.

UNITED STATES DEPARTMENT OF AGRICULTURE
FOREST SERVICE

Address Reply to
THE FORESTER
and refer to

Washington

L
Recreation, Superior

February 20, 1923

Mr. Paul B. Riis, Secretary
Department of Wild Life Preservation,
American Institute of Park Executives,
301 Shaw Street,
Rockford, Ill.

Dear Mr. Riis:

In further reference to your letter of January 24 and of my reply of February 13:

The wide-spread objection now being expressed against any step which might possibly impair the value of the Superior National Forest as a game sanctuary or as an area within which natural conditions are scrupulously preserved for the lover of wild life, particularly the canoeist, makes it apparent that the people who hope or plan to use this area and the organization charged with the responsibility for its protection, maintenance and development have need for a fuller understanding of mutual ideals and wishes than now appears to exist. The immediate problem of the Forest is the proposal to construct the three road projects which I discussed in my previous letter but it is obvious that from time to time other forms of use will be proposed or applied for over which similar differences of opinion may arise.

The problem is a much greater one than has been as yet outlined in our correspondence. As you have been told, 411,000 acres of the land within the Superior Forest is privately owned, as is most of the land surrounding the Forest. Would it not be to the public interest to bring much or all of this land into public ownership? The only way the private holdings could be extinguished would be by purchase or by acquisition through exchanges involving the grant to the private owner of mature timber standing upon the publicly-owned lands. Such exchanges would, of course, mean the ultimate exploitation of the timber resources with at least temporary impairment of the value of the area as a game sanctuary and of its scenic beauty. On the other hand, if not acquired in this way, would not such private lands be exploited in the not far distant future and upon them, at least, arise the conditions which you are seeking to avoid on the Government lands?

It is our understanding that some of the wood-using industries of the region have predicated their plans, in part at least, upon the eventual utilization of the timber resources of the Superior Forest and applications for the purchase of timber may confidently be expected in course of time. Here, again, economic utilization would come into conflict with the values of the Forest as the habitat for wild life and as a recreation area. Is it possible to arrive at an understanding as to some middle ground preventing wholesale exploitation but preserving a large share of all economic values, both material and spiritual?

It is understood that some parts of the region are mineralized to an extent which will eventually result in considerable mineral development. Probably most of the mineralized lands are in private ownership but it is quite possible that some of the public lands may also prove to be mineral bearing. The exploitation of the mineral resources, unless carefully regulated, will develop another conflict with the wilderness principle of management.

The State and Counties may reassert their legal rights to extend their highway systems over the public lands and adequate protection of the Forest resources may demand better transportation facilities than those now present. Forms of special use, as, for example, hotels and modern summer resorts, may be applied for and strongly supported by local commercial interests plus considerable parts of the population which may look to the Superior Forest as its natural recreation area.

It would be an admirable thing to bring together in a conference the representatives of the wild life organizations who advocate the wilderness type of management, the State and County officials in charge of highway construction, game protection, forest management, etc., the local wood-using industries who look to the Forest as a source of raw material, the local business men whose plans contemplate the commercial development of resources within or near the Forest, and officers of the Forest Service who must formulate and carry out the agreed plan of management. I am sure that such a conference would strongly develop and, to a large degree, harmonize the views of the different elements interested in the Forest and would probably result in agreement upon the essential principles of organization and the use which should govern the Forest Service in its administration of the area. It should clearly bring out the great public importance and real economic value of the game and recreational resources which now exist and by doing so might lead to material modification of the State and Counties' present plans for road development and game management.

It is quite essential that the conference, if held, should be rather well attended by intelligent representatives of the various interests which may have a stake in the future use of this region. Otherwise the decision is in danger of being based upon a partial or faulty presentation of the case. Such a decision would not, of course, stand the test of time. As a matter of convenience to all concerned, the conference should be held at some point not far removed from the Forest. Off hand, Ely, Duluth or St. Paul impress me as the most desirable places of meeting. The date should not, in my judgment, be much after March first.

Do you think such a conference worth while and practicable? If so, would there be any assurance of a substantial attendance by representatives of the wild life organizations? Would you yourself find it possible to attend? What in your judgment would be the most convenient place and date of meeting? I shall greatly appreciate a prompt answer to this letter so that we may make necessary preparations for a representative at the meeting if one is held.

Very sincerely yours,

(Signed) E. A. Sherman
Acting Forester.

INDEX